RIDING FOR THE BRAND

LAWRENCE H. LEE

Personal History of

Lawrence H. "Larry" Lee

During the Airline Years

1943-1986

DEDICATED

To

Phillip E. Peirce,

Cloyd Hollingworth and most of all

My dear wife, Marjorie A. Lee

As I look back over the forty-three years of my airline history, these three played the key roles in my rise from junior stock clerk to the chairman and CEO of Western Airlines, Inc.

Cloyd gave me the basic training in management. Phil Peirce offered the support and encouragement that motivated me to advance and rise to the level of corporate officer. Through all of this, Margie was at my side, sustaining each transfer and advancement. When I retired, the board of directors of Western gave her a plaque that read:

Marjorie Lee
Without Your Support, Where Would We Be?

That plaque is a continual reminder to me of the importance of this wonderful woman in my life. I could never have achieved what I did without her love and support.

Last, but far not least, I acknowledge the hand of the Lord in all that I was able to accomplish at Western Airlines. My life is dedicated to Him and at every pivotal point of my career, He was at my side.

-Lawrence H. "Larry" Lee

Table of Contents

PREFACE

With all of the negative examples of reckless and greedy corporate leaders in America that we hear of these days, a leader occasionally comes forward who is motivated not by what or how much he can get, but what he can give. Such a man was my good friend, Lawrence H. Lee.

Larry, as he preferred to be called, was an individual who had worked up through the ranks of Western Airlines as a line employee, manager, director, senior VP, and finally CEO and chairman of the board. He was a man who had truly "earned his wings."

Larry was a renaissance man, a man for all seasons, raised up and cast from the forge of sweat, hard work, and tireless hours. He had faced disappointment, but never gave up until success was achieved. He was a visionary leader and so organized his vision as to easily describe it to others with such conviction and clarity, that we embraced it as our own.

Yes, we were all filled with his grand vision of what Western Airlines could again become; the nation's senior airline, the best on-time record, the safest, the most innovative, serving the best food, flying the youngest fleet of aircraft, the best trained pilots and flight attendants, etc. Yes, all employees became totally immersed in his grand quest to the point that we were sold on it and each became a critical member of a "trusted team" and part of the solution. Each of us felt a part of the heart of Western Airlines.

Maggie Walker once made a statement suitable to this occasion:
Make not small plans, for they have not the magic to stir men's souls

Larry was the kind of leader who could stir men's souls. He was low key, unselfish, charismatic, enthusiastic, self-disciplined, and an exemplary leader in every way. He always instilled confidence, integrity and trust; they were not just important to him, they were essential!

Larry could not only paint a vivid picture of his grand vision to return Western to its previous and much envied stature, but he followed his words with appropriate and timely action.

He worked tirelessly to save Western Airlines when it was on the brink of bankruptcy and did it not for monetary or political gain, or to bolster his ego, he did it because it was the right thing to do and he had prepared himself and instinctively knew how. Many, many employee's jobs, futures and lives were saved by Larry Lee's unselfish and dedicated leadership qualities.

Larry believed in "miracles" and convinced others that miracles could happen, but not without hard work and long hours. He worked hard enough to make these miracles happen. When he "circled the wagons in Salt Lake City," or whatever was left to circle, he created a miracle indeed. Utah Governor, Scott Matheson, said, "This hub will be the biggest thing to hit Salt Lake City, since the covered wagons." Elder Victor Brown, then Presiding Bishop of the Church of Jesus Christ of Latter-day Saints, added that; "This is the most significant thing for Utah since the coming of the railroad." All of this was happening while many battles were being lost in the mounting debris of the newly deregulated airline industry.

During the critical last three years of Western's history, which could have been the company's darkest hours, he created and organized a "Competitive Action Plan" that was brilliant, detailed, and addressed every conceivable issue. It was participatory for all departments and created unity and solidarity even in our fully unionized groups. As you will read in this history of Larry's "Airline Years," it gave Western employees an ownership in their beloved airline and created great pride and esprit-de-corps. At this time of commercial aviation history, such a thing as employee ownership and employees serving on the board of directors was unheard of. Larry created a fatherly relationship with the employees and from top to bottom it was "one for all, and all for one."

An example of his refreshing leadership style was reflected at this critical period when he asked his esteemed employees to take heavy pay cuts. He lead by example and took the heaviest cut himself; at times working without pay - and he did this until his retirement.

Larry spoke to the employees, the unions and the corporate officers with frankness, but always with sincerity and sympathy and his deed always followed his word. He was a man with whom honor and integrity were sacred. With the corporate culture that Larry carefully wove into the fabric of Western Airlines, we indeed felt that we were in it together. It was a culture of pride, confidence and determination and we were once again the grand and glorious airline that its history decreed.

Yes, these were the days never to be forgotten and now finally the details have been recorded in Larry's "Riding for the Brand." This tells it as it really happened; especially Western's critical last few years. With each page you read of trials and trouble, success and failure, and then you realize what a miracle it was that Western survived at all, let alone reestablishing itself as the great airline that she once was.

Larry Lee was pivotal to that miracle. When our pilots were "junior manned" and called to fly a trip on Christmas or New Year's Eve, they referred to it as "Riding for the Brand." Larry inspired the trust and dedication of all to "Ride for the Brand" and Western Airlines was again "The 0-o-o-only Way to Fly!"

Captain Duane B. Gerrard
Vice President Flight Operations Western Airlines, Inc.
(Retired from Delta Air Lines, Inc.)

Chapter 1

47 CENTS AN HOUR

In the early spring of 1943, at age sixteen, I had already labored in two jobs that were significant enough to note on an application for employment and obtain a good reference. After a stint at Helms Bakery in Los Angeles, at that time the largest bakery of its kind in America, I returned to Salt Lake City which had been my place of residence for the past four years. My objective was to find work that I would enjoy until I would enlist in military service. World War Two was still in progress.

All of my life I had been in love with aircraft and the aviation industry. One day I saw an ad in the newspaper for a stock clerk at Western Airlines at the Salt Lake Airport. I called and asked how to get an interview and the lady said to come on out to the office of the station manager, Mr. Joe O'Neill. I filled out an application, lied about my age, was interviewed by a couple of people and got the job.

I began working for Western on May 31, 1943. The pay was forty-seven cents an hour, eight hour days and six days a week. Training lasted one week on the day shift. Then, I started on my own working on the midnight shift - midnight to eight in the morning handing out tools and parts to the mechanics and keeping up the inventory.

At that time we flew Douglas DC-3's and a Lockheed "Lodestar." One of the DC-3's and the "Lodestar" would overnight in Salt Lake City. The maintenance on the aircraft began when they arrived that night and if necessary would proceed until departure time in the morning.

The length of the work depended on what type of maintenance "check" the aircraft required. Most of the mechanics worked the midnight shift so they could carry out whatever maintenance checks were necessary during the aircraft down time. In the morning the mechanics would get the two aircraft out of the hangar and position them at the gates. They would then load the mail and baggage for the two departures and go home.

When I started work with Western Airlines, we had three flights a day between Salt Lake City and San Diego, California. The southbound trips would stop at Las Vegas, Burbank and Long Beach. The morning flight was an example. The flight would leave Salt Lake City at 8:00 a.m. and arrive in Burbank, California at 10:50 a.m.; a three-hour and fifty-minute trip which included a ten minute Las Vegas stop. That was the southern part of the system. The flight north left at 7:00 a.m. en route to Lethbridge, Canada. It stopped at Pocatello, Butte, Helena, Great Falls and Cut Bank, Montana. It was the Lockheed "Lodestar" and arrived in Canada at 12:40 p.m. That was the extent of the Western Airlines System on June 1, 1943. Western was the oldest airline in continuous service; having inaugurated flights in 1926 between Salt Lake City and Southern California as Western Air Express.

When I went to work in Salt Lake, the base had a wonderful bunch of people. The mechanics there worked hard and played hard. Practical jokes were part of the routine and I could recite twenty pages of the fun and funny things they did. No one was ever hurt and no one was exempt from a "trick." Some of the mechanics names I recall are Ray White, lead mechanic, and Bob Gallagher, inspector. There were the Deeter brothers, Ralph and Lou, Tony Carpino, Art King, Rex Wood, Don Larson, Don Pitt and a fellow named Ed Chapman. I bought my first car from Chapman. It was a Model "A" Ford sedan that set me back twenty-five dollars.

I will recall a couple of these pranks. Because of gas rationing, certain of the group chipped in and bought an old limousine. They had installed a third-row seat which was a wooden bench. The mechanics who rode home would vie to see who would get the soft seats. The routine was to punch out at the time clock, go past the lunch room to pick up their lunch bucket and then head for the limo. One of these fellows was always first at the time clock to punch out. The others tired of this routine, so one night they bolted his lunch box to the table. As he rushed by and grabbed his pail, the handle came off in his hand and he was half way out the door before he realized what had happened.

This same fellow was always inciting the group to play a trick on others. Where the mechanics washed up, there was an eight-foot long sink with multiple faucets on both sides. Our instigator was plotting to take the night janitor and stuff him in the sink and turn on all the faucets. For several nights he had been trying to get others to join him in this prank. One night they agreed and hauled the big janitor into the wash room. He was a very strong man and he grabbed the pipe holding up one end of the sink. The bunch would pull one way and he'd laugh and flex his muscles and pull them back. At a given signal everyone but the prankster let go, rushed out the room and held the door shut. Left alone in the room were the janitor and the instigator. We could hear the gleeful laughs of the janitor as he picked up his tormentor and stuffed him under the running faucets.

The youngest mechanic in the crew was "Tink" Thiese. He was several years older than I, but we hit it off well. He drove a blue 1939 LaSalle coupe which was in mint condition. We did some fishing, hiking, camping and played pool together. Tink seemed to enjoy the out-of-doors and was a fun guy to be around. He later was named director of maintenance for Frontier Airlines in Salt Lake City.

I met another person at the airport who became one of my closest friends in Salt Lake. Her name was Ima Russell Gout. Ima was a cook on the night shift at the airport cafe, which was owned by Western Airlines. In addition to the coffee shop, they did all the inflight food service. This consisted of doughnuts on the morning flights and sandwiches later in the day. Ima was like another mother to me.

After nearly a year, I found my job in the stockroom to be dull at best. It was interesting at first because it required knowledge of the various parts, rivets, nuts and bolts that it took to keep an aircraft operating. However, I was more interested in what was going on with the other, more exciting parts of the operation. So, I applied for a "ramp" job.

Tony Favero, who was in charge of Salt Lake maintenance, was also the acting station manager. Joe O'Neill, the manager who hired me, had transferred to San Francisco to open Western's new operation there on May 1, 1944. Mr. Favero approved the transfer to "junior cargo clerk." My primary responsibility was the airmail and doing the "weight and balance" on the aircraft. I had two days training from the senior cargo clerk, Joe Meek. I was to then work the midnight shift with an experienced lady named Mabel Rasmussen. The very first night, she called in sick. I was on my own, which meant I had to balance the aircraft and make certain we did not exceed our maximum takeoff load. I had to do this on two different types of aircraft. I was scared to death that first morning.

One of the pilots was captain Ray Ellinghouse, a great big guy that I didn't think would even fit in the Lockheed "Loadstar." He looked over my shoulder as I worked with a funny box called a "Libra scope." This was supposed to tell us how much weight to put in the tail pit, among other things. Captain Ellinghouse told me not to worry. He said it didn't matter what we did, the plane would still fly. One of the mechanics had worked the weight and balance before and offered to help.

My stock-room job at Western had been paying about $80.00 a month, before deductions. I rented a room from a widow lady up on Sixth Avenue. There were no cooking privileges, so I had to eat out. Ima knew that I always ran out of money about three days before pay day. She'd do two things. First, she'd call me in the stock-room and tell me there would be a hamburger sitting on the cement wall in back of the coffee shop; second, she would increase the frequency of invitations to "drop by for a meal."

When I transferred to cargo service, I got a nickel an hour raise. That was appreciated, but not as much as the change to a forty-hour week. This was done without a pay-cut. Having two days off was a real treat.

Shortly after this move, Richard P. Ensign was transferred to SLC as the new Station Manager. He was a jovial fellow and would often be there in the evenings to watch over the operation.

A man named Woody Campbell managed the coffee shop. Woody and Dick would play the pinball machine in the corner of the shop by the hour. They played "dollar ball." The winner was the person who could get the highest score in a game; that is without "scratching." (Going into the bottom gutter or "tilting" the machine.) Woody was a poor loser and Dick loved to "rub it in" when he won. A crowd would always gather and cheer on their champ.

I enjoyed my relationship with the passenger service personnel and also the girls who worked in reservations. It was a small terminal and the reservations office was directly across from the ticket counter. Many of the girls in reservations were from the top families in Salt Lake City. Working for an airline was a prestigious job at the time. One of the girls was engaged to the heir of the Kearns family. She had a four carat solitaire engagement ring. Some of the others were kidding her and said it was not a real diamond. I said that if it was, it would cut glass. She took it off, handed it to me and said, "Cut glass." I went to the window and scratched a large, deep triangle. She said, "Any more questions?" There was silence.

When the first good snows were on the ground, the winter of 1943/44, I was working the midnight shift. Several of us asked for this shift so we could participate in winter sports during the day. Three of the girls in reservations and one female radio operator got off at 8:00 a.m. and we five drove to Alta to ski. We would ski until around two in the afternoon and then sleep in the evenings.

On one of these trips, I had gone to Rustlers Lodge with the others for a sandwich. They were sitting by the window playing bridge. I said I'd make one more run and then we'd go. As I skied down the slope toward the lift, I hit a spot where someone had taken a spill. My left ski dug in and I twisted around on that knee. I could feel something tearing when I went down. One of the girls was watching from the window and they alerted the ski patrol. By the time the patrol got there, the girls were hovering over me and extracting me from my skis. I was loaded on a toboggan, taken to the car and driven to the hospital by four lovely chauffeurs. I was the envy of the lodge. It was almost worth the two weeks on crutches. However, that ended my skiing and ice skating for the rest of the winter.

One day I saw an ad for a 1940 Harley Davidson sixty-one OH motorcycle. The "bike" was in mint condition. I finally made a deal with the owner. He would take my saddle and bridle and four hundred dollars. Mother loaned me the four hundred. It was to be paid back within a year.

My car had "given up the ghost," so, this was my only means of transportation - which was fine, except for the days when it snowed. In late June of 1944, when I was seventeen, I decided to ride my motorcycle to California and visit my dad and Tom, my brother. I had saved enough gas rationing stamps to barely get me to Los Angeles. After putting a suitcase on the flight to Burbank, I left. The plan was to sell my "bike" in L.A. and fly home on a pass. I worked the midnight shift, climbed on the Harley and zoomed off for Los Angeles. My first stop was my old home town, Santaquin, where I gassed up at the station where I was remembered. He didn't want the stamps. This gave me the edge I needed to relax on the road. I got to Las Vegas by late afternoon, had a bite to eat and went on. By the time I got to Victorville, I was so sleepy that I ran off the road twice. It was late at night when I walked into the lobby of a small hotel. There was no one on duty at the desk. I sat down in a large, comfortable chair to wait. Next thing I knew a person was tapping me on the shoulder asking if I wanted a room. I looked outside and found it was daylight. So, I just climbed on the "bike" and went on. Best night's sleep I'd had in three days.

I mention this experience as I don't want anyone to think there was nothing else but work in my life. Dating was rather difficult with just a motorcycle, however, I managed.

I worked the evening shift that last fall. When I got off at midnight I would hang around to see if they were going to use the DC-3 for pilot training. When they did, I'd fly along as a passenger while they would "shoot landings." We'd take off and then circle the field and land; that was it and I loved it. The rougher the landing the student pilot made, the more fun I'd have. Funny, I never had much desire to pilot an aircraft but loved to be around them. In those days it was a pleasure to just ride along. Captain Bud Brown was one of the training pilots and always welcomed me on board.

After working the midnight shift, some of us would occasionally stop at Decker's Pond to skate on the ice for an hour or so and then stop at a little coffee shop for the best chili in town. I wasn't much of an ice skater as my ankles were too weak for the shoe skates I had. Nevertheless, anything that was free was great.

The only time I worried about getting fired at Western was on a morning that we were inaugurating service into Ogden, Utah. This occurred on November 3, 1944. I was told to be at the Salt Lake Airport at 6:00 a.m. and assemble the ground handling equipment that had not yet been moved to Ogden Airport. I was threatened with everything but bodily harm if I did not get to the airport with the stuff by 8:00 a.m.

I loaded a pickup truck with a battery cart, wheel chocks and locks for the wings and tail. It was so foggy that morning I couldn't see the road and crawled along all the way to Ogden. I was happy to hear the inaugural flight was late because of the fog. There exists a picture of me in my white overalls leaning against a DC-3 nose stand. I have a disgusted look on my face which reflects my feelings on that particular morning.

Richard P. Ensign is in that picture. He was Western's station manager in Salt Lake City at that time. Dick was to supervise my activities once again before the end of my career. He was a very young manager for such a large location. His manner was easy going, but he was well respected by all.

When I went to work at Western, I had informed them I was nineteen years old. I'm not sure that Joe O'Neill believed me, but he never asked about my "draft" status. You couldn't find too many people around who were over eighteen, the minimum hiring age at Western, who would accept a job paying forty-seven cents an hour. So, the question of age did not arise. It was during this winter that I was fast approaching eighteen and would be eligible for military service.

The government was offering a six month deferment to airline employees because they felt they were engaged in an essential service. The closer I got to eighteen, the more I thought about my goal of "joining up." So, about a week before February 8th, 1945, at which time I had to register with the draft board, I enlisted in the U.S. Navy. I explained that I wanted to get in before my birthday and they set me up for a physical the very next day.

When I took my physical, I was informed I was a few pounds underweight for my height. The old Navy Chief who was working my papers advised me to eat hearty for a couple days and come in again to get weighed. I spent three days eating fresh banana double-thick egg malted milks at Snelgrove's Ice Cream Parlor. The second time I weighed, I was two pounds to the good.

After the appropriate notice and goodbyes at Western Airlines, I left Salt Lake City for "Boot Camp." The band of recruits was divided, and our group boarded an old steam train in a railway car that must have barely survived the First World War and we headed for the Naval Training Station in San Diego, California. The other half of the new recruits went to the Great Lakes facility, the coldest Naval Training unit around.

During the last weeks of training, we were interviewed and given some intelligence tests. Having worked for the airline for nearly two years, it came as no surprise that I was assigned to Naval Air Transport Service, known as "NATS." They said I would be located somewhere in the Pacific Theater.

NATS had a large operation out of John Rogers Field, which is now the Honolulu International Airport. It included both land and sea-based aircraft which were used throughout the Pacific. After completing boot camp and arriving in Honolulu, they assigned me the job of plotting the "point of no return" for the flights to the mainland, and the flight monitoring of some of the flights. As I recall, it took an R4D around nine hours to get to the Oakland Naval Air Station. The "seaplanes," as they were called, took about twelve hours and landed at Alameda Naval Air Station, wartime home of one Marjorie Lewis - later to become Mrs. Lee.

There was a formula we used to select a point where the flight would proceed to a destination if it had an engine failure. If the engine went out before this point, the flight would turn back. It was not unusual to have at least one flight a week return during my shift. These were the days of piston engines which were not as reliable as our current jet engines.

The work was very mind-numbing and I spoke to the personnel officer, Mr. McNally, about other assignments that might be available. He called me one day and said they were short a flight orderly, which was similar to a flight attendant except they had to work weight and balance and the weather data. I told him I'd be ready to go that day. The next evening I found myself working in the flight kitchen. The training program for "flight orderlies" consisted of just two things, how to open doors and how to serve the food to the passengers. One learned all of this in the flight kitchen. I was also in a new squadron, VR-11.

On September 13, 1945, I received my leather flight jacket. That was "big stuff" in the Navy. When the supply officer presented it to me, I was instructed that if I didn't turn it in when my tour of duty ended, I would probably face a firing squad; or words to that effect. It must have impressed me for I think I was the only one in the Navy to turn in his flight jacket at the end of the war.

I spent the next six months on many great, and some scary, adventures on both land-based aircraft and a four engine PB2Y2 seaplane called the "Coronado," that was assigned to the 5th Fleet in Shanghai as the Admiral's

Flagship. In fact that seaplane adventure caused me to have no desire to ever fly again; I think the Admiral felt the same way.

When I arrived back in Honolulu from the Shanghai adventure, I reported to the personnel office at the VRJ Squadron. I was ushered into the office of the head of personnel. Sitting behind the desk was Lt. Cmdr. Johnson, our plane commander on the China venture. I said: "... when did you get back and how come you are the Personnel Officer?" I won't burden you with the stories that kindled the kind of relationship that allowed a Petty Officer to talk to a Lt. Commander in this manner; in private that is. Suffice to say, our crew of eleven on that Coronado seaplane was so closely inter-dependent and served together for so long that rank was ignored when we were alone.

He said he had returned a week earlier, requested ground duty and they gave him this job. Then, Commander Johnson went on to say that the trip we had to Shanghai and back was all the flying he could stand for a while.

Commander Johnson asked what I'd like to do. I told him I'd take anything on the ground. I added that I didn't ever want to get on another airplane. "I'm through flying," I said. Johnson said: "That's great; I've a job for you running our officer's ward room." I asked him what that entailed. He responded: "You will supervise the cooking of breakfast and lunch and then make sure the crew gets the place cleaned up for the next day. You'll also have to supervise the procurement of the food and beverages and, as long as I have anything to say about it, you will have this job until you accumulate enough points to get a discharge from the Navy."

About six weeks later, Commander Johnson called me to his office and asked if I'd take a flight to the Oakland Naval Air Station. I said that I wouldn't, unless it was an order. Johnson said he would not order me as he knew how I felt about flying. He then proceeded to tell me that I was a month away from having enough points to be discharged. He asked if I knew how I would be going home. I had no idea. He said it would be aboard ship, and he proceeded with a description of what a troop ship was like and what conditions prevailed on board these over-crowded vessels. It was not a rosy picture and that was the way I would be returning if I didn't fly off the island.

The Commander then gave me the details of what had happened. There was a VRJ flight coming in from Johnson Island. It was carrying some members of Congress that were going to overnight in Honolulu and go on to Oakland the next evening. The cook had been taken off at Johnson because of appendicitis. There were no other cooks that would be available by tomorrow. He said all I'd have to do was cook breakfast for them. The aircraft was a specially configured R4D. I had never even seen a galley on a VRJ land-based aircraft.

When he saw I was still hesitating, he dropped the last shoe. "If you'll take the flight, I'll arrange a two-week leave for you and transfer you to a temporary assignment at the Oakland Naval Air Station. There you can await discharge from the Navy." I said I'd take the flight. The next day, after saying goodbye to a couple of friends, I went on board the aircraft, put in the supplies we'd need, and got acquainted with the galley. A tall, handsome Navy Lieutenant came on board by the name of Kenny Nelson. He was the plane commander and welcomed me to the crew.

It was an uneventful flight and most of the passengers didn't even want to eat. We arrived at the Oakland station midmorning and everyone unpacked his gear. It seemed this was the crew's last flight together as most of them were getting discharged. They had been together for some time and Lt. Nelson invited them to his family home for an evening together. He was kind enough to extend the invitation to me, even though I'd known him less than twenty-four hours.

The reason I've mentioned all this Navy stuff is that this was the night I met my future wife - future being a month later when we eloped to Reno, Nevada. Marjorie Lewis was Lt. Nelson's date that night and the minute I saw her I fell madly in love. I am now writing this 62 years later and that night is just as precious to me now as it was then - and, I'm more than ever, "madly in love" with her.

My application to USC had been accepted and I was due to begin classes that fall. Marriage changed this plan and I decided to return to Western Airlines; even though I felt I would never get on an aircraft again.

Larry Lee in his flight jacket. Shanghai, China, circa 1945

Chapter 2

AFTER THE WAR

At that time the only flight operation Western had in the Los Angeles area was at the Burbank Airport. Our Corporate Headquarters was in Hollywood and I went there for an interview. Ernie Brown was head of the personnel department and after we talked a bit, he took me to see Paul Sullivan - his boss. They were most cordial, congratulated me on my tour of duty in the Navy and asked when I wanted to start. They said I'd have more opportunities for advancement at Burbank because it was the largest operation. I told Mr. Brown it would take a few weeks to get reorganized and make the move.

Western had purchased some new DC-4s from Douglas Aircraft; in fact we were the first to receive a postwar DC-4. We also bought a few C-54s, which was the Air Force version of the DC-4 and they were converted to forty-four seat passenger aircraft. The work at Lockheed Air Terminal in Burbank was just not to my liking.

It was good to see some familiar faces as several of the mechanics from Salt Lake had moved to Burbank. I also knew many of the pilots. However, there were mostly new faces and new ideas of how the job should be done and I longed for a smaller operation. The break came when they announced we would begin service into Oakland, California, on September 1, 1946.

Our ground services division was located at the Burbank Airport and the key people were Harry Karst, Tom Runner and John Good. I went to see them and asked for a transfer to Oakland. The airline was somewhat unionized at the time, but the bidding procedure was still a rather informal process. A few days later, I was notified they had approved my transfer to Oakland as a cargo clerk.

When I reported at the Oakland Air Terminal, I was directed to the corner of a small waiting room for passengers where there was about twelve feet of ticket counter space. Behind this was a little cargo room which opened onto an area where light delivery trucks could pull up and unload. There were three tiny offices; one for the manager, a "walk-through" office for the passenger service operation and one for cargo service. When I went into the back room, I found the new station manager standing in the middle of a pile of ground equipment with a look on his face that spelled, "guess this is it?" I introduced myself and he said I was the first to arrive. He then handed me a list and said, "Inventory the ground handling equipment." It took five minutes.

We had portable DC-3 steps, one set of aileron locks, one elevator lock, one rudder lock, a set of wheel chocks, a battery cart, one large fire extinguisher, a nose stand and two baggage loading carts. In those days, that is all it took to run a ramp operation at a small station.

When the aircraft arrived, we'd put the "chocks" under the wheels; plug in the battery cart for power and put in the aileron locks to keep them from flapping in the breeze. While this was going on, another person would put the locks on the tail-rudder and elevators. Then you'd signal the captain that he could let loose of the brakes and the controls in the cockpit. We'd push the steps to the main door and the nose cart to the front of the aircraft. While the passengers deplaned, the pilots would help unload the cargo. Airline life was simple in those days.

The station manager's name was Cloyd W. Hollingworth. He was from Burley, Idaho and began working for Western in Pocatello, Idaho. His most recent assignment had been to open the El Centro, California, operation on January 1, 1946 as the station manager.

Cloyd had served in the Merchant Marines during the war. I always called him "boss," as though it was a nickname. Even in social settings I can't remember ever calling him by his first name. Years after he left Oakland I was still calling him, "boss."

One could not have asked for a better trainer. Cloyd had a rare quality of being your friend and your supervisor at the same time and conducted himself in a way that you never had to spend time delineating between the two. I watched these qualities in action and emulated them as I matured in the business. He was one of the two men who would shape my future success at Western Airlines.

In those days, even in small stations, we had personnel with the title of "passenger agent." It was their job to work the ticket counter and board the passengers. The rest of us were "cargo agents." My pay was $1.20 an hour and I never worked the ticket counter, for which I was very thankful. I handled weight and balance, air mail, air express and baggage. We were just in the process of getting a system together for "air freight." Up until then, all cargo outside of air mail moved as Federal Air Express. The only piece of equipment we had in common with passenger service was a teletype machine by which we sent and received our passenger and cargo load messages.

Western's reservation office was located in San Francisco and it served both San Francisco and Oakland. Our sales office was in the Leamington Hotel and the sales manager was Norm Kidd. Norm reported to Art Kelly, vice president sales division and we reported to Marvin J. Landes, VP service division. The reservation department was part of the service division.

In July of 1947, Western Airlines began handling the American Airlines operations in Oakland. At first, we had a morning departure to Dallas and an evening flight returning to Oakland. The flights originated and terminated in San Francisco. A little later, American set up an "interchange" of equipment with Braniff and National Airlines which provided single aircraft service from Oakland to New York, with stops at Dallas, New Orleans and Washington, D.C.

At certain times of the year, we used a National Airlines four engine aircraft. One day I overheard a passenger say, "I bought my ticket at American Airlines, Western checked my luggage and gave me a boarding pass and I'm now boarding a National Airlines aircraft. I sure hope they know where they're going."

By virtue of our handling the total American Airlines operation, I received a great deal of training in other types of procedures. This also gave me a broader picture of our industry as American was larger and, at that time, more highly organized.

During this period, I was promoted to a lead cargo clerk. My pay was increased ten cents an hour. That raise amounted to $17.33 a month which today seems an insignificant amount, but at that time had much more purchasing power. For example, our gas, electricity, water and telephone bills for one month came to a total of $16.23. Does that make the point? If it doesn't, try this one. Dinner for two at Bertola's Restaurant at Fisherman's Wharf in San Francisco was $3.25. This information was taken from the budget book we kept during the first few years of our marriage. One item in the book that jumps out at me is: "Ice cream soda at Edy's; 20 cents." Edy's was the top of the line ice cream parlor.

Western Airlines began service from the Los Angeles International Airport on December 9, 1946. I remembered it as Mines Field, where "air shows" were held when I was a young child. The next time I visited Mines Field was on occasions when Burbank was forecast to be below landing minimums and a crew of us would drive over to Mines Field and be on standby there in case our flights had to use it as an alternate. Our heaviest passenger offering was on the Los Angeles, San Francisco route.

Oakland had started receiving DC-4 flights as well as the DC-3's. In those days, people from our side of the bay seldom drove across the Bay Bridge and down the peninsula to catch a flight from the San Francisco Airport. Therefore, some flights made an Oakland stop or would "tag-end" from San Francisco to Oakland. This was a pattern that would continue for many years. I really enjoyed working the DC-4's. There were two upper cargo pits; one in back of the captain and one behind the copilot. Both were open areas surrounded by webbing. They wouldn't pass safety muster today.

Most of the pilots helped load and unload the upper pits. I'll give you one example. As the aircraft stopped at the gate and was secured with wheelchocks , I'd push out the nose-stand and Captain Sam Moser, wearing his ubiquitous baseball cap, would have the upper cargo door open, the webbing down and would be hollering at me to get a "move on" or he was going to throw the stuff out on the ground.

Many of the pilots had a strong drive to have an on-time departure. If the ground time was fifteen minutes, they wanted the wheels rolling in that time. That was a challenge when you had to unload, load, clear the ground equipment and start four engines within that allotted time; but, with the whole team pulling together, we'd do it.

We handled a lot of airmail from Oakland. The Post Office was not supposed to load over fifty pounds in a sack, but they'd put in as much as it would hold. Many would exceed the limit, especially around Christmas. I must have been in good shape in those days. I can recall standing on the ground and tossing those fifty-pound mail sacks, basketball style, from the ground to the doorway so the pilots could load them and save the time of working them up the platforms of the nose-stand.

The Civil Aeronautics Board (C.A.B.) granted Western authority to serve both Portland, Oregon and Seattle, Washington on August 1, 1947. This was a big move for us and put us "head to head" in competition with United Airlines. We began flying the route with DC-4's.

Western acquired ten Convair 240's in 1948. The first three were delivered in June. These were to replace the DC-4's which were not pressurized. They were used on the Pacific Coast route against United four-engine DC-6 pressurized aircraft, and I might add, not very successfully. They didn't carry enough cargo or enough gas. It seemed we were always restricted on the load we could carry, especially between Oakland and Portland. Working the "belly-pits" on this aircraft was a real test for a six-foot-four inch ramp person. I was often thankful I was both limber and skinny.

In those days, the fog in the Bay Area was a big problem. We were often the "alternate" for San Francisco when it fogged-in and, if we both closed, Half Moon Bay was used. We kept a lot of Greyline Buses in business during the winter operations. It was not unusual for San Francisco to close around eight at night while Oakland remained open. By midnight, the whole airport would be covered with various airlines' aircraft and most of us would work a sixteen-hour shift.

In January of 1949, Cloyd Hollingworth, the boss, decided to change all classifications at Oakland to station agent. The union allowed a station agent to work any position and therefore would give Cloyd greater utilization and flexibility in manpower scheduling. The "rub" was that an existing cargo clerk had to be approved by a station manager and the division vice president at corporate headquarters as a person with the qualities to work in passenger service, or, he must transfer to a station which utilized cargo clerks; for me, that would be San Francisco with a very long commute.

I had no desire to work the ticket counter. In fact, I was scared to death at the thought of having to work face-to-face with the passengers. I expressed this to the boss and he advised me to wait and see how things developed. Being somewhat panicked about my future at Western led me to seek work elsewhere. I applied at several places, one of which was the Metropolitan Life Insurance Company. They gave me a battery of tests, which I passed, and I was offered a job. Mentioning this to the boss got me a stern look and a lecture. He said, "I thought I told you to sit tight." The "lecture" contained a few other choice words of admonition and advice.

Cloyd Hollingworth seemed confident I'd be approved to fill one of the station agent positions and read me a paragraph from a letter he'd sent to Marvin Landes, VP of services, at the general office. Years later, I found a copy of this correspondence in my personnel file. Cloyd wrote:

January 21, 1949

Mr. Lee is well qualified for a station agent's duties due to his lengthy experience with the Company and has been doing station agent-type work for the past two years. His conscientiousness and his ability to apply himself to his duties make him, by far, the most valuable person I have at this station.

On February 1, 1949, age twenty-one, I was finally out of white overalls and into a uniform. Our uniforms were mocha brown with tan shirts and a dark brown tie. We also wore a cap with an emblem and wings over the pocket on our jackets. Big stuff! I was not totally convinced that I was progressing when I found my salary would stay the same, $225.00 a month and, I must pay for my own uniform.

Those who worked the ticket counter had to be familiar with all the American Airlines ticketing procedures as well as those of Western. I worked hard and Cloyd was both patient and helpful. I quickly realized that our passengers weren't that scary and began to look forward to my "turn" at the ticket counter.

The work performed in our reservation office was totally unfamiliar to me; therefore, on some of my days off, I drove to San Francisco and spent the day working in the office to become acquainted with their procedures. Looking back, I realize how helpful this was to me as it gave me the broader vision of our total "ground service" activities.

By the fall of 1949, Cloyd Hollingworth convinced the staff at the General Office that he needed to appoint three senior station agents to increase the supervisory coverage. On November 11, 1949, now twenty-two years old, I was appointed a "senior agent." With this came a $32.00 a month raise. I was the most senior employee of the three and chose to have weekends off. This was the first time I was off on the same days as my wife, Margie.

Western Airlines' early history has been recorded in several publications, which are well worth reading. As of this writing, there is not much recorded of the last ten years of Western, from 1976 to 1986. Therefore, I will try to be a little more comprehensive in writing about that period. Until then, there will be only short details of what was happening to Western as a company. This is not easy to do for I am tempted to talk about the industry as a whole.

The history of the airline industry is very exciting. By 1950, I knew it would be my lifetime career. I enjoyed every day at work and every new challenge offered to me. I used to tell Margie, "The first week I don't enjoy my job, I'll quit." This did not happen until the fall of 1982, but that's another story.

American Airlines was still relying on us at Oakland to take care of all their services. They now had two flights a day in each direction. Western had a morning departure to Los Angeles that left at the same time as the American flight to Dallas. One morning we got a call from the American Dispatch Office that one of our Los Angeles passengers was on the Dallas flight. A few days later, I spoke to the American Airlines stewardess who was on board that flight. She said they were on a southern course, and the pilot came on the cabin speaker to call attention to one of the points of interest. He then commented that they were expecting to arrive in Dallas on schedule. Our passenger leaped out of his seat, upsetting his meal tray and started shouting, "Dallas! Dallas!" As carefully as we checked gate passes, this repeated itself several times.

In April of 1950 we had a "night-coach" flight that went from Los Angeles to Seattle with stops at Burbank, San Francisco, Oakland and Portland. This was a heavy cargo flight inbound from the south, and we had a large passenger load boarding at Oakland, to go north. The southbound flight was a heavy cargo flight, but mostly shipments of flowers, which were easy to handle. The reason I mention this is that the southbound and northbound flights were often on the ground at the same time - that was around 2:15 a.m. I supervised the handling of the flights three nights a week, and that was enough. What a challenge! These were DC-4's, and they scheduled the ground time for fifteen minutes on each flight.

We received a lot of military personnel that had come in through Travis Air Force Base and were on their way to Seattle. Each person carried a huge duffle-bag. Since we were the last boarding station in the chain, we got all the "overage" problems. It was the "senior's" job to handle the oversold passengers. This really bothered me at first, but I quickly learned that most of the Army personnel were more than happy to wait for the next flight as long as you gave them dinner, a hotel room and a letter explaining why they were late.

The only time I can remember getting panicked was on a night when we got the passenger load out of San Francisco and found we were oversold twenty-seven passengers. Our people had all checked in. There were no passengers off at Oakland and just three empty seats. I called the Leamington hotel, booked rooms and got a Greyline bus on its way to the field. I then pulled three "emergency" type civilian passengers to one side and told them to go to gate five, which was way down in the non-scheduled airline area. The flight would not be called for arrival or departure. The other oversold passengers were paged to the counter and told the flight was cancelled. They were all military personnel returning from Korea who looked like they could use a good night's rest. We put them on the bus with their baggage and got them on their way to the hotel while the flight was being worked down the field at the "non-sked" gate. We never received a complaint. It set the record for handling the greatest number of oversales on one flight during that year.

In today's environment, we have a whole different set of methods and procedures for handling oversales. Some of our present resources were not available in those days - such as, the "buy-off" programs, where the passenger can get a free ticket and catch the next flight out of town. With more competitive schedules and greater frequency, passengers are quick to volunteer. Back in the early 1950's, there were occasions when we had flights with one person standing in the aisle, no empty seat and not one volunteer to deplane. There was a night when we had to get airport security to remove the last passenger boarded so the flight could depart. We had one such experience with a Dallas-bound American Airlines flight where I threatened to cancel it in Oakland if the "two-too-many-in-the-aisles" didn't get off. Other seated passengers were getting ready to do them bodily harm.

The challenges did not always pertain to our passengers. We had some interesting challenges handling cargo. Each station did not have the same ground-handling equipment. Los Angeles had a forklift to get a heavy piece of cargo in the pit, and all we had was a "nose-stand" to get it off. We finally got a hydraulic lift, which was out of service half of the time. Our reputation as a "quality cargo-carrier" didn't improve much when we had to drop a couple of four-hundred-pound pieces of freight from the aircraft door onto the ramp to get the flight out. Our advocate at the General Office, John Good, got this under control by getting us a "belt-loader."

We carried a lot of animal shipments in those days, from baby chicks to alligators. There were dogs, rats, hamsters, birds, etc. At one point in time, we handled the cargo delivery for Philippine Airlines. They would receive some large shipments of "fighting roosters." There was a mesh across one side of the cage and a printed notice, "Do Not Face This Cage toward Another." Our first alert that a shipment was on our dock was loud squawking and feathers flying. The delivery boy took delight in facing two "fighting roosters" toward each other, and we had to settle them down as you could hear the ruckus all over the terminal.

Cutter Laboratory, in Berkeley, got a lot of shipments of mice, rats and hamsters. I opened the rear "belly-pit" one day and a large box of hamsters had sprung a leak. There were fifty or sixty brown balls of fur scurrying around the cargo. We unloaded, got a broom and swept the pit clean. Reports came in for the next few days that there were loose hamsters showing up in the cargo bin. We believed it as we were chasing them around the ramp for a week. The same problem occurred with a shipment of parakeets, and for a long time we saw them in the trees.

One day, we opened the pit to find a four-foot alligator looking at us. He was a gift to a little zoo in Oakland. It had been in a wooden crate, which he demolished during the flight. A snapping alligator is a thrill to unload!

Dog shipments often created problems. As much as we schooled the personnel in not giving food or drink to a dog, unless they were inside with the doors shut, someone would let the dog out of the crate and it would escape; usually onto the wide open spaces of the airfield.

One such event was a dog that was some sort of champion, and she was shipped to Oakland to be bred to another champion. She got away and headed across the runways. There was a pack of wild dogs that roamed the airport and chased rabbits. This bitch, which was very much in "heat," joined the pack. We finally got clearance from the tower to go out on the field in the jeep to try to catch her. This was not as hard as we had thought as she was totally bushed from running from most of the male dogs in the pack. We put her back in the cage, and several hours later she was picked up by a kennel. When her pups were born, it was obvious the champion had not been the sire. We were threatened with court action for not protecting the dog. The case was dropped as it was obvious they could not prove where this mating event had happened. The dog had seemed happy.

Another such incident involved a puppy that had been shipped to someone whose good friend back east had a dog this family adored. They had been promised a puppy the next time the dog had a litter. The puppy got loose and disappeared. We never did find out what happened to it. Creativity kicked in and once again permission was obtained to access the dog-pack on the field. As luck would have it, there was a young dog running with them. It was somewhat mangy, but of the right gender. The dog pack was chased until the youngster tired and fell behind, at which time an employee threw a blanket over it and the dog seemed delighted to stop. We put the dog in the vacated crate and it was delivered. We never heard a word about it. My guess is the party receiving it did not dare say anything to the sender, and his kids probably fell in love with the mangy critter.

If I could assemble a half-dozen of the old "ramp-personnel," we could write a very long and funny book on those early days of the shipment of animals; but, enough of that for now.

On June 1, 1953, Cloyd Hollingworth asked me to come to his office. He'd asked several of the others to step in. He handed me an Annual Pass on Western, which an employee received after ten years of service. He then handed me a small box to open. Inside was my "ten-year" service pin and a hard rubber head of an Indian in full headdress. I thanked him for the pin and asked about the small bust of the Indian. Cloyd said, "He's a 'chief and so are you." It finally started to sink-in. "You mean I am now a chief agent?" "As of today," he responded. The boss had asked for approval of one assistant manager and, while I was the youngest among those considered, he had sold Phil Peirce, our director of stations, with the fact that no other person contending for the job knew anything about American Airlines.

I was to work a day shift on the weekends to cover for the boss and then work evenings on Monday through Wednesday. This wasn't much different from what I had been doing before becoming a senior station agent. I was given a $30.00 a month salary increase, but was told I would not be receiving overtime or shift differential. It was below the dignity of "management" to receive such things. The net result was a pay cut. That's the way it was in those days. If you expected to get ahead, you were obliged to sacrifice. Marvin Landes, our VP, ran a "tight-ship," and he alone approved all salary adjustments.

This made a change in vacation-relief coverage for the boss. Until my promotion, when he'd gone on vacation, they sent in someone to relieve him. Now I was the relief. This made Cloyd happy, for every time we had another management person in the station, he seemed to get American upset over some trivial thing. Example: Bruce Pickett was the acting manager and we received a "crisply" written note from the manager of cash receivables in Tulsa. Bruce had written "sour-grapes" across one of his letters of complaint and sent it back to him. When Cloyd returned, the roof was falling in and Bruce was merrily on his way to open the Palm Springs station for the winter.

Early in 1953, Western began flying Douglas DC-6B's. This was a sixty-six-passenger aircraft and a definite upgrade of the DC-4 as it was pressurized. Six of the seats were in a horseshoe configuration in the rear of the aircraft. These seats were never sold so our customers could use the area as a lounge. It was an excellent aircraft, and we were proud to have it begin service into Oakland. We had been using a DC-4 on flight 301 that originated at 8:00 a.m. for Los Angeles, with a stop at San Francisco. This came back to us at night as flight 336. The equipment overnighted in Oakland. This flight sequence was replaced with a DC-6B and became 601 and 636. We also had a "6B" on a flight through to the Pacific Northwest.

You may have noticed I have not mentioned any flights I had taken on Western. That's because I hadn't taken any flights on Western, or any other airline. One day Cloyd received a teletyped message from Marvin Landes about a meeting two days hence in Seattle to discuss the DC-6B cargo loading problems up and down the coast. He said, "Any management person at a pacific coast station who handles the DC6B is to attend." Cloyd left it in my file that evening with a note saying, "Do you think you can make it up and back by car without missing work?" I could see his grin written all over the note.

I took my first flight in nearly seven years from Oakland to Seattle and it was as frightening as I had imagined it would be. Fortunately, the "jump seat" in the cockpit was open on the return, and I flew up front with the pilots. This was much better. Much of the fear seemed to stem from my being in the back and not knowing what was transpiring up front. In those days any employee could fly in the jump-seat; so long as the captain approved.

That broke the ice and I was once again in the air; but very reluctantly. I did gird up my loins and take every newly-hired employee down to our General Offices at LAX (LAXGO) for an orientation visit. This was done on the one day of the week when we had double supervisory coverage. We'd leave on flight 601, returning that night on 636.

Dick Ensign was now director of inflight service and had designed a great meal presentation for the San Francisco/Los Angeles flights. He and Bert Lynn, director of advertising, collaborated on this program. They called it the "Californian" service. It is well described in Bob Serling's book, The Only Way to Fly. The only problem was for the flight attendants to find enough time to perform the whole service between these cities.

On every flight I took I would wind up helping pick up the meal trays or pass out orchids and cigars. But, it was a tremendous advertising advantage and, without a doubt, the best food service in the sky. Dick Ensign was a very creative man and demanded the best from those that did the catering. The two flight attendants who had to get this meal service completed were absolute geniuses in their delivery. The passengers quickly learned the routine, and it was not at all unusual to see one of them handing out the after dinner cigars.

On the night of April 20, 1953, I was getting ready to leave the coffee shop to prepare for the arrival of flight 636, when one of the agents came running in. I'm sure he meant to whisper in my ear, but it came out as a shout. "Flight 636 just crashed in the bay!" I was stunned. The control tower was on the phone and said they had lost his radar "blip" on the screen and assumed he'd crashed. They had called the Coast Guard and given the approximate location of where they had lost him.

When I got to the counter I paged anyone meeting passengers arriving on the flight and no one showed at the counter. The passenger-load message out of Los Angeles showed there were over a dozen Oakland-bound passengers. San Francisco called about that time to say some of the Oakland passengers had deplaned there. I heard later that there was a group of employees from the Kaiser Company returning to Oakland and some of them had cars at the San Francisco Airport. They had offered rides home to the Oakland passengers that worked for Kaiser. We began double-checking the actual count and determined there were five passengers on board.

By then, Cloyd was involved and he began working with the Coast Guard. Two of my favorite stewardesses were on board, Barbara Brew and Beverlee Nelson. I had also worked with Bob League, when he had been a mechanic. League had become a flight engineer and was married to one of the world's most wonderful ladies, Pat League; she later went to work for Western as a passenger agent in San Francisco. I had met Captain Clark but didn't know the Copilot. This was one of the longest nights of my career. I knew Cloyd would call as soon as he had word. We finally heard there were survivors, but we didn't know who or how many. Finally he arrived to tell us that there were survivors, Bev Nelson and a couple of passengers.

Much later, after all the investigation by the government agencies and safety boards had ended, one of the investigators told me two of the people that survived were doing things that were against "safety rules." Bev was sitting in the "lounge," which was not supposed to be used on landing. A passenger that survived was walking up the aisle when the plane hit. He had told the investigator that he looked out the window and could tell by the reflection of the lights on the water that they were practically in the water. He didn't know what to do, so he'd started up the aisle to bang on the pilot's door when the plane hit. He said the plane had banked to the left and the wing must have dipped into the water which threw the nose down. The front end separated and he found himself in the water. The tail section, where Bev was sitting, also separated.

I think one of the hard things for Bev Nelson, one she had a difficult time ever talking about, was that Barbara Brew got out of the crash alive. She was in the water near Bev clinging to a seat cushion. She told Bev she had no feeling from the waist down. Shortly after this, Bev looked over and she was gone.

We had a new employee that I was supposed to take to the LAXGO, (our General Offices at Los Angeles Airport). He'd only worked a short while when this happened. We had been scheduled to go to the LAXGO on 601 and back on 636, April 20th. He had called in sick, so I worked my normal shift that evening. He telephoned me after hearing about the crash on the morning news. He said, "Wasn't that the flight we were supposed to come home on?" I told him it was. We never saw him again.

There were several other accidents around Oakland, but this was the only one involving Western. United had one in the Hayward Hills, almost within sight of the airport. It happened on a clear moonlit-night. They never could figure out what happened. The UAL pilot just ran into the top of the hill and scattered down the other side.

The only serious accident at the Oakland Airport occurred in a very dense fog. The military had a GCA, (Ground Control Approach), system where they would watch the aircraft on their radar screen and talk the pilot right onto the runway. They'd bring them in very fast so they could "abort" the landing more easily if they got off course. They were set up for the left runway, and when I heard them on the tower monitor, I went out on the ramp to see if I could get a glimpse of the aircraft landing. I did this quite often as I couldn't believe they could come in under "zero-zero" conditions.

The day of the crash, the field had been closed all morning. It looked like we were "socked-in" for the day. I went out to the ramp and could hear the plane approaching. It was a DC-4. As I looked, I saw a flash of fire, heard the sound of an impact and then saw another flash. I had already started running across the field. When I got closer, I could see the major part of the aircraft in the sand, just off the left runway. Bodies were strewn all over the ground. As I got closer, the bodies started getting up. I couldn't believe my eyes.

Oakland Airport was a very small operation and the coffee shop was the only place to eat on the field. Therefore, all the news of what was happening, or what had happened, was disseminated there. One of the men working radar at the "GCA" station told me of the conversation he was having with the commander of this Navy aircraft. It had taken off from Moffett Field, on the San Francisco Peninsula, and was landing at Oakland to pick up some additional passengers. The controller began telling the pilot that he was too low on the "glide path." The pilot did not correct. He again said that he was too low. There was still, no correction by the pilot. The controller finally said he was too low and to pull up and go around. The pilot said he could see the runway and was going to land.

What the pilot saw was the mud flat, short of the airport. The tide was out and the mud was the color of the runway. There was a large "dike" built around the airport to serve as a "sea-wall" to keep the bay water out during high tides and high winds.

I put on my rubber boots and walked out onto the mud flat the day of the crash. I could see where the aircraft had "touched down" with the main landing gear. Then I could see where the nose wheel made contact with the mud. It was at that point where the pilot probably saw the rock "dike." You could see where the nose wheel left the mud; this was when he pulled up the nose of the plane to avoid contact. It was this last move that saved lives.

With the nose up, the aircraft hit the "dike" in an upward position and it bounced on over. One landing gear and a wing came off at that point. This was the first flash I had seen through the fog. The aircraft was then just to the left of the runway. It made contact again and the fuel tanks in the other wing exploded. That was the second flash I saw. What was left of the aircraft proceeded to slide along the sand in a "sideways" position and was moving away from the burning fuel. The whole side of aircraft seemed to peel back exposing the cabin. The passengers were spewed out of their seats and onto the sand. They were muddy and sandy, but alive. There were some injuries, but I was amazed at how they had fared, especially considering how fast those aircraft were required to land. Come to think of it, the extra speed probably saved them as the nose may not have otherwise raised enough for the aircraft to bounce over that high "dike."

The fire truck and ambulance from the base got to the scene of the accident about the same time I did. Shortly, there were other vehicles and a couple more ambulances to haul people off the field. There was one Navy enlisted man in his "blues" with muddy shoes. He was no dirtier than I used to get when walking through the fields in China to find our aircraft. I asked him if he had remained inside the aircraft until it had stopped. He replied, "No sir, nobody did." I said, "Then how come you're so clean?" He replied, in his southern drawl: "The plane hit something and the next thing I knew I was hurled toward a bulkhead, but the bulkhead disappeared and I was in the open. I said, legs get a movin' - we're in trouble. I lit a-runnin' and never fell down."

Sadly, there was one fatality. One of the female flight attendants had been buckled into what we called a "MacArthur Chair." Somehow, it had been thrown out at an odd angle and came down in the middle of the runway. I was the first to reach her and she was still strapped into the chair. She was killed on impact. It was a great miracle that the others were spared. Pieces of aircraft were strewn all over the south end of the airport.

These experiences did not dampen my enthusiasm for the airline industry, but I only flew when I had to. I'm sure there are fewer "Pass Requests" in my personnel file than any other airline employee.

On January 11, 1954, Western's president, Terrell C. Drinkwater, called a general conference of all management personnel. It was held at the new Statler Hotel in downtown Los Angeles. It was the first time in the history of Western Airlines that all the management team had been brought together at one time. The conference lasted three days. One of the great tributes to our employees was that the whole Western Airlines system ran flawlessly during those three days.

There were a few familiar faces from the service division, but most of the folks who attended were only names that were occasionally mentioned. Our president, Terrell C. Drinkwater, was in rare form. He was at his best in and around a group of his employees. He made a point to shake the hand and have a few words with each person there, and I doubt that he missed anyone. As usual, I was the youngest person at the conference. Drinkwater gave the opening address. In his remarks, he outlined the organization of the "Executive Staff." At that time the Company was small and the corporate officers were few.

Following is the lineup:

OPERATIONS - under vice president Shatto, with 797 people.

SERVICE - under vice president Landes, has 730 people.

TREASURY - under vice president Taylor, has 119 people.

SALES - under vice president Kelly, numbers 109.

ADMINISTRATION - under vice president Paul Sullivan, 47.

Stan Shatto and Marvin Landes were on the board of directors and represented the company along with Terry Drinkwater. At that time, there were nine other members of the board. It was Drinkwater's strategy to have the nine selected in such a way that Western was represented in our major geographical areas of service.

The main thrust of the conference was for each member of management to become acquainted with the responsibilities of the others. The five division VP's gave presentations and called upon their department directors to do the same. The secondary objective was to "rub elbows" with one another during the evening socials and planned dinners so that we could feel more like one big family. In my estimation, both objectives were met. This was to be the last system-wide meeting of this sort. Everything within the industry was changing too fast to pull all the management into such a setting.

Cloyd Hollingworth told me that I had made a favorable impression on several of the key people in our service division and in sales. He knew how uncomfortable I felt at being the "newest and youngest" member of the team.

Western leased a "nose-hangar" for our one overnight flight. This was located at the entrance to the airport, just south of the "non-sked" terminal. After the night flight was unloaded, we would tow the aircraft to the hangar and then clean it for morning departure. The crews would sleep in the upper two rooms of the hangar, pilots on one side and the two flight attendants on the other. There were a couple of major complaints; only one bathroom and no shower, and, the city dump for San Leandro was right across the street. The fires lighted the sky all night and there were only slatted bamboo curtains on the windows. We finally got better drapes, but still no shower.

It wasn't long before we had a mechanic assigned to Oakland. He was on the midnight shift and, if there was a major problem, he would get reinforcements from San Francisco. The mechanic would try to be as quiet as possible, but that's tough to do when you're messing around with a metal aircraft. I don't think the crews got much rest and this wasn't a very popular "line of flying."

The only time I had trouble towing the aircraft was during a fog operation, and we had to get two planes into the hangar area. The asphalt apron sloped up on the south end. I pulled the plane up on the slope and made a left turn. The employee who was watching my wing tip yelled for me to stop. I was now heading down hill and the tiny tractor, one that was only meant to pull baggage carts, finally slid to a halt. No one rode the brakes in the cockpit on these nights - it was a Spartan operation.

The wing of this aircraft was almost against the top of a lamppost that was next to the sidewalk on the other side of the fence. I tried to back up. It was impossible; the little tug wouldn't budge the big aircraft. We were too proud to call for help and, finding a sledgehammer in the mechanic's shop, I proceeded to knock the top off the street light, glass and all. I positioned the other employee on a ladder to watch the wing to make sure I had clearance when I released the brakes on the tug. The wing had only an inch or so of clearance, but we made it. I was wringing wet and it was a cold night.

When our mechanic drove into work that night and saw the top of the lamppost had been knocked off, he nearly had a heart attack. He was sure he'd find an aircraft with a damaged wing tip. Where was the flight crew while all this was going on? They'd been shown pity and were now staying at the Alameda Hotel.

Cloyd Hollingworth was notified that he was to transfer to Denver as the new station manager. This was a fine promotion for him. Cloyd was told to go to Denver immediately, and I was asked to be the "acting station manager" at Oakland until a new permanent manager could be selected. This was a blow to me for I enjoyed working with Cloyd and, while I knew he was qualified for more than he was doing, I just hadn't faced the possibility of his being transferred.

Phil Peirce, director of stations, called me from Los Angeles and said I was one of four people under consideration for the job. Somehow, Cloyd found out who the other three were and shared this with me. They were all older and senior to me in their management experience. I had pretty well resigned myself to having a new boss.

At that time, we had a procedure in place whereby any passenger complaint made to Western's headquarters would go to the VP, Marvin Landes, and his assistant, Merrill Morris, would "register" it, meaning that this file would have a number assigned and was then sent to the local station manager where the problem occurred. These were to be handled immediately and personally by the manager. He was to make a personal call on the individual who made the complaint, offer apologies and then send in a report to the division VP outlining the highlights of the visit. One of these arrived shortly after Cloyd left for Denver. It was from a Mr. Blue who was an Oakland attorney. Seems we didn't hold a flight for him. He claimed to have been at the airport ten minutes before departure. I tossed it in the file for the new manager to handle when he arrived.

That night, I couldn't sleep and was very apprehensive about something that I could not identify. This was unusual for me, as I was one who could fall asleep on a "two-by-four." The next day was more of the same feeling of discomfort. I went over all my activities and the only thing that kept popping into my mind was the "registered" file from Merrill Morris. I decided that it was not proper for me to delay the handling of the file and I called Mr. Blue for an appointment.

I'd never been on such a call as this and was uncomfortable when his secretary took me into his office. There was no need for concern. Mr. Blue was impressed that I'd take the time to come see him. As we parted he smiled and said he'd get to the airport earlier and that he really did appreciate our "on-time" performance. Back at the office, I made some notes on the file and tossed it in the basket for the new manager. That night I was as restless as before and knew by now there was something special I was supposed to do with this file.

The next day was very busy as our secretary was on vacation, so I took the file home that evening and wrote a letter to our VP, Marv Landes, outlining the call I made to Mr. Blue and the favorable outcome. Margie typed the letter for me and it was in the mail pouch the next morning for LAXGO. That night I slept like a baby.

A few days later, August 8, 1955, Phil Peirce called me and said: "Congratulations, you're the new manager at Oakland." He asked me to delay a vacation I had planned until I could select a new chief agent, but wanted me to come to LAXGO to visit on a few matters. I saw him a couple of days later and he went over my assignment. He then asked me to go visit with John Good and Ed Hallgren, the superintendents of stations.

As I was leaving his office, Phil said: "By the way, you might be interested in the background of how you happened to be selected for this job." He said: "The committee on the new management appointments was meeting in the conference room, and we had made our decision on the Oakland position - we'd passed you by because you lacked depth in management experience. The meeting was about to adjourn when Merrill Morris came in and said we should look at a 'registered file' that had just arrived from Larry Lee in Oakland. We read it and saw a side of you that none of us knew existed; the very thing we felt you were lacking, which was the absence of any management training or experiences beyond the direct operation of the airline. Your handling of this file was discussed and the prior decision regarding our selection for the new Oakland manager was reversed. The way you handled that complaint got you the promotion to station manager Oakland."

As I now look back on the pathway of my career with Western Airlines, I can see there were higher powers involved in my obtaining this assignment. The handling and timing of my actions were no natural coincidence.

This was singularly the greatest "pivotal-point" in my career. Later I could see that without this appointment, I would not have been in the right places nor had the unique opportunities to develop the skills that played such an important part in my future.

American Airlines treated Western's operation in Oakland as one of their own; therefore, we were on the station mailing list. We also kept a full set of their manuals. American was lagging behind Western in certain areas, but organizationally was well ahead. For example, they did a lot of passenger-service training and had some good training materials. Fare construction was becoming more complicated and American had an excellent outline of how to train a new employee in the procedures of ticketing. I adapted this to Western's system and began using it as a refresher with all the agents. Our ticketing errors decreased. They also had some good material on how to improve customer relations. These, too, became the basis for our station training. This did not happen all at once. It took a great deal of evening writing, typing and printing to get it up to speed.

Ed Hallgren was our regional superintendent at the time and had heard about some of the materials we were using. He came up to see them and asked if he could have copies. I continued to develop new methods and, from the comments made by others, felt we were well ahead of the rest of the system in the training we did at Oakland.

The supervisors that reported to me were fine men and did a good job of training. They found me to be a bit "over-structured" in my communications. I admit that I was, and always have been an "over-communicator." An example of this was the problem I had making contact with the supervisor on the late shift who didn't come in until 7:00 p.m. There was a filing cabinet just inside the cargo-room door and each person had a file for personal mail. I'd leave notes in the file folder of the evening supervisor relating to things that had to be done. One night I came back to the office just as the senior station agent, Doug Brown, was pulling the day's notes out of his file. As I approached the door, I heard him say: "That note-writing-son-of-a-bitch." My momentum carried me through the door. He looked at me, smiled and said: "Well, you are!"

Doug and his wife had a lovely home in the hills of Castro Valley. He was proud of his garden. Knowing we often went to the mountains, he had once asked if I'd pick up some big rocks for his yard. When we hauled some building logs up to the cabin, we had a hydraulic lift on the back of the truck we rented. On the way back, my friends and I rolled a huge rock onto the lift and brought it home. It was late at night when we arrived and we quietly backed into Doug Brown's driveway and left the rock right in front of his garage door. He had to get the neighbors to help move it so he could get the car out. I think I left a note in his file saying we were now even. In any event, he was so happy with his rock that he decided not to retaliate.

My access to American's materials stopped suddenly when our non-management employees, those represented by the Brotherhood of Railway Clerks, went out on strike.

On January 10, 1956, I came out early to open the operation - having been called by LAXGO regarding the strike. I found the door open and three of the agents were standing in the cargo room reading the messages on the teletype machine. I asked if they were working. They said that they were on strike, so I ordered them off the property. Ken Ford, the chief agent, came in and Bill Patz, who had been a station agent and was now in our sales office, showed up to help out. The three of us got the morning flight on its way. American's San Francisco manager sent some help for their flights.

The next day, Fred Friedli transferred from American's Los Angeles Regional Office to be the new station manager for American at Oakland. They had been considering taking over their own operations and Western's strike made up their minds. Fred had been a regional auditor and we had met on a couple of occasions. I worked with him to get their operation going and we became close friends.

The strike lasted two months and it took a while to regain the connection with the rank and file. We slowly brought back the team as we gained more flights, but some were not to return because of our loss of American's flights. Several of our people tried to get on with American, but they would not hire our strikers. As I remember, we settled the pilot's contract during the strike and Western was back up to a full schedule by April 1, 1956. It was tough to lose the American operation. It had created a great deal of extra work for me, but also provided a real edge on some advanced industry practices.

I suggested that Fred Friedli and I have lunch together each Friday at The Cottage; a local family restaurant in San Leandro. We finally invited the other two managers to join us. Charley Lovett, the UAL manager, replaced Hunter Manson about the time Cloyd left. Since Fred, Charley and I were new managers, we had much in common and developed a good rapport with one another. There was never a problem between our operations that lasted beyond the Friday luncheon.

Hunter Manson of UAL had been somewhat of a "bear," but he had a great sense of humor and loved to be "one-up" on the other managers. For example, one of our new employees reported to United by mistake. He was sent to Hunter who then put him to work in cargo. That afternoon, he came to us and said, "We appreciate your sending us some extra help today. He's welcome to stay as long as you'll let him, but he's on your payroll."

Charley Lovett later transferred to Monterey, California and retired there. Fred went to manage American's big flight training center in Texas and finally retired to the coast of Oregon. Those guys, and many more like them, were the unsung heroes of the aviation industry during its period of post-war growth.

Chapter 3
THE MOVE TO PHOENIX

Midway through the summer of '57, Phil Peirce called me and said the Civil Aeronautics Board examiner had recommended Western as the carrier to begin serving Phoenix to Denver and Phoenix to Los Angeles, by way of San Diego. We did not presently serve Phoenix. He went on to say that I was currently the "front-runner" to open that location if we received the final go ahead from the "CAB." Phil wanted me to be thinking about the possibility of a move. I held the information until Margie and I went to our mountain cabin for a one-week vacation.

When I gave her the news, it was received with the enthusiasm of a care package full of menus. She had never thought of having to move away from the environment we had created during the past eleven years. My salary was now more than the two of us earned when we bought our home and we were "debt-free," except for the very low house payment. Our lifestyle was about as comfortable as one can get.

Margie asked what I thought of the move. I responded with a longer-range view of my situation. I reminded her of the goals I'd set when I was made the manager of Oakland station. One of those goals was to be in the General Office in Los Angeles in five years; preferably in a position where I could develop a training program for Western. I reminded her that the realization of this goal would require a move. Also, the chances of my achieving this would improve if I were given the opportunity to start a new operation.

It would be a more challenging environment to test training theories and develop new procedures.

The answer I gave was obviously not the one she wanted to hear. There were several reasons she could see for not making a move at this time. First, she was pregnant. Second, we had never been to Phoenix and she was picturing a town full of "wigwams" with streets full of cowboys. Last, and possibly of most importance, we would be leaving her family. She had never been separated from them for very long and now was depending on her mother to help with the children.

Cloyd Hollingworth was taken into my confidence. He was very close to Jerry Brooder, regional VP of government affairs at Western Airlines. Jerry resided in Denver and kept an office at the airport. He told Cloyd that he felt we were a "shoo-in" for the route. He said the City of Phoenix honchos and the Airport Manager, Bill Ralston, were pulling for United Airlines, but we'd get it. I called Phil Peirce and asked if it was all right to take Margie to Phoenix and see what was there. He agreed. I went down by way of Los Angeles to get some business out of the way. Margie flew in the next evening on TWA.

I had carefully mapped out a route to get to our hotel that evening; leave the airport, turn right to Washington and left to Central and then drive up Central to see the city at night. As we left the airport, I turned left and wound up getting lost in the middle of the stinking pig farms. Margie was not impressed. I was able to recover my status as tour guide the next day with lunch at Camelback Inn and a trip around Scottsdale to look at housing. She was still not completely sold but felt much better about the city.

Western received the "go-ahead" to fly out of Phoenix and Phil Peirce confirmed that I was to open the Phoenix Airport operation. He said that he wanted me to get started as soon as possible. There was no suitable space for us at the airport, therefore I'd have to be involved with a construction job to get things rolling.

My appointment was official on October 16, 1957, and we were to begin operations on the first of December. I immediately left for Los Angeles to meet with a few people who would be involved with the "start-up." When I stopped by Phil's office he said he had confirmed my salary as $555.00 a month, a $45.00 raise. By this time, Margie was making nearly $400.00 a month. This was to be the biggest cut in income I would ever experience, percentage wise, that is. Margie never returned to work.

As I left the office of Phil Peirce he said, "Would you stop by public relations and go over the press release they are sending to Phoenix. They've gone through your personnel file and find three different dates of birth. Tell them how old you are and get your records straightened out with Ernie Brown in Personnel." I was thirty and was still the youngest manager on Western's system, but I decided it was time to confess. I had to get an up-to-date picture taken for the press release, and I remember putting on the sternest look I could get away with to signal that I was not some youngster who could be pushed around.

The day I arrived in Phoenix, I was greeted by a headline in the local newspaper stating that Western was battling with the airport manager over where they were to be located in the terminal. Our VP, Marv Landes, had been to Phoenix ahead of me and told Bill Ralston, the Airport Manager, that he wanted Western located in the "Game-Room." This was a small room to the left as you walked in the front door of the terminal. It contained a bunch of pinball machines and was the single biggest money maker, per square foot, at the airport. My first job was to peel Bill Ralston off the ceiling.

We finally settled for a much better area at the end of the present ticket counters. It would give us a larger cargo room and was closer to the gate for any late check-ins. There was no space for a manager's office, so one was made available at the other end of the terminal. I was never in the office when flights were on the ground, so it didn't matter.

To get the construction finished and the equipment in place required ten to twelve hours a day, seven days a week. The last bits of our space came together within a few days of the first flight. I remember that the baggage scales arrived late. They were put in place and then, the day before our first flight, I discovered they must be "certified" by some agency or other. I got in touch with one of the inspectors and asked if he could meet me that evening. All I got was a chuckle. I told him we were the "Champagne" Airline and that a case of our samples would be used for testing the scales and whoever happened to be around could take it home. He was there that evening and we were ready to go the next day.

The original schedule was all DC-6B's, one turnaround and four through flights; two to San Diego and two to Denver. The Denver flights went on to Minneapolis and those to San Diego went through to Los Angeles and then on up the coast. We started with a goal to have the best "on-time" performance on the system and we were always near the top.

The days of the pilots helping to load the aircraft were gone. We had two ship-cleaners to take care of the aircraft that "overnighted" in Phoenix. On the first morning, we were loading the aircraft and two of them were sitting on the fence watching. I went to the "lead," George Creason, and asked that they help load the cargo. He said that they didn't do that work. Later in the day I called their boss, Tony Favero, and asked him to get these guys out of Phoenix; they were just costing us money and we could handle the cleaning. Tony flew over the next day and there was no more "fence-sitting." George told me later that he got in a bind with the union but didn't want to let Tony down.

The other members of the Phoenix team were Bill Kellogg, sales manager, and Max Petty, reservations manager. They were both located at the Sahara Hotel in the middle of the downtown area. Max Petty was moving quickly to have the reservation Office up to speed. Much of the success in filling seats out of Phoenix was depending upon his ability to get the phones answered.

When the staffing for both the field and reservations was approved, we were not overly surprised to see a very senior group of people bidding for the vacancies. To this day, Phoenix is one of the most "senior" stations on the system. My secretary, Janet Weller, was the only local person I hired. Our maintenance was contracted out to TWA. Sky Chef, a subsidiary of American Airlines, handled the food service. This was the first time I'd worked with a caterer and it proved to be a very rewarding experience.

Western's inflight department, under the direction of Richard P. Ensign, my old boss from Salt Lake City days, was in high gear with its "Champagne" flights. Freeman Fish, Sky Chef's Catering Manager at Phoenix, was the best draw I could have made to start a new station. He really went out of his way to teach me the finer points of food preparation and equipment handling. He also ran an excellent dining room in the terminal. Our quality control standard was to get feedback on the meal service within twenty-four hours. I'd review these personally with Freeman. The comments from the stewardesses helped more than anything else. They would take the time to write-up any suggestion that came to mind, and it was most always "constructive criticism."

For the first few weeks, I worked all seven days. A smooth start meant a strong foundation for the future. I was later to learn from my secretary that the employees had given me a nickname, "The Hawk." It was because I was always hovering around. Well, "The Hawk" deserted them on the 23rd of December. Mother Lewis called me at the airport to say I now had a little daughter. I took the next westbound flight to Oakland.

Early on, there was a board of director's meeting held in Phoenix and a stewardess graduation. This provided a lot of good public relations. Ray Silvius had returned to work for Western. Earlier in his career, he had worked for one of the Phoenix newspapers. He always got good press in his "hometown paper."

The airport manager, Bill Ralston, finally came around. It took him awhile to get over his disappointment at not getting United Airlines into Phoenix. The managers of the other airlines were not as close to one another as I had been used to in Oakland. There was a lot more pushing and shoving to get the job done. This was partly due to the cramped quarters we were in at the Terminal. Phoenix was growing rapidly and the terminal was far too small to accommodate the expansion.

We had no more than developed a smooth routine when I received a call from LAXGO on the night of February 21, 1958, advising our pilots had gone out on strike. I was told to give furlough notices to everyone in the station. Within days, there were only the three managers employed at Phoenix. My boss, John Good, regional superintendent of stations, told me to lock up everything at the airport and start answering the telephones at Western's Sahara Reservations Office. It looked like this was going to be a long strike.

After a month of this, we were advised to take our full vacations on a rotating basis as we had to keep the reservations lines open. Max Petty went first. Bill Kellogg and I split the remaining time. As Margie and I were trying to decide what to do for vacation, and considering the fact that we were told we might have our pay reduced, we had pretty well decided to stay home and get acquainted with Arizona. This changed quickly when we were advised that Jim Montgomery, ex-Western employee and now one of the marketing heads at Pan American Airways had worked out a package for any of Western's management who had been pushed into taking an unplanned vacation. The place was Hawaii.

So, off we went on Margie's first trip to Hawaii. We flew over on a Pan American Boeing "Stratocruiser" which had sleeper seats and a lower lounge area. It was the plane with a "built-in headwind." As I recall, the flight took about eleven hours.

Pan Am had arranged for a free "lanai-room" with an ocean view at the Reef Hotel on Waikiki Beach. We were there for eight days. Our Hawaii vacation ended all too soon and I was back in the reservations office in downtown Phoenix.

One memory I have of working in that office is during the period that Max Petty, manager of reservations, was on vacation. He had set up a telephone message that played when the office was not staffed. Bill Kellogg called from home and said, "While Max is gone, will you change that telephone message? Max must have been in a bad mood when he made the recording for it sure sounds somber." That night I got out my bass ukulele and wrote a song. An Academy Award production it wasn't - but, it had a very catchy tune and the lyrics portrayed the various things Western was doing at that time to market our service; these included free champagne for all adult passengers and Hawaiian orchids for the ladies onboard. Here are the lyrics:

"Dear Sir, or madam, if it be, our date to fly, is still a mystery,
But this I promise, we're saving for you
A glass of champagne, an orchid of purple hue.
So friend, we ask you 'please call again,' and then
We may have some news that won't give you the blues."

The next morning, I took my ukulele to work and sang the song into the answering machine. We were only getting six or seven calls a day, so this was just a joke. I called Bill Kellogg and told him there was a new message on the machine and to call in to hear it. I hung up the phone and turned it to automatic answering. I heard it click on. When it had rewound, I turned it off.

The phone rang and I said, "Well, what do you think, is it less somber?" A female voice said, "Hello, who is this?" I responded, "Oh, this is Western Airlines Reservations, may I help you?" The female voice continued, "When I called a minute ago, there was someone singing a song." "Sorry about that, we were just testing equipment." "Well," she said, "my neighbor doesn't have a phone yet and I asked her in to listen to it, would you mind playing it for her?" I turned it back on and it went through its cycle. Finally, the phone rang once more. I answered, "Western Airlines Reservations." It was Bill Kellogg and his voice was a bit edgy. "What's going on down there, I can't get anything but a busy signal." "Bill," I said, "let's just forget the whole thing." Neither he nor anyone else at Western ever heard what might have been one of the first airline singing commercials.

The strike ended on June 9, 1958, and things soon settled into a routine pattern. We were granted permission to fly non-stop to Los Angeles. This improved our competitive product a great deal.

We at Phoenix had some flights dropped that first summer because of light loads. Our heavy periods were now early morning and late afternoon. The two times were too far apart to be covered by one shift. Our employee contract allowed management to implement a number of "split-shifts" in such a situation. To the dismay of the employees, I used that provision to solve my coverage problem. I had a few station agents working four on, four off and four on; rounding out a twelve-hour day.

At that time I went to some of the local hotels and asked for a free room and swimming privileges for the employees and their families. I didn't have one refusal. This gave those on the "split shifts" a chance to be with their families during the period when they had four hours of slack time. The complaining stopped and when the employee union negotiated that the "split-shifts" be eliminated, our Phoenix employees were screaming louder than when I had implemented the program. They had found the hot summer months went by more easily with the mid-day leisure time with their families.

Freeman Fish, of Sky Chef, was transferred to Denver and while I missed his quality management, the catering equipment balance improved on the flights from Denver. Freeman did not forget his friends. We had three good senior station agents running the operation; Grady Martin, Jim Merrigan and Lou Dooley. Lou Dooley and I had worked together in Oakland and the other two were worried about favoritism. This was quickly dispelled when they learned we were a team, not individuals. Later on, it was decided that we needed a chief agent in Phoenix. I felt Grady Martin was ready, but others thought there were some more senior people to be considered. Woody Larson was the finalist and proved to be an excellent lieutenant.

Our training program and station procedures continued to have my highest priority. Jack Slichter, director of reservations, toured the system with a presentation on "personal appearance and passenger relations." This was followed by a test. Before his arrival I had set up training sessions to review the basics of what I knew to be his objectives. Following his visit to Phoenix, I received the following letter from our division VP, Marvin W. Landes:

It is noticed that Phoenix now has the highest test score in the Passenger Relations Program. Congratulations! It is understood that you have an extensive training program underway. The score indicates this type of training pays dividends. Keep up the good work.

This was the first real "test" of how we would measure against the other stations on the system. It was a "red-letter" day.

By now, we had introduced the turbo-prop Lockheed "Electra" to the fleet. Phoenix didn't get them at first. They began service in competition with United Airlines on the Pacific Coast. I had mixed emotions when Phoenix inaugurated the "Electras." It was an electrical "monster," and we had no maintenance support at Phoenix trained to handle the problems that developed. Our on time performance went down. However, we soon got a couple of well-qualified mechanics from Los Angeles to train the TWA maintenance group on how to fix some of the basic troubles. Our maintenance service in Phoenix was contracted to TWA. Tony Favero, director of maintenance, also set up a "hot-line" for us to communicate with the electrical technicians in Los Angeles when things went sour. It all worked out and our performance improved.

We had a turbine "air-start" unit for the aircraft that was built in Phoenix. One day we couldn't get the aircraft to accept the air from the turbine and the engine wouldn't turn over. The flight engineer happened to be an ex-mechanic. He came out and said he thought the valve that was supposed to open to accept the air had frozen shut because of the high heat in Phoenix. He asked if I had a hammer. I got him one. He told me to crank up the ground "air start" unit. When it was up to speed, he gave a spot inside a little door a couple of taps with the hammer and the engine started turning over. He closed the flap and they departed.

A week or so later, this same plane was through Phoenix and the engine wouldn't accept the air. The captain told us to call TWA maintenance. I went in and got my hammer, opened the little door, and when our ground "air-start" was up to speed, tapped on the valve. I asked the captain to try it again and the propeller started turning and the flight was out of there. The captain was giving me a weird look as he taxied away, but I never heard anything about my hammering.

It was fun to watch the "Electra" takeoff. It would rise like an elevator and its engines made a very distinctive sound of power. It was much faster than the DC-6B, but we still enjoyed working the older Douglas aircraft; it was, and always will be, my favorite. The book, The Only Way to Fly, is full of tales about the "Electra" and its subsequent problems. It also documents the serious effort that was going into Western's bid for a route to Hawaii. Therefore, I'll only make a few comments about this.

Boeing 707's were introduced to our fleet when we leased two that Cubana Airlines was not able to finance when Fidel Castro took over Cuba. These were to be used to fly to Hawaii; but until that case was decided, they were flown on the Pacific Coast.

Jerry Brooder, VP government affairs, and his wife, Wanda, were frequent visitors to Phoenix; that was after their daughter and her husband moved to Scottsdale. Jerry and I often had lunch or dinner together. One day I asked Jerry if he'd seen what was happening to an area north of Scottsdale called Carefree. He hadn't even heard of it. I told him he should see it, and the next day Margie and I drove Jerry and Wanda out for a preview of what was to become their retirement home. It was all dirt roads with building lots selling for as low as $4,000.00. They both saw the potential of the area and were ready to pick a lot.

On one of these visits, Jerry told me that T. C. Drinkwater, Western's president, was too deep in cement on our application for Hawaii and this was really disturbing Jerry. He told me he had gotten a call from a high-ranking person in Washington who said, "If you had your choice of a major part of the Southern Transcontinental Case or the route to Hawaii, which would you take?" Jerry said that he had responded that he would take the "Southern Routes," but doubted that made any difference because Drinkwater was going "all-out" for Hawaii. The person then asked Jerry to contact Drinkwater and offer him the choice. He did, and received the answer he had anticipated. Jerry said this was a major error in Western's strategy. He had no reason to be sharing this with me, but I had the feeling that he was so frustrated he had to talk to someone.

Many times over the years, I have thought of this "unauthorized" offer and the decision that was made. I wondered what Western's future would have held if Drinkwater had listened to Brooder and Renda on this matter; Jerry said Dom Renda felt as he did. Continental got a large piece of the Southern Trans continental Case and began service to Phoenix from Los Angeles with flights that went on into the south and southeast sector of the United States.

Western got C.A.B. approval to fly to Hawaii, and it was immediately rescinded by a "request" from President Eisenhower on his last day in office; the rumor prevailed around the industry that he was taking care of his friends at Pan American Airways. We did not receive permission to fly to Hawaii until 1969. At that time, Continental also received authority to serve Hawaii. The Southern Transcontinental award gave Continental a new vitality and also put them in a better position than Western to receive permission to fly to Hawaii. History would have taken a much different "tack" if Drinkwater had listened to Jerry Brooder and his staff. Also, Continental would have been in a much weaker competitive position in the 1960's.

The City of Phoenix had finally cleared the way for a new Airport Terminal. I was on the committee and Jim Keefe, director of property, was supervising our efforts from LAXGO. I had worked with Jim on a new terminal for Oakland, so this wasn't virgin territory for me. With Continental coming into Phoenix, we were really functioning in a "shoe box." Still, we ran a solid operation. Phoenix was reassigned to John Good, regional superintendent, and he came over to see how the station was operating. We had an afternoon departure that was our best on-time performer. We, in Phoenix, had put a real team effort together to design a "split-second" on-time departure for each flight. It took a great deal of cooperation between the ticket counter and the gate. John had heard me brag about the team and was betting we wouldn't make schedule; we had nearly a full load for Los Angeles.

All our employees synchronized their watches with the electric clock at the ticket counter. I told John to set his watch to match this time. We watched the ticket-counter activity and then walked out to the gate to watch the boarding and loading. It was three minutes to departure and things were not all folded up and ready to go. He said, "You lose." Then, as if by some automated system, doors closed, steps rose and the engines were starting. I said to John, "Look at your watch when the wheels begin rolling." Just as the second hand was coming up on the departure time, the wheels were in motion.

The team knew what was going on and came off the field beaming from ear to ear. I don't know that we could have done it that well twice in a row, but John Good was impressed and I was sure proud of my people.

The employees decided to have an annual picnic at a park on South Mountain. The first year it was a "trial-balloon" but went smoothly enough that they did it again the next year. That was the fall of 1960. I volunteered to do some "pit-roasted" potatoes and got the steaks from Sky Chef at wholesale. We had a good turnout that evening and, after dinner, they had planned to do some singing around the campfire. Without saying anything to anyone, I brought along my guitar. When the time came for the singing, I got it out of the car and offered to start off with a song. Their mouths dropped open. They had never heard me sing nor did they think I'd do anything so "earthly." It was great fun.

When Janet Weller, my secretary, came in the next morning, she said: "Well, you sure blew your image last night." I asked what she meant. "No one had seen that side of you before and you are no longer the 'stuff-shirt-boss' they thought they had." I wasn't sure if this was good or bad, but it was fun, and the only difference I noticed was a more responsive BRAC Union Representative who had been one of the key organizers of the successful affair.

During the winter of 1960/61, I talked with Art Neff, of Avis, and we worked out a plan to have some Western Airlines folks move cars to Denver. He would pay them for the fuel and enough to cover an overnight stay en route. He would also allow four days to get the car to Denver. This event was big enough to warrant a special announcement. My son, Richard and I drove out past Mesa where there was a wide, rocky stretch of the Salt River. He put on his "back-pack" and I loaded it up with some colorful, smoothly polished rocks; no larger than a small fist. I painted them with eyes, nose and mouth and called them, "Howling Stones" - they had a big painted mouth.

I sent one of these stones to each of our key sales and service people with a letter, encouraging them to come to Phoenix on their vacations and drive through Arizona to become better acquainted with the beautiful State we'd been "howling" about. Bill Kellogg, our sales manager, thought it was great. I quickly received a call from Art Kelly, VP of sales and was ready for his commendation, but all I got was a "chewing-out" for not coordinating this with his staff. Well, it was good to be humbled from time to time. It kept me in line. We had a fair turnout of drivers and they loved the scenery. I saw the "Howling Stones" on desks around the system being used for paperweights. If I'd just called them "Pet Rocks," our future might have been different.

During that winter, P. E. Peirce, director of stations, sent a few managers out into the field to address some specific problems that needed improvement. I was given "baggage service." This project was finished in a week and a full report of recommendations documented to Mr. Peirce. The results of these tasks were reviewed at a special ground services department meeting at the Miramar Hotel in Santa Monica. I often thought that this would be an excellent way of testing those who showed interest in "staff" work to check their analytical and documenting skills. I found a copy of my report while preparing this autobiography. I think I'd have flunked the test.

Life started to settle into a wonderful routine. My salary was now to a point that we could eat more than tamale pie; we had a nice group of folks around us, and as Bishop of the Scottsdale Ward in the LDS Church, I was contributing my time to a community beyond just Western; things couldn't have been better. I should have known this was all too comfortable.

Jack Slichter left Western to join the Air Transportation Association in Washington, D.C. When this happened, Marv Landes, our VP, decided to do some reorganizing. One of the items on the agenda was to form a training department for the ground services division. Phil Peirce came over to talk to me about it. He indicated there would be a manager of this new department who would report to him and, if the job were approved by our president, Terrell C. Drinkwater, the job would be mine. Was I interested? He asked me to think about it.

This job was right on target for my long-range plans, and the timing wasn't bad. Margie said she was ready to go. It seemed to her that she had been ill with one thing or another ever since we had arrived; mumps, "mono" and miscarriage. She called them "the three M's." Of all the places she had lived, Southern California was the area she enjoyed the most.

After a week or so of vacillation, I called Peirce and told him I would take the job as long as it was considered a promotion. In August of 1961, I was promoted to system manager of training procedures for the ground services department.

There were five of us reporting to Philip E. Peirce. With the additional cities we now served, there were three regional superintendents of stations; Ed Hallgren, John Good and Jack Neel. Jack was formerly the station manager in Salt Lake City, and then Los Angeles. Bob Leinster, who had been Jack Slichter's assistant, was responsible for all the staff work for equipment and procedures, and I had the staff responsibility for training. Phil referred to us as his "five horsemen," and we would stay together as a team for six and a half years. That's a long time, when you consider the dynamic changes that were taking place in our industry.

I had mentioned earlier that I had two bosses who had made the most significant impact on the shaping of my career. Cloyd Hollingworth was the first, and Philip E. Peirce was the other. He brought out a loyalty that had to be the envy of every other department director. I once told him, "Phil, don't give me one more compliment on my performance or I'll work myself to death." Drinkwater called him "coach" for very good reason. He broke down all barriers between those with "line" responsibilities and those who were "just administrators." We all worked as one in our planning and in the execution of those plans.

Our offices were scattered at LAXGO, but this soon changed when the new terminal was completed at Los Angeles International Airport. Marv Landes chose to move his whole division to the mezzanine of the terminal. The theory was that we would have much better access to the people coming in and out of the office from around the system. To this day, I still think Marv was escaping the politics of the general offices. It was terrific to have all of us in one place; we were just steps from one another. Bob Leinster and I had side-by-side offices and shared the same secretary.

After accepting this new position, I developed a set of personal goals for the next five years. The primary goal was to establish the best training department in the industry and then move to a "line" position, hopefully within the general offices. My former long-range goals had been more "staff" oriented; however, I now knew that I wanted to ultimately work directly with the employees who were delivering our services to the customers. These were private goals that I shared with no one except my dear wife. I knew I had to earn the right to lead and that meant doing the very best to support those who performed these heavy "line" tasks.

Phil Peirce gave me one minor task when I began this training position; one with a high priority as it related to our rapidly expanding operations. He wanted to improve our greeting and guiding of the passengers in front of the ticket counter at the larger locations. We decided to have a "special agent" work the front of the counter. They would not supervise anyone but would be the type of person who could handle any problem or, would know where to direct the person to get the problem resolved. We called them "Special Agents" and put them in a unique uniform with white gloves and a fresh carnation in their lapel. No one else in the industry was doing this at the time.

We announced this new program and Paul Harris, manager of what is now called Human Resources, and I designed a testing plan to determine which employees had the right attributes for the job. The Union kicked up a bit of a fuss, but it settled down when we agreed to pay them a nickel more an hour. I have a picture of the original group in my album. Many of them moved up into management. Phil was delighted with the success of this program.

My first major task was to analyze the various station training programs that were presently being used throughout the system. This didn't take long. They were as varied as the size of the operation, and there was very little to assure continuity when a passenger, reservations or ramp agent transferred from one location to another.

First, we established what Company orientation we wanted every new employee to receive, no matter where he or she was to work. It quickly became obvious that the volume of hiring warranted a centralized orientation class that would dovetail with the requirements of the personnel department. I worked closely with Paul Harris and we came up with basic standards that needed to be met by all employees in ground services. I had no authority to speak for the other departments or divisions of the company. We did a basic time study to see how long this would take to administer and then presented a proposal to my boss, Phil Peirce. Simply stated, it was to create a central school to handle the training that was in common to every ground service function.

The Central Training School was approved and established in the basement of a new Tishman Building which was located right across the street from our General Offices. It was a solid operation with fine classrooms, visual and audio equipment and hand-picked training administrators to start the new employees off on the right foot. The three-day orientation classes were soon expanded to include reservations, ticketing and customer relations training. Ramp training was best accomplished on the job.

We were using some of the latest techniques in the training world. United Airlines was leading the industry in training methods and programs. I visited them at their corporate headquarters in Chicago on several occasions and they were most helpful. Some of the competitive atmosphere found in other departments did not find its way into training. We all shared a great deal in those days. "Programmed instruction" was the new thing and I introduced it at Western. We were the first airline to use it as a methodology for many of the basic courses.

United was interested in our new training techniques, and I was able to return some of their favors by sharing our work with them. American had begun falling behind in their customer service training. They were concentrating their efforts on "management development" programs. At that time I was not impressed with the employee training of either American or TWA. Delta was living in the dark ages and Northwest was acting like a "lone wolf." The aura at Pan American was, "We're above it all and you domestic carriers really don't have anything to offer." So, UAL and Western led the way. We two airlines received the most invitations to share what we were doing in the field of industrial training. I accepted all the speaking engagements I could handle, but time was limited as our own airline had increasing challenges and opportunities during that period.

As mentioned earlier, Western had entered the "jet-era" with the Boeing 707's and we were now adding the new Boeing 720B, which was much better suited to Western's system. With the change to larger capacity jets came a need for a whole new look at the way we approached customer service. It was a "New Challenge" and that is exactly what we called the training program. We committed to take it to every ground services employee on our system.

With the help of Phil Peirce's immediate staff and with the input of key station and reservation managers, we established the training objectives that were to be achieved. This was difficult as the whole complexion of "service" was changing, and we still had a great gap in applications between the small locations and large airport terminals. In years to come, this would change through automation. A boarding procedure at Helena, Montana would be no different from that in Los Angeles. At this time, there were many differences.

To schedule and present the "New Challenge" program was a major undertaking. The manager of our Central Training School, Gene Shannon, had joined me in Chicago to see an audio-visual presentation by Eastman Kodak. They used three screens with three projectors. This "multi-screen" presentation was the hit of the National Audio-Visual Convention. We adapted it to meet the objectives of our presentation which, for its day, was outstanding. Gene did an excellent job of visually and verbally presenting our "new challenges" and outlining the goals we must meet to be a leading competitor in our changing environment. These meetings were held in small group sessions, and the regional superintendent for the station didn't miss one. Phil Peirce came to some of the meetings so he could feel the pulse of the employee reactions. This was the biggest budget item we had ever had in training and every dollar was well spent. It was a definable bridge between the old days and the new "jet-era."

Gene Shannon had some custom-made wooden boxes to haul the equipment around the system. One held the large screens. It was dubbed "the coffin." When the program was completed, we had a small staff party at the Marina Hotel, mainly for the secretaries who had been the backbone of the scheduling and shipping. One of the secretaries, Grace Herbert, had decorated the room, and at the head of the table was "the coffin" with a sign which read: "Gene Shannon, may he rest in peace."

About that time, Phil asked me to begin training our senior agents. We had been doing "management development" work with the station managers and their assistants. He felt this was not being pushed down to the "senior agents." The weakness of that classification was that it was within the union ranks and anyone could bid for this supervisory position on a seniority basis. The large turnover we were having was a drawback to using this approach. As we discussed this with the others, the consensus was that the training would add prestige to the position and this might cut down on the "turnover."

We put together a package of some of the programs we had given to management and took them around the system. After the first year, Phil Peirce observed that the attention we were paying to the group had meant more than the learning outcome. As usual, he was right-on. We worked with several outside management trainers; Howard Watts, Dr. Adam Diehl and Dr. Alan Katcher were among them. I learned many of the finer points of personal communications, interpersonal relations and good organizational development from these gentlemen.

On April 21, 1964, my title was changed to "superintendent, training procedures." This change put all five of Phil Peirce's staff on the same level with the title of "superintendent." The name didn't fit a staff job, but it got me a raise in pay. At this time, we couldn't be called "directors" for that was Phil's title.

Western had been one of the first carriers to automate their reservation offices. We had chosen the Teleregister System which, for its day, was a quantum leap for this department. However, with current and projected growth, Bob Leinster could see the need for another big shift.

IBM was working on a new program called "PARS" - Passenger Airline Reservations System. Western formed an evaluation team comprised of Gene Olsen, data processing; Pete Wolf, communications; and, Bob Leinster, reservation and passenger procedures. While it was to be "driven" by the data processing department, Bob Leinster was the major evaluator of the applications from the standpoint of a "user." It was quickly apparent that this was the program for us. We were the first to buy into it. To convert to this new system would require major changes at all of our reservations offices in equipment, procedures and training. These three things had to be carefully coordinated as they so closely interrelated.

With the decision to purchase and implement the new IBM Passenger Airline Reservations System, it became obvious to all that Bob Leinster would have to devote the major part of his time to the work on the new equipment and software. We discussed this with Phil Peirce and decided that I would take over the "procedures" part of passenger, reservations and cargo services. This was logical as the training group would have to be totally conversant with every action that needed to be taken by any person involved in any way with PARS. On April 25, 1966, my department was renamed, ground services procedures and training. Then, Phil Peirce was made an assistant VP which opened the way for my title to be changed to a department director. This was done on June 30, 1967 and my salary was raised to $17,000 a year.

The new PARS system presented an interesting challenge. IBM claimed we had met it with one of the finest organizations ever put together to deal with procedures and training. The changes would require re-training of 2700 ground services personnel.   Equally important was the identification of new procedures and the documenting of these in the various manuals.

The new reservations system was called, "ACCURES." We had a contest that was open to all employees to come up with a name and this was the best we could do. The employees liked the name and the "in-house" press made it sound like the greatest thing since jet engines. We chose a self-pacing program for our training. It was composed of a "programmed instruction" manual, an audio tape and a training module built into the new computer software. Using our largest reservation office as an example, we set the training room in between the old office and a new section containing the "ACCURES" system. The transition training would take five to eight days -- depending on how fast the agent got through the self-paced training modules. We found that almost everyone completed the course and passed the tests in a week.

The employee would then move to one of the new "ACCURES" desks, never more to see the old system. Bob Leinster was in charge of the new desk design and the environmental aspects of the new offices. He and I worked closely on the design of the desks. They were built without any space for a person to write. With the old system, the person would converse with the customer on the phone and write all the information on a piece of paper. After the customer got off the line, the employee would transfer all the reservation data to the "Teleregister" equipment. The new PARS system required teaching them to work with their fingers on the keyboard to make all the necessary transactions in the computer while talking to the customer.

Most reservation agents said it couldn't be done and they'd still need to make notes to be completed after hang up. The only way we had to fight this old habit was a desk just large enough for the CRT and keyboard and a training program guaranteed to convert the employee to type and talk at the same time. It worked. We all held our breath through the first training class, but a week later they were "patting their heads and rubbing their stomachs" at the same time - a similarity they had come up with.

The major part of the "cut-over" was accomplished one location at a time. "Topper" Van Every was in charge of the scheduling and logistics. He had, what he called, bubble-charts all over his office showing the time path of each location and how the cut-over interacted with other events.

Folks at IBM were very pleased at how smoothly it all went. One of our biggest compliments came from their head office when they literally pleaded with us to let National Airlines use our training package; they were next to go on-line with "PARS." We sold it to them for enough to recover our out-of-pocket training equipment costs. It was worth ten times what we got for it, but IBM had been very helpful in giving us the computer programming expertise we needed for the training phase.

A small committee was established for the completion of the documentation, which was so important to us in writing our "standard operating procedures." Joy Anderson represented our training and procedures department. One day Bob Leinster charged into my office and said: "I've had it with that 'nit-picker' you've put on the committee." It only took me a few minutes to persuade him to leave it alone. My convincing remark was that the "nit-picking" was exactly what we needed to make sure we had covered every step a person must take when using this new and complex system. Joy was one of the best people on my staff to identify anything that did not link up properly to the required behavioral objectives. When both Bob and I looked back on the success of the program we thanked the Lord for the "nit-pickers."

Richard P. Ensign, who was now VP of inflight service and reported to Marvin Landes, senior VP service division, received an offer from the Marriott Corporation to head its growing "inflight food division." Even though I did not report to Dick, I had enjoyed being around him again and continued to learn a great deal from our association. When the rumor got around that he would be leaving, my friend Jerry Brooder, regional VP government affairs, who was close friends with our division VP, called me to say he thought Marv Landes would give me the job if I asked for it.

On this, I "sand-bagged"; I didn't talk to Landes for that was the last job I wanted at Western. It was what I'd always called a "can-of-worms." You are in charge of food and everyone is your critic; each thinking he or she is a gourmet chef. You are responsible for the aircraft interiors, and everyone becomes an authority as an interior decorator. You must select the flight attendant uniforms and you quickly discover that the majority of the employees are clothing designers and color specialists. Got the picture? Anyway, the whole thing died down and Ensign decided to stay put at Western.

Chapter 4
LABOR RELATIONS AND
CORK-LINED ROOMS

In 1966, T. C. Drinkwater got together with Art Woodley, president of Pacific Northern Airlines, and worked out a merger of the two airlines. It was approved by the Civil Aeronautics Board on June 2, 1967. Western was to be the surviving carrier and we now had access from Portland and Seattle to Anchorage. We also had the rights to serve many of the smaller locations in Alaska. Unfortunately, many of these stations were later closed. Alaska and Wein Airlines moved into the vacuum. This was to give them much of the feed they needed to be stronger competitors; especially Alaska Airlines; Art Woodley's arch enemy. I was appointed to the "transition training team" and enjoyed meeting and working with these great Alaskans.

Late in 1967, Bob Six, president of Continental Airlines, made a "full-court-press" to get Dominic P. Renda, VP legal and governmental affairs, away from Western Airlines. In December, he succeeded. Ill will had developed between Drinkwater and Renda after Western's initial loss of the Hawaii route. It grew worse as the years went on, and this move came as no surprise to many of us. Jerry Brooder had told me of problems between Terry and Dom; these had to be resolved. I've always believed the condition of the company at that time was the final factor contributing to his departure. We were still recovering from the effects of the well-warranted bad press on the safety of the Lockheed Electra and had made huge financial commitments to equipment and facilities. Both Brooder and Renda felt that Drinkwater got lost in Hawaii and never found his way back.

At this time, the industrial relations department reported to Dom Renda. It was headed by Terry Shrader who had been brought in from Eastern Airlines by Stan Gewirtz, then VP administration. Reporting to Shrader were two directors, one heading labor relations and the other had personnel services. Within a week of Dom Renda's announced departure, Shrader informed Drinkwater that he was leaving to go to Braniff Airlines. He thought he should be reporting directly to the president and when informed he could not, Shrader left.

The relevance of all this is that I got a call from Drinkwater's office and was told to get over to the other building as he wanted to visit with me. I had no idea what was going on. When I arrived, Stan Shatto, senior VP operations, was with him. After a few questions relating to my department, Drinkwater said: "Shrader is leaving the company and I want you to replace him - you'll report to Mr. Shatto in the operations division. The operations division now included ground and inflight services. I told them I knew absolutely nothing about labor relations. Drinkwater's response was: "That's one of the reasons I have selected you for the job. I want someone who knows how to get along with people and not make a 'federal case' out of every labor dispute." I was soon to learn that this may have been Drinkwater's desire, but it wasn't to work out that way; Shatto was a confrontationist of the first degree.

I asked if I could have a few days to consider changing jobs. Drinkwater said he wanted to know the next day. That night I had a long talk with Margie and advised her that this was probably the biggest step I would take in the company as it was a whole new field for me. The end result would mean working ten to twelve hour days, six days a week for a couple of years while I learned the "trade." She was supportive and told me to accept the new position. The next day I informed Drinkwater of this and on January 15, 1968, I became a corporate officer with the title of assistant VP industrial relations. This meant moving from the terminal to the LAXGO. It also meant inheriting some angry guys in labor relations who didn't get the job and would not accept me as a labor leader. On hindsight, I should have fired two of the three and promoted the other, who was a relative "new-comer."

I had not gotten a full vote of confidence from all the senior VP's; the first indication being the title of the department having been downgraded from VP to assistant VP, which left room to put a full VP over me if things didn't work out. Shatto was more concerned about my lack of labor experience than was Drinkwater. Jud Taylor, senior VP finance, had voted against the move because, "I knew nothing about pension administration." Therefore, I thought it best to work with the group I had in the labor relations department and isolate their sphere of influence by not adding any responsibilities that they did not presently hold. Hopefully, my decision would avoid any more corporate turmoil. We had been through enough trauma in the labor department; first, with the departure of Gewirtz, and now losing Renda and Shrader.

While this period of my career was somewhat miserable, it was also the most helpful in preparing me for what I would ultimately achieve for Western Airlines. It was a terrific training ground for all the work we did with our five unions.

Terry Shrader had handled all the pension planning and administration. When he left, he said I should turn this over to the labor relations department as ninety percent of it was the result of negotiations with the unions. The pilot pension program was very costly and complicated, the others weren't so tough. Fortunately, I decided not to take Shrader's parting advice and notified everyone that all matters pertaining to the pension area would be handled through me until they were ready to be administered by the personnel department. This did two things; first, it put me in the key position to be educated on pension administration; second, it forced the labor relations group to work more closely with those who had to perform the day-to-day tasks in carrying out the provisions of the plans. This was very important as we had five different union plans to administer and the provisions of the plans were always a major part of every negotiation.

Roger Patrick of Hewitt Associates was accepted by the pilot union and flight attendant union as being a strong leader in the pension actuarial field. I brought Roger on board as a part-time consultant and our actuary. After briefing him on my personal goals and concerns, we formed a wonderful relationship. He was a good teacher, and because of my interest in his field, he became my mentor. Within two years, I was more knowledgeable in the area of pension administration than most of my counterparts in the industry. Even Jud Taylor admitted he'd been wrong in his fears of my inadequacy in this field. Nevertheless, it continued to cause ego problems within the labor relations group; these would erupt from time to time.

The "ego" problems in the labor relations department were fueled by the lack of faith Stan Shatto had in my overseeing this activity. This was a very costly mistake by Shatto. Ultimately, it not only cost him his job, but sadly led to the demise of our president, T. C. Drinkwater. Had Shatto managed labor through me, rather than around me, history would probably have taken a much different course. Having said that, who is to say it would have been any better.

During this period we were in the processes of re-negotiating the agreement for the Western pilots and, at the same time, reaching accord on the merging of PNA pilots into the Western contract and seniority roster. This particular negotiation was further complicated by the Boeing 737 issue which involved a "third crewperson in the cockpit." The aircraft was designed to be flown by two pilots, but the Air Line Pilots Association wanted three pilots up front. We had temporarily resolved this issue within weeks of my taking the new job. We agreed to put the third person in the cockpit, but Stan Shatto made it clear we would not "bargain" on the duties of this person; they would be assigned as the company saw fit and that was to be a lookout for other air traffic. The pilots rejected this.

The initial delivery of our 737's arrived and, on the morning of the first scheduled flight, the spokesman from the Air Lines Pilots Association said they would not fly it under the conditions we had specified. Shatto's orders were to follow normal procedures and, if any pilot refused to fly, fire him and go to the next pilot on reserve. This was to continue until someone flew the plane or all the pilots were fired. The union representatives were at the gate and so was the pilot management. The first pilot refused; he was held out of service and the first reserve pilot was called forth. The union caved in and the flight left without the passengers even knowing what was going on.

The whole airline industry and the people at Boeing were closely following these actions. The 737 was to be a big factor in the short to medium-haul market and it was not economic to fly it with three pilots. Western and United seemed to have been chosen by ALPA as the "guinea pigs" of the airline industry; Western was first up to bat.

With this problem temporarily out of our way, we were back to resolving the full open pilot contract. We met for nearly two weeks in Miami. We were now under the direction of a mediator. No progress was made. The

National Mediation Board finally released us and the thirty-day cooling-off period began. Lev Edwards was one of the three members of the NMB and had a home in Fort Worth, Texas. He was a specialist in handling the airline industry problems, especially when they reached the cooling-off period. He would bring the parties together in what he called "super mediation." His favorite place to meet was at the Worth Hotel in his home town and, if it was summer, so much the better. The Worth Hotel was not fully air conditioned, and what was there lacked operating consistency. The negotiating table was surrounded by hard, old-fashioned fold-up chairs. One wasn't highly motivated to spend much time there when it was a hundred degrees outside.

It was late summer when he called us together in Fort Worth. The hottest day I recall was one hundred and two degrees. Lev had a sleeping room that connected to the negotiation room. He would get things started and excuse himself to his adjoining room where there was a bed and a fan. He had a book with all the "open items" that were yet to be resolved. As we agreed on an open issue, he would highlight it in red and have both parties initial it. This got to be known as his "red book." Lev Edwards seemed to be a firm believer that nothing really important happened with pilot negotiations until the midnight hour of the last day of the "cooling off period." Therefore, if he had all the loose ends tied down in his "book," last minute progress could move more rapidly. This helped in the case of Western.

Captain Joe Swan was heading the negotiating committee for ALPA. He was a real "hard-nose," but still had problems keeping his committee on track. There were a lot of problems to be resolved from the PNA merger and there were a couple of contentious PNA pilots on the negotiating committee. All this was compounded by their belief that until Stan Shatto showed his face at the "negotiating table," there would be no contract. In fact, the pilots had stickers printed for their flight bags which read: "Only The Shatto Knows." I knew he would not meet with the pilots under any circumstances, so we spent a lot of hot days in Fort Worth and made little progress.

One of my pilot friends let me know the extent of the "infighting" going on between the PNA and Western pilots. We needed someone to come in that was well respected by the group to break some of the deadlocks. This had to be done quickly or we'd have a strike on our hands. A few days before the clock ran out, Captain Denny Seavey came in from the San Francisco pilot base and did the "head-knocking." Things started to improve and I knew we were close. It was now obvious to them that Shatto was not going to enter the negotiations. It was equally obvious that the PNA pilots were not going to be satisfied until they saw that the company was ready to take a strike.

Two hours before the magic midnight hour when the pilots were free to strike, we made a final proposal. We recessed while the pilots considered it. Everyone reconvened shortly before midnight and the union spokesman began telling us everything that was wrong with our offer. Our spokesman was Dan Zaich, the director of labor relations. We also had three of our pilots from management on our committee; the VP flight operations, his director and a chief pilot from LAX.

The protocol, up to that point, was that only the "spokesman" talked at the negotiation table. This changed a few minutes before midnight as the pilots were droning through the faults of our final proposal. When there was an appropriate pause, I banged my fist on the table and said: "This is outrageous! We have made you an excellent offer and you are treating it like it is a piece of dirt." I reminded them it was our final offer, arose, and said we were leaving. The rest of our Western committee looked shocked for this had not been rehearsed. As I started to leave, our mediator, Lev Edwards, jumped up and said, "I'm calling a recess." I said, "Call it what you want, Lev, but that's it."

I walked down the hall to our private room with the director of labor relations chewing on me about walking out without clearing it with him. An hour later one of our committee, Bud Caward, VP flight operations, called Los Angeles and was told the pilots were out in front of the building with picket signs. Lev Edwards stayed with the pilots and, at four a.m., he brought Captain Swan and a couple of others to our room - they had a few questions - mostly related to pensions and passes. I answered them in a way that did not add to what we had given them and Captain Swan then said we had an agreement.

We shook hands, freshened up in our rooms, signed off Lev's "Red Book" and we were on our way back to Los Angeles on an eight o'clock flight. The director of labor relations was seething because my actions, not his, had broken the deadlock. I could see what was needed and was willing to gamble. The rest of the committee was not much more affable; the pilot types treated me like I had just put too much baggage in their tail pit.

I knew Stan Shatto was going to get a warped version of what happened, but I decided to let things develop as they may for that way I could find out how much faith he had in his new man. Turned out he didn't have the trust I'd hoped for. When the dust settled, Shatto pulled me into his office and told me I should always work through the "labor spokesman" and not to repeat what I had done. I said my actions were necessary to break a log-jam, but he didn't back off.

This was only the beginning. One of the open items the pilots had agreed to defer related to the pensions of twenty PNA pilots; they claimed they were being disenfranchised. It looked like the whole pension issue was going to arbitration, which was usually very costly. A pilot for whom I had a great deal of respect came to my office for a visit. He was on the pilot pension committee. Indications were that we could settle the whole deal and finalize all the open items if we took care of these few PNA pilots. (I was personally to learn later how it feels to be "disenfranchised.") I called Roger Patrick of Hewitt Associates and asked him what the annual cost would be to give the pilot pension group what they had suggested. He said about twenty-six thousand dollars. The current open items that would wind up in arbitration were worth several hundred thousand. I called the pilot pension committee together and settled the matter.

My labor relations director told Shatto I'd "caved-in" to the pilots and Shatto gave me my second verbal workout. I told him that I would do the same thing again as it made the most economic sense and set no new precedent.

The 737 issue had been a real "sticky-wicket" and what we did was seen as the temporary benchmark for the industry. In the final contract language, we agreed to put a low-paid pilot in the jump seat with limited duties. He or she was referred to as the "GIB" - meaning the "Guy In Back." This didn't cost as much as had been predicted, but sure caused some major trauma in the company.

The reason I have been referring to "he or she" is that we had begun hiring female pilots. This, too, was a major milestone in the industry. One of our first hires was the daughter of Clint Walker, a movie actor. She was from a mold that was hard to duplicate and she would be a strong confidante to me on some line pilot matters much later in my career.

I mention all this labor strife to set the scene for what I have always considered to be the "death knell" for our president, Terrell C. Drinkwater. Robert J. Serling, author of *The Only Way to Fly, the early history of Western Airlines*, seemed to agree. He records:

"Terry's grip on the airline was loosening visibly with each new setback ... By far the most crippling blow came only four days after inauguration of service to Hawaii. On July 29, 1969, Western's mechanics began what would be an eighteen-day strike - a walkout that cost the airline an estimated $18 million. With all its difficulties, WAL might have made money that year except for the strike; losses in 1969 totaled $12 million, and much of the red ink was directly attributable to the effects of the walkout ... For Terry, it was more than just another labor fight; it meant the end of the line as far as the presidency of Western was concerned."

The mechanics were represented by the Teamsters. They were as tough as their reputations led one to believe. The contract with the mechanics had been open for some time and when we finally reached the "crunch," there were two items left that were not considered "major" to the "rank and file," but were of very high priority to the Teamster organization. One was the demand that they take over the pension and medical benefit funds; the other was a demand for an additional nickel an hour. The Teamsters had to be a nickel an hour ahead of the International Association of Machinists, who was by far their biggest competitor in the airline industry.

The company prevailed on these two issues. Our position being that the employees wanted to get this settled and they didn't care about this "chicken stuff." Our labor relations group was positive that the agreement would be ratified by the mechanics. I left for Atlanta to attend an ATA Personnel Relations Conference. I was on the executive committee and expected to participate at that gathering. Even more important was my getting together with the vice chairman, Charles Hopkins of American Airlines and Percy Wood of United. These were my counterparts at their airlines, and the three of us had been quietly working to see if we could break out of the Air Transportation Association and form a coalition of airlines to combat the rapid rise in labor costs. We had planned to have dinner together in Atlanta and spend the evening discussing our strategy.

When I left Los Angeles, I had asked our labor relations director to let me know immediately if the contract did not ratify or if he was contacted again by the Teamsters. During dinner, around 9:00 p.m., I was paged in the restaurant at the hotel and advised to call my office. Our labor relations man answered. He said: "The mechanics didn't ratify - what should we do?" I said: "If necessary, give them another nickel and see if they'll take it to the membership. If they won't, give them the pension and medical benefits." He started to laugh and said: "That's exactly what I thought you'd say. I talked to Stan Shatto and we told them to get lost - we're now on strike."

I had known exactly what was needed to resolve this dispute and so did the director of labor relations. This was a pure "power play" on the part of my labor relations head without regard for anything but his "ego." Before I flew to Atlanta, I had set up a means by which Stan Shatto could reach me at any moment - day or night. He never called. Shatto did what I feared most, he relied on his past practices and called the shots without adequate counsel and without fully considering either the timing or the consequences. Had he called me for advice, the strike could have been eliminated and we'd have saved more than $18 million dollars. We ultimately had to give the Teamsters what they wanted in order to settle the strike.

As I flew home on the 6:00 a.m. flight, I couldn't help recalling the words of Terry Drinkwater when he asked me to take the job: "I want somebody who knows how to get along with people and not make a 'federal case' out of every labor dispute." Stan Shatto had different ideas. If someone were to ask me what really pushed Drinkwater out of his job, my response would be: "A nickel an hour." This event was "the last straw" for our new major stockholder, Kirk Kerkorian, and he had the Western's board of directors replace Drinkwater as the CEO. Kirk had stacked the board with some of his cronies and now had enough clout to do this.

The ensuing events are written in Bob Serling's book. I have no idea how accurately they have been recorded, but from what I can recall, the results of the Kerkorian takeover are well reported.

J. Judson Taylor, the senior VP finance, reluctantly accepted the job of being president and CEO. Fred Benninger, Kerkorian's right arm, was vice chairman and came to Western a day or two a week to assist Taylor - this was at Jud's request.

T. C. Drinkwater remained for a while as chairman of the board. Soon, he was replaced by Fred Benninger. Stan Shatto kept his executive VP title, but industrial relations no longer reported to him. When Drinkwater finally resigned as chairman in May of 1970, the wind went out of Shatto's sails. His office was moved across the street to the Tishman Building and the saddest day of my career was when I had to go over there and advise him of his pension package. We'd had some rough years together, but I would be willing to live through them one more time. I learned a great deal from him in a very short time. They were often tough lessons but they groomed me for what was to come. My only regret was his lack of faith in my ability to work our contracts with the labor unions. I took no delight in knowing that this lack of confidence in me was what caused him to lose his job.

The seeds that Percy Wood, Chuck Hopkins and I had planted in Atlanta quickly sprouted and George Keck, UAL's president, called a meeting of the CEO's of the major airlines. It was held in his board room at their headquarters in Chicago. Jud Taylor was just getting underway with his new job and he asked me to represent Western at the conference. I was met by a UAL limo at O'Hare Field and taken to a lunch that was prepared in a private dining room. It was there that I realized how much weight this matter had been given by the airline chiefs.

On that day, I was the only industrial relations officer present; the rest out-ranked me. Among the airline presidents attending were some that I had met before; Tillinghast, from TWA; Nyrop, NWA; Spater, AAL. There were others I didn't know from the regional carriers. The meeting went through the afternoon and the consensus was that we should have a new association called the "Airline Industrial Relations Conference." This would later be referred to as "AIRCON." We would bring in a strong head from the labor relations field. Each CEO would be a member of the board of directors and each VP industrial relations would be on a steering committee to do all the grunt work. A "mutual aid pact" would be formed to financially assist those airlines that were targeted by the unions to be struck for "bench mark" pay or work rule changes within the industry.

It took several months to get this organization under way. I made weekly trips to Washington, D.C. to meet with the other industrial relations officers to get the program structured. Delta stayed outside as they were mostly non-union and did not want to offend anyone; however, we allowed one representative from Delta to attend the meetings so they were at least in some form of correlation with the rest of us.

Harding Lawrence, CEO at Braniff, on the advice of Terry Shrader, would not get onboard and that started some deterioration. Airline labor costs were exploding and I was amazed how few at the top were willing to really address the problems they were facing. This situation was a perfect "catch 22." The unions could make unreasonable demands and, with all costs rising so rapidly, the airline could not pass the costs through to the consumer because the fares were regulated by the Civil Aeronautics Board, which was so political it could never keep up with the real world.

We hired Conrad Cooper, "Coop," to be the president of AIRCON. He had been a top negotiator in a couple of big conglomerates and knew how to work in such a diverse environment. He would spend most of his time with the VPs committee and met once a month with the board of directors to review the status of industry negotiations.

Once again, Jud Taylor said he didn't have time to attend the board meetings in Washington, D.C. and asked that I fill in. Shrader of BNF was always there without his boss. Even though BNF did not join AIRCON, Terry Shrader was invited to attend so we could find out what was going on there and could apprise him of what the others were doing. Toward the end, he was more impressed with the tight line we were holding at AIRCON.

Regional carriers, such as Braniff, Continental, Eastern, National and Western had the most to gain from this new organization as they were the usual targets for "bench mark" salaries, work rules and fringe benefits. The reason Terry Shrader held out at Braniff was his firm belief that the group would fragment the minute there was a major challenge.

The airlines were very vulnerable to "slow-down" tactics by employees - especially the pilots. "Flying by the book" could cost a carrier all its annual profits, and most in top management were unwilling to take the necessary steps to combat it. There were ways to handle this but no one, outside of Don Nyrop at Northwest, had the nerve to do what was required to stop these tactics. In spite of all the haranguing, AIRCON got off the ground and sent a strong message to the unions that they could not expect to continue the economic course they were pursuing with the airline industry.

George Spater, president of American Airlines, had approached Drinkwater in December of 1968 on the possibility of a merger. This was shortly after Kirk Kerkorian had made a "tender offer" for Western Airlines stock. Talks continued between the parties into the fall of 1969. Progress was slowed for several reasons; one of which was a new "power play" between Drinkwater and Kerkorian. These conversations were kept very quiet and, since no formal proposal of merger had been made, were not divulged to the shareholders. This situation blew loose at the Annual Shareholders' meeting in April of 1970. It was following this meeting that Drinkwater got the final ax.

After Drinkwater left, Kerkorian warmed to a possible merger and talks ensued with several airlines. American Airlines was finally selected as the "groom" and on October 30, 1970, Western and American signed a tentative merger agreement. Within a few days, I was in New York City at American's headquarters with Charles Hopkins and his staff. We discussed the teams that would need to work on contracts, pensions, etc.

When Stan Shatto's authority was restricted to the operations division, my department was transferred to the service division, where I reported once again to P. E. Peirce, now a senior VP. Also reporting to Phil were Richard P. Ensign, VP staff and Jack S. Neel, VP line. This was obviously a "holding pattern" for our group while awaiting the merger decision.

During 1971, I had many meetings with American Airlines in New York City. Teams and coordinators were established in all major functions and, with everything else that was required to keep Western moving ahead on its own, the merger workload became tough to handle. Fortunately, several of the meetings were in Los Angeles. Once, we met as a large group with our counterparts in American's Flight Attendant Training Center near the old Fort Worth Airport. My old friend, Fred Friedli of Oakland days, was now the director of that center.

By now, it was obvious to me that this merger was just what Western needed and would fold us into what I had always considered to be the best managed airline in the USA. Of course, I was somewhat biased by all the years I had handled their operation in Oakland, California. The Los Angeles Airport functions would be larger than United Airlines, which operated out of two terminals. The fact that Western and American had terminals side by-side was a big bonus. The routes blended well and, since there was very little overlap in our route structure, I could not see any reason for the regulatory agencies being concerned about the merger; but they were.

The merger dream ended on July 28, 1972 when the Civil Aeronautics Board made the stupid decision to kill it. There was just too much opposition on the political scene for this marriage to be consummated. Western's financial position had improved and American's had temporarily worsened. No one at the top seemed too displeased that the merger was off.

We had been going through some rough negotiations with the pilots during the merger period. Our pilot union, ALPA, did not represent the American pilots and therefore they were demanding all sorts of protective clauses in their open contract. They even pulled a major "slowdown" to force the company to give them what they wanted. Fred Benninger called all the shots. Fred sat at the negotiation table when the crucial issues were decided and he directed every issue pertaining to the economic package.

Benninger had a good friend who was a pilot at Flying Tiger Airlines and who was presently head of their flight operations. His name was "Pinky." One of our pilots said he had seen "Pinky" and Benninger together in the evening and the word was out with the pilots that "Pinky" was feeding Benninger what would be required to resolve the contract. I don't know who was the most generous, Fred or Pinky, but that was one of the most expensive contracts we had ever negotiated.

Kerkorian did not want a labor stoppage at that time and was unwilling to do what Don Nyrop was doing at Northwest; which was to use the Mutual Aid Pact and shut down the operation rather than intensify the already high cost of piloting the aircraft. Nyrop made by far the best use of this program; others in the industry didn't have the backbone to do what he did. In this respect, Terry Shrader of Braniff had been correct.

The merger had ended and I was now a full VP of industrial relations; my labor relations department was headed by an assistant VP. I had three other departments: personnel, wage and salary, and consumer affairs. The latter didn't fit too well in my organization, but it served the whole company and at the time there was no other reasonable place for it to reside - in addition, no one else wanted it. I tried to convince our president, Jud Taylor that it should report directly to him. He wouldn't even listen to the rationale. Not long after the CAB decision on the merger, J. Judson Taylor decided it was time to retire.

On February 1, 1973 Arthur F. Kelly, then senior VP of marketing, was elected Western's new president and CEO. Fred Benninger stayed on as chairman of the board.

Another major change in the "senior officer lineup" was the return of Dominic P. Renda to Western. He came back from Continental on January 1, 1973 as an executive VP. On April 22, 1976, he was elevated to the office of president and chief operating officer as Art Kelly moved to chairman of the board and CEO.

Richard P. Ensign left Western in 1971 to join Pan American World Airways as senior VP marketing. During the merger negations with American, he informed me that if he had to move to New York City, it would be on his terms, not Western's. At that time, Ensign's department was moved under Phil Peirce.

After the merger attempt, Kerkorian lost interest in Western and within a few years sold out. Western bought his remaining stock for a little over thirty million dollars - money the company would soon wish they had as a cash reserve.

With the assurance that our headquarters was to remain in Los Angeles, I had a strong feeling that I should spend the next few years improving my formal education. Beyond my high school instruction was a hodge-podge of courses taken at various times; nothing that tied together in any reasonable discipline. I had discussed this several times with my step-mother, Margaret. She said I should sit down with some department heads at one or two of the local universities and get their recommendations.

I spoke with Pepperdine, UCLA and our local State University. Each would accept me if I passed certain tests and my score in the ATGSB, (now the GMAT) was acceptable.

The summer of 1972 was spent taking tests and studying for the ATGSB. All tests were satisfactorily completed and I was accepted into the Graduate School at all three universities. I felt that at the present time UCLA offered the best program. Unfortunately, their classes began at 5:30 p.m. on the campus in Westwood, and I saw no way I could finish my work at Western and fight my way through the cross-town traffic to get on campus by that time of day.

Pepperdine was not using a "course curriculum," but was running a two-year small group session involving more research than problem solving. I chose our California State, Domiquez University for two reasons. First, I needed the type of individual course curriculum they were using. This would force me to "rub knuckles" with each phase of the education I would receive so I could meet my over-all objectives. The other reason being, I could get to school on time.

Margie had asked me about these educational objectives, since I was already a corporate officer. My answer was: "I want to get back into higher level line management and be in position to take on more responsibility. To do this most effectively, I'll want to think within the educational vocabulary of my staff, many of whom will have MBA degrees." I had a firm belief that you can only think within your vocabulary; a precept emblazoned on my mind by G. Homer Durham when he was president of ASU. How could I demand the best from employees if I did not know how to draw on the skills they had gained in graduate school? Also, and maybe of most importance, was the very strong impression from within that I should move ahead with this academic program. I had learned to pay attention to these feelings.

After receiving my MBA, one of the highest compliments I was to receive, relating to above mentioned objectives, came from an employee who had been a young refugee from Cuba. Carlos Hernandez received a master's degree in finance and also an MBA from the University of California at Los Angeles. One day he said: "You demand more from me than anyone I've ever worked for at Western, and yet I enjoy it. The reason is that you are the only one who knows how to draw on all the knowledge and skills I gained in college." He really made my day.

In the spring of 1973, I was reporting to Dominic P. Renda, executive VP. Dom asked me to do a compensation study of the officers and all of the non-bargaining employees. He wanted recommendations on a full compensation package that would be commensurate with what others were doing in the industry.

Dom and I discussed bringing in an outside consultant to assist in this project; Henry Golightly's firm was selected as he had just finished similar studies for two other airlines. This project was to be completed by October and would be presented to the board of directors for their approval at that time.

The pay and benefits for the non-bargaining group were running far behind in many areas. The mission was completed on schedule and approved by the board. We had closely scrutinized the over-all compensation being offered by the regional and transcontinental carriers and this package put us a little below the middle of the range. It was still a problem in some areas as the employees represented by the unions were above the mid-point of the industry - some at the very top.

With this program behind us, both Kelly and Renda had increased their interest in making some major structural changes in the organization. I suggested we not bring in an outsider as a consultant for it would be a waste of time and money. It was apparent the two of them had agreed on the major objectives they wanted to achieve and that's usually half the battle.

In early 1974, we set aside a small "war room" for the project. I had the only key to the room. The four walls were lined with cork board, with draperies mounted over each section for privacy. After establishing the first line of report to both Kelly and Renda, I then placed the current organization under each division, using the current titles. I would then invite the incumbent division head to view his organization and suggest changes that met with certain pre-established parameters. Kelly and Renda came in to review these recommendations and make adjustments they felt to be appropriate. No names were yet on the board, only titles. Over a period of two months we worked and reworked each division and department to get the cleanest possible organization that fit the separation of "turf" between Art Kelly and Dom Renda.

After we had established the titles and pay grades for each of the non-union positions in the company, we then began putting in names. This was done in the "war room" with each division head, along with either Kelly or Renda - no one else was permitted in the room. Also, no individual could see what was going on in the other divisions unless it was with the approval of the president. In that way, we had the fewest cooks "stirring-the-pot" and still allowed the president and executive VP to handle the "politics" of their senior staff without my being involved.

This proved to be a very interesting exercise and one that was long overdue. It turned out well, with the exception of one area. While we were running the company with ten percent less management employees than most of the other airlines, our new organization had too many corporate officer titles. This was to become a real sore point with the unions and would label Western as being a "top-heavy" airline.

Jack Slichter had been director of passenger service when I was in Phoenix. He left Western in 1961 to become a VP of the Air Transportation Association in Washington, D.C. Early in 1966, Drinkwater had rehired Slichter as VP of government and industry affairs. I mention this as he was to play a prominent part in this reorganization.

One of Art Kelly's prior goals had been to merge the sales and service divisions under one head; at the moment this was Phil Peirce. Phil took on the assignment and did a great job of reorganizing these two divisions into one.

Kelly now wanted more authority pushed out to the field locations and felt this could be done by forming ten regional divisions, each headed by a VP. He wanted them to report to a corporate VP at headquarters who would report to the senior VP - marketing. Renda felt Jack Slichter was under-utilized in his government and industry role and suggested he head up this team. It was a bold move for an airline the size of Western. United had used this method under Eddie Carlson, but they were a carrier that was much larger. This was one of those organizations that looked good in theory; however, Western at that time was too centralized and compartmentalized in their thinking, as well as their practices, to allow any significant authority to move to these regional VP's. This act was to produce a major battle ground within the company over the next five years, primarily in the area of marketing.

Back in the "cork-lined" room, we had reached the final stages of putting the names with the titles. Only one remained open in the marketing division. Both Kelly and Renda had insisted that we recreate an inflight department, including the flight attendant group, rather than having it remain a part of "passenger services." Kelly stated that it hadn't received the attention it deserved since Dick Ensign left.

The last day the three of us were together in the room, I asked who was going to fill the slot of VP inflight service. They turned to me and said they wanted me to take it. That caught me by surprise. They both knew I wanted back into the "line management," but I said this was not what I was looking for. Each gave persuasive reasons for my being in the job and offered to make it a pay-grade higher than my present position; they would also authorize a promotional increase.

I had my usual twenty-four hours to decide. Having just graduated from college, I'd planned on more time at home and this put me right back in the learning mode - meaning, long hours. Margie gave it a "thumbs-up" and, with the final wrap-up of the company reorganization, I moved to the position of VP inflight service, reporting once again to Phil Peirce, senior VP marketing; which now included all passenger services. I had a great deal of admiration for the flight attendants in their role of passenger safety and service. I was concerned about not living up to their expectations with all the economic constraints I could see on the horizon. My marching orders, which came directly from Renda, were to concentrate on establishing stronger controls, better accountability throughout the department and, the toughest of all, cutting costs.

Chapter 5

Inflight Service and Tragedy in Mexico City

There was little I could accomplish in the way of "cost cutting" with the flight attendants. That was more of a long range project as we considered the food service and staffing on each flight. Much of their cost was driven by their contract and the FAA requirements for safety. The one area I could get under better controls was the food and beverage service. I brought in Carlos Hernandez, the Cuban lad I have previously mentioned. He had been working with the cost analysis group in the finance division who policed our budgets.

We set about re-identifying cost centers and the amount of control we had over each. As I thought, our greatest opportunity to cut cost was to re-evaluate each of our catering units with whom we contracted our food service and "re-bid" our agreements with those whose unit costs were the highest. This was consuming a great deal of my time; however, we reaped a good harvest of savings when it was completed.

The reporting of these savings created the biggest thorn in my side over the next few years. I was working with Dom Renda's financial hatchet team, and they expected me to produce the same type of reductions in food and beverage each year. I did too good a job in the first year. That so often happens and causes folks to play games in the budget area; "I'll spread these savings out over a few years so the downward slope will not be so great." I've never believed in that gamesmanship.

The re-evaluation of our caterers and the rebuilding at certain cities put me in touch with Bill Marriott. He had built a new flight kitchen in Phoenix for Western and we failed to move into it. The facility was sitting empty and Bill had lunch with me to see if we would consider shifting from Sky Chef. Evidently the planned move had been aborted when some of the former inflight management left the company. I told him the savings would have to be substantial enough to offset the inconvenience of having to make the move. In the re-bidding process at several other units we achieved the same savings and, before many years passed, Marriott inflight service was our lead caterer.

From the pure point of organization, the marketing division was as near perfect as it could get. If asked today to re-evaluate what we had done, I would make one change in the structure – the regional heads would have been directors, not VP's. Our union employees were counting the number of officer titles in Western's Annual Report and they didn't like the number.

Within a year of the reorganization of this new marketing group, there was a move that caught just about everyone by surprise; Phil Peirce announced that he would take early retirement on July 1, 1975. This action on Phil's part came as no surprise to me. During a marketing meeting in San Diego, within a year of his leaving, Phil and I were out for a stroll to get some fresh air. The subject of Western's retirement plan entered our conversation. Phil made what I thought to be a strange statement. He said: "No one will pick my retirement date for me; I'll decide when the time is right."

On the evening I returned home from the meeting, I told Margie that I felt Phil was going to take early retirement. She asked how I came to that conclusion. I said he had achieved the success he desired and, with the merging of the sales and service groups, he would be leaving at a pinnacle of that success. I spoke of this to no one else, but later told Phil of the impression I had received from our San Diego conversation. He said I was on track with his thinking at that time. He was a great man in so many ways. He practiced what Peter Drucker and Tom Peters were preaching at that time and he accomplished it by doing what came naturally to him, as there wasn't a phony bone in his body.

Many in management give their words lip-service, but few are willing to put their advice into action. Phil was a true "coach" in every aspect of that title. Those of us who could feel what was shaping up in the marketing arena, especially with the new challenges brought on by deregulation, were greatly concerned with this announcement. On the other hand, this was the ideal time for Phil to step out; that is, if he was not willing to stay for another four or five years. He was not!

In the fall of 1985, Harry Gray, one of the nation's top executives, sent me the following message:

DO YOU REMEMBER WHO GAVE
YOU YOUR FIRST BREAK?

Someone saw something in you once. That's partly why you are where you are today. It could have been a thoughtful parent, a perceptive teacher, a demanding drill sergeant, an appreciative employer, or just a friend who dug down in his pocket and came up with a few bucks. Whoever it was had the kindness and the foresight to bet on your future. Those are two beautiful qualities that separate the human being from the orangutan. In the next 24 hours, take 10 minutes to write a grateful note to the person who helped you. You'll keep a wonderful friendship alive. Matter of fact; take another 10 minutes to give somebody else a break. Who knows? Someday you might get a nice letter. It could be one of the most gratifying messages you ever read.

On October 18, 1985, having read the above message, I wrote this letter to Phil Peirce, who had now been retired from Western for several years:

In 1955 when Cloyd Hollingworth was transferred from Oakland to Denver, you gave me the chance of taking over that station even though I had less experience than the other candidates. While that might not have been my first break in life, it was certainly the biggest for it gave me the opportunity to put into practice some of the principles that a larger airline, American, was establishing within their company and, as you remember, we handled their total operation. That was the beginning of my experience in the training field.

In 1957 you gave me another break, again passing over some of the more experienced people available to you, when you sent me to Phoenix to open the operation. That gave me four years to hone my skills with a brand new growing operation. It also gave me the opportunity to be selected as Bishop of the fast-growing Scottsdale Ward where I learned my new leadership principles.

Then, in 1961 you chose me to head up your training operation in the ground services department and establish a centralized training program. I could not imagine receiving any greater support than I had from you as we launched our many new and innovative programs during that period of time.

In your gentle way you demanded perfection and I gave you the best that I had. While doing so, I learned from you the greatest principle of all which is that of human kindness.

You also gave me the opportunity to make mistakes and you recognized that I punished myself for those mistakes more than you would have allowed. That was the "coach" in you. Obviously, someone gave you a break when they allowed you the opportunity to become a coach, and those fine principles you gained followed you all your life and through your actions, you transferred those attributes to others. That, in my estimation, is the greatest achievement one can attain in this life.

I'm sure these comments could be made by countless others who have had the opportunity to work for you through the years, but I think only one of us has the opportunity of saying to you that without your guidance, training and direction and the example that you set, Western Airlines would not be alive and well today.

The things I have done in the past several years, and especially since becoming C.E.O., can be directly traced to Phillip E. Peirce. It is such an honor to have been a member of your team.

I want you to know that I think of you often, continue to admire you very much, and hope this finds you in good health.

With love,

Larry

On October 28, 1985 Phil responded to my letter with a handwritten note. Fortunately Phil did not lose his fine hand of writing in his later years. I'm going to share this with you:

Larry:

Ede and I have read and reread your letter and will keep it close at hand so that we can inflate our egos at any time. You and I both know that you have overstated the facts, but it's not my intention to return the letter for revision. To illustrate, did you ever stop to think that my track record depended on your performance and others like you? Further, you have served with distinction as president, CEO and chairman; positions unfamiliar to me, and long after I was out of the picture.

My impression is that we were intensely loyal employees, working our butts off, and had a good time doing it all together. Those traits usually produce positive results, but never less than lasting friendships.

You remember our interest in Arabian horses. We continue to raise champions and they all have one common trait. Let me bore you with an example. This year we put our first, a three-year-old filly, into racing. Always competing "up in class," she progressed from finishing dead last in her first race to running in the money in her fourth outing. She has talent, but far more heart. She thrives on challenge and never quits.

Horses, I believe, are comparable to humans in some respects. Give me individuals with that will to win; Larry Lee fits that mold.

Our best to you and your wonderful family.

Phil Peirce

When Phil announced his retirement, there was some internal elbowing for the top marketing job. Art Kelly wanted Bill Balfour, whom he had groomed for a top job, to move up. Dom Renda was pushing Jack Slichter, his favorite from day one. It was obvious that this conflict was not going to be resolved. The compromise was to bring Richard P. Ensign back from Pan American Airlines to fill the top job in marketing. At the time, he was an executive VP at Pan Am.

Dick Ensign arrived on June 1, 1975. He kept the same basic marketing organization in place. There were the five VPs reporting to him - four with departmental responsibilities and one taking care of all marketing administration.

Prior to the reorganization, Kelly, Renda and I had discussed labor relations. It was decided that each major division of the company would have someone who would be responsible for the union negotiations in their area and work with the VP of industrial relations and provide all costing data on work-rule changes. The VP industrial relations would act as "facilitator" and spokesman for the Company. The end result would be that the head of each division would have the obligation of achieving a contract with the union or making the decision to take other action, not the labor relations group. In the marketing division were two unions; the Association of Flight Attendants (AFA) and the Air Transport Employees (ATE), which represented the ground service employees.

Jack S. Neel had been chosen to be VP marketing administration and was the key person in all negotiations. This provided more free time for the department heads to concentrate on planning, as well as the controls necessary to the system-wide operations. The other three VP's were: Willis R. (Bill) Balfour, VP sales and service; Bert D. Lynn, VP advertising and sales promotion; Jack M. Slichter, VP field management; and I remained VP inflight service. The division covered most aspects of selling and providing the personal service to our customers. The scheduling of the aircraft was not included in this division. This activity was driven by the economics of the operations division, which proved to be a constant irritant - especially to Jack Slichter who was correlating the demands of his ten regional VPs.

Slichter had a very good grasp of the scheduling process and sat on the Scheduling Committee. In a regulated environment, the company could afford to have the operations division in the driver's seat as they represented such high costs; pilots and maintenance. At this juncture, it was unwise.

After Phil Peirce left, problems developed within the marketing division. It was not immediately apparent, but was like a sore that began festering between those who "planned the product" and those who "implemented the plans." As in most cases, it was not the fault of the organization as much as the behavioral characteristics of those involved. It centered mostly in a tug-of war between two people, Balfour and Slichter.

There were three major planning functions in the sales and service division; Bert Lynn and Bill Balfour each had one and I had the other. Lynn had been in the advertising and sales promotion job for many years and was well respected by everyone in field operations. He also had a history of strong controls over the allocation of his product which was hard to challenge. Therefore, his functions presented little conflict within the ranks of the regional VP's; and when it did, Bert was a master at handling the problem.

One of Bill Balfour's primary responsibilities was "pricing and allocating" Western's product among all the corporate and field entities; such as travel agents, wholesalers, etc. This allocation process was a constant battleground that raged on between the staff and the field.

As previously stated, my personnel area was pretty well defined by the requirements of the FAA and flight attendant's contract. However, food and beverage was a clear field for constant debate. Most of the regional VP's envisioned themselves as gourmet chefs and each wanted to be involved in the menu planning. Additionally, they felt they should determine on which flights we would board food and how much of the same.

Coming from the other direction were Dom Renda and his minions asking for major cuts in these costs. The annual food and beverage budget was around thirty-five million dollars. As I mentioned, our over-all costs were reduced during the first couple of years with the implementation of better control systems and improved negotiation strategies with the caterers. By 1976, we could no longer provide the reductions that Renda demanded without removing food from many of our flights. This was where the regional VP's really started to get "up-tight." Thanks to a first rate staff, improved evaluation programs, that included the regional VPs and a good relationship with Jack Slichter, we got the emotions under control.

Our biggest demand for a cut came in the year of Western's fiftieth anniversary. This was unfortunate for Bert Lynn, VP advertising, who wanted to do something special that year to attract attention to this event. We got together and explored an idea I'd had of calling the event, "Fifty-Fair." We would spin off as many things as possible from these words and create an air of celebration. Our inflight group developed picnic baskets with festive accoutrements and, at the same time, cut our costs considerably - lots of hot dogs and beer that year.

Bob Keller had been the genius behind much of what was done to add the "sizzle" to inflight meal service. He retired early and I was fortunate to be able to persuade Marriott inflight service to hire him to coordinate Western's food design and implement it within the various Marriott Flight Kitchens.

Pat Glowe was the flight attendant base manager in San Francisco and showed a real talent in both food design and control. I brought her in to direct our internal design function. By this time, we were in a tie with Eastern Airlines for being the carrier with the lowest cost per passenger in food and beverage - a statistic published by the CAB. Thanks to our staff, we accomplished this and still had some of the best food.

The food service departments of the various airlines had banded together for the purpose of keeping up to date on what was happening in the world of airline catering. Once a year a seminar was held at a different city in the USA; one year we met in Chicago, the next in Tampa, another time in Monterey, California, etc. These large gatherings included the airline caterers and the primary vendors from whom they, or we, bought equipment and food. There were many excellent speakers on hand from the various fields and the vendors were always vying with one another to see who could host the best dinner in the city. It was the airline catering highlight of the year and, in addition to gaining weight, much was gained from the one-on-one visits with the department heads from other airlines.

Breaks, such as the catering seminars, were very welcome as life in the inflight service department seemed to be losing its ability to satisfy the creative talent we had assembled - those now involved in constant budget cuts. If the Federal Government could get in the same mind set, we'd be a healthier nation. Nevertheless, there comes a time when you need a respite from swinging the ax. After two years of this regimentation, the staff was getting stale. In 1976, we were awarded the route from Vancouver, B.C. to Hawaii. Cara Catering in Vancouver had a great "international" kitchen.

This was one route that would not have a high profile for the usual Los Angeles general office critics. So, I turned the staff loose to use their best creativity on the food and beverage design. They were thrilled to get a chance to show their level of expertise. The inflight service they designed would challenge any international carrier. This was an emotional bonus for all of us. Kelly, Renda and several board members, including Cary Grant, were on the inaugural flight. While on board, I explained to Renda and Kelly that this flight would have a special food presentation. There were no complaints then, or in the future.

Our first-class service had deteriorated on the DC-10's; this had happened when we took out some first-class seats and added a coach section in front of the galley elevators. We would be flying the DC-10 on a new route Western had been granted from Los Angeles to Miami. I used this as leverage to get a change made in our first class service. This required a major modification in the arrangement of the first class cabin. The food on a DC-10 was stored downstairs and had to be brought up in an elevator and then wheeled down the aisle. Therefore, the first class service carts had to be wheeled through the coach section to reach the passengers seated in first class. The present configuration of the DC-10 was giving the flight attendants fits for a variety of valid reasons. One of the reasons was that two sets of first class seats, those in the front row, were right by the aircraft doors and the passengers sitting there felt like they were half way into the lavatories; plus, they couldn't see the movie. With the backing of Tony Favero, VP maintenance, and help from McDonald/Douglas engineering department, we removed these four seats and put in a first-class galley. This would isolate the FC service and the two flight attendants who worked that area need not be concerned with the lower galley. This also improved the speed of both services. The design was terrific and we inaugurated it on the Miami/Los Angeles non-stop.

There were problems with the way we were packing the items in the new galleys. I called a couple of flight attendants who had been flying the Miami route and told them to redesign the "packing diagrams" for our caterers. After two check flights, everyone was happy. You have to listen to those who work the service. I don't know that our first-class business improved that much, but our passenger complaints disappeared and we were more competitive with United's 747 service to Hawaii, where most of our DC-10's were used.

This gives a sample of the kinds of things in which I was involved that had a day-to-day impact on the regional VP's. I found, if you told them your objectives, listened to their point of view and explained your constraints, the environment between "planning" and the "line" operation was much more harmonious; especially if you kept Jack Slichter informed.

Unfortunately, Bill Balfour did not learn this lesson and, for whatever reasons, did not keep Slichter in touch with all his plans. Bill was not used to this type of organization and couldn't seem to make the paradigm shift that was necessary to work within the new structure. This was exacerbated by Slichter isolating his group from Balfour in order to make him work through his office. As an example, Slichter would have a meeting in Los Angeles with the ten regional VP's and would not invite Balfour to attend. Bill would come into my office fuming over this apparent "slight." I would offer some suggestions, but Bill did not want to hear them. The "festering sore" was becoming an open wound.

Even though I was relieved of my primary responsibility for flight attendant contract negotiations, Ensign still wanted me to serve on the negotiating committee. Having occupied my position at one time, Ensign recognized the need for the department VP to be in agreement with any work-rule changes. Jack Neel did an excellent job of handling our end of the program; as mentioned, my role was to provide the technical data needed for pricing the contract proposals.

The first negotiation we had was rather drawn out and a mediator was finally assigned from the National Mediation board in Washington. Susan Edwards, a Western Airlines flight attendant had become Chairperson of the

Master Executive Council. She called the shots on the property for the AFA, Airline Flight Attendant Union. There were three flight attendants on the committee, Susan being one of them, and she was the key to getting a contract. One of the other two union members was Helga Lahnert. We finally reached the point where we knew the mediator was about to "cut us loose" - meaning the thirty-day cooling off period would begin. After the thirty days, they were free to strike. We wanted a contract, but it was obvious that Susan Edwards wanted to be set free to go right down to the "midnight hour." She had a belief that the last nickel would not be offered by the company until they saw the picket lines forming.

We went to Phoenix for one last try. In those days, it was important to do everything possible to avoid going into the "thirty day-cooling-off period" as the travel agencies would start booking away from your airline. We arrived in Phoenix just before the Labor Day weekend. Late that afternoon, Jack Neel went out to play tennis and fell on his arm, receiving a severe break at the wrist. I spent the evening with him at the hospital and tried to get him to fly home, but he wouldn't go.

We didn't accomplish much during the first couple of days. I was worried about Jack as I knew he was in a lot of pain; but, he never let on in the meetings.

Saturday, we made progress. Dick Ensign flew over that evening with marching orders from Renda to get a contract, but not to exceed a specific dollar amount. Close to midnight on Sunday, we gave the flight attendants a final package. They countered with a proposal that was too rich for our blood. We told them they could take our final offer and move a few things around, but we'd spent all we could afford. Susan Edwards said that was not satisfactory and would not move off her position.

We caucused, returned to the table and told the mediator that our final offer was as far as we could go. The meeting was about to be adjourned when Helga Lahnert said she wanted a short recess. They came back within the hour and said they would accept our offer. I could tell Susan wasn't happy about this turn of events. By four o'clock, Labor Day morning, we had signed off on the mediator's agreement. Margie and the two children flew over and we spent the rest of Labor Day weekend at Camelback Inn, swimming and resting.

I mention this particular negotiation for a reason. Shortly after I took this new job, we had a flight attendant collapse right after boarding her flight in Los Angeles. Her name was Dixie Duncombe. I went to the hospital as soon as I was notified and found that she had been diagnosed with an aneurysm in the brain. Her parents were in Salt Lake City and we brought them to Los Angeles as quickly as possible.

Dixie had been Helga Lahnert's room-mate. I first became acquainted with her when she served on the flight attendant grievance committee. Helga spent as much time as possible in and out of the hospital with the parents. Dixie was plugged into a life support system but never regained consciousness. After a few days, she was pronounced "brain dead" and her parents were faced with the decision to take her off the life support system. I was with them at the hospital each day and could tell they were really struggling with this decision. Dixie looked beautiful; she just appeared to be sleeping. Finally her parents gave instructions to "un-plug the machine." Helga did a magnificent job in helping Dixie's family through this crisis.

We flew Dixie to Salt Lake City for the funeral and burial at the Salt Lake City Cemetery. Helga asked me to speak at her funeral. By now, I was so emotionally involved that I wasn't sure I'd be able to do it; however, I agreed. The service went well and one of our pilots who was an LDS Church Patriarch in Thousand Oaks, California, dedicated the grave. Helga held together very well until after the burial, then she let the tears flow. I ran into Helga on occasion, but did not see her again as a union representative until this recent negotiation. We never mentioned Dixie as it was just too painful to relive the event.

After that memorable Labor Day morning, when Helga requested the last minute recess with her committee, I asked her what had occurred in their caucus room. She replied that she would not discuss their conversation, but said that she felt our proposal was fair and she believed we wouldn't go any further. The position she took must have persuaded another member of the committee to vote to accept our proposal and I guess it was a majority rule and the two of them out voted Edwards, the Chairperson.

Helga was a real professional and I knew she would never discuss what went on behind closed doors at a negotiation, but I always wonder how deeply she felt about the events surrounding Dixie's death. Helga had later said to me, "Larry, I have never forgotten what you did for Dixie Duncombe and her family." I guess that answered my question.

In this, and subsequent negotiations, I learned some things about Susan Edwards that would serve me well in the future. She was a very skilled negotiator and I had a great deal of respect for her intelligence and her tenacity. Her only problem was her desire to back you in a corner and push you halfway through the wall before she would believe the Airline Flight Attendant Association had drained your last ounce of blood. While I had this admiration for Susan, I never forgot the lessons I had learned in dealing with her in matters pertaining to the union. Later, this information would help me break a log-jam that almost put the company into bankruptcy.

It was very difficult to build a relationship of trust with the flight attendant group. They felt they had been "jerked around" by a culture that had evolved from one individual who was no longer with the company. Bob Leinster had tried to resolve these concerns when he was over the department, but he did not have the time to do what was needed. Bob's scope of responsibility was too broad to concentrate on the communications problems within that sector.

I held meetings with the flight attendants at every base. These were attended by Jack Slichter and the regional VP for that area. The flight attendant schedules made it tough to catch them all, but it was well worth the effort. In the very first meeting in 1974, I became aware of the high level of their hostility. They believed they had not been treated as professionals and so they acted accordingly. I told them at the beginning that I knew I must earn their trust and I didn't expect them to give it freely. I asked them to give me a chance to show we could improve their work environment. They put me on probation. A year later, the attitude in the meetings was better. By the third year, I had earned a trust that would last until my retirement. Words cannot express the enjoyment I found in working with this particular group of professionals. They were capable of creating rainbows in clear skies.

There are a few highlights from these years that I'd like to mention. It seems there is always a tough lesson to be learned by any new manager, and it usually involves making a decision without checking with the team. I had brought in a key planner who had worked with me on the reservation "ACCURES" project; Charles "Topper" Van Every. Among his responsibilities were inflight supplies. We were having difficulty at that time with "hijackers." Topper brought to my attention that we were carrying a "lethal weapon" on the aircraft called a "swizzle stick." It was a long plastic stick with our airline symbol on one end and a sharp point on the other. We decided to put a ball on the end so no one would get stabbed by the swizzle stick.

The new "sticks" hit the field at the same time as my first meeting with the flight attendants. When I opened the session for questions, the first was: "Who was the idiot that put the ball on the end of the swizzle stick?" I responded that I was that idiot. She said: "Don't you have any idea what we do with these things? We stab them into the fruit that goes in the drink. Have you ever stabbed a piece of pineapple with a ball?" Obviously I hadn't.

The swizzle stick episode could have been a symbol of idiocy; however, by admitting to my error in the rest of the meetings, prior to the question and answer period, I was able to turn it into an example of why we had to be more conversant with the flight attendant's environment. Two years later, at one of these meetings in San Francisco, the group awarded me "The Royal Order of the Swizzle Stick." It had been made into a medallion on a necklace.

For some reason, the San Francisco Base was the toughest. They would keep me alert. If I ever wanted to know what was really happening out on the line, I'd spend a day hanging around the San Francisco flight attendant lounge. By the end of the day I could pretty well predict the attitude of the group and where the "hot spots" were on the system.

One night Margie and I were flying down from San Francisco and were seated in back of two San Francisco based flight attendants. They were headed to Los Angeles for recurrent training. Halfway down, they leaned over the back of their seats, grinned at us and one to the other said, "Should we tell him what happened on the flight out of Anchorage this morning?" "Oh yea! He'll want to hear this one."

The story unfolded as follows: "Anchorage boarded a strange breakfast menu that we have never seen before. It was a small Belgian waffle and some fruit stuff. We had served this big husky Alaskan and had started down the aisle with another tray, when he bellowed out: 'what is this s_?' He then proceeded to tell us in detail why it was the worst breakfast he had ever seen. All the while he was busy roaring at us, the syrup from the Belgian waffle was running down the leg of his pants."

There was a pause for my reaction and I couldn't hold back the laughter. We all four had a good laugh. I found out the regional VP in Anchorage, where we owned the flight kitchen, had decided to design some new meals. I called Ken Downs who managed the kitchen, and things were back to normal the next morning. But, I'll never forget the description of this big Alaskan and the dripping syrup.

Most Alaska passengers, especially those coming off the North Slope oil rigs, were known for their enormous appetites and their capacity to drink everything in sight that was alcoholic. On our Anchorage to Honolulu flights, we'd double pack the "booze" carts and they'd be empty on arrival. I once called a flight attendant, who had bid the route, to see if we were putting on the right mix of alcoholic beverages. She said, "Doesn't matter - when we run out of one thing they switch to another and never complain." I asked our Honolulu station manager if they had to carry any of them off the plane on arrival. He said: "Are you kidding, they charge off the flight and head for the airport bar like they'd just come from a 'dry' county."

The older Pacific Northern flight attendants taught us a few things about passenger handling procedures for some of these rugged northerners. I was party to one such lesson on my initial "check-ride" down from Anchorage to Seattle.

I was sitting in the last row in first-class and there was a ruckus in the aisle in back of me. Standing in the middle of the aisle was this six-foot-four resident of Alaska. He towered over the little female flight attendant. She was hollering up at him: "Joe, you son-of-a-bitch, if you don't sit down right now, you'll never get on one of my flights again." Joe sat down.

When we arrived in Seattle, I decided to wait on board and have a talk with the flight attendant. She was up at the front door as the passengers deplaned. As Joe came by her, he lifted her up, kissed her on the forehead and said, "See you next trip, Hazel." I got off the flight with the others and thanked the Lord I had said nothing to Hazel. I later learned that she was so popular with the old PNA crowd that some of them would call our reservation department in Seattle and ask which flight she was on so they could take that trip. In 1993 I heard that Hazel was still flying and she had to be pushing seventy-years old.

We had a very special flight attendant named, Nora Jeroue. She had been in supervisory jobs and had conducted training; however, she mostly enjoyed just "flying the line." Nora had open heart surgery when she was in her fifties. When she came back to work she bid the Honolulu turn-a-rounds. This meant she would fly from Los Angeles to Honolulu and then return on the same aircraft. It was a long day of flying, and with large loads, could be a mighty tough two flights. After she had flown for a couple of weeks, I asked her to stop by my office for a visit. "Nora," I said, "I'm concerned about your health flying these turn-a-rounds." She replied: "Don't be concerned about me, but you better figure out what to do with these youngsters who are flying 'reserve' - they're dying on their feet half way back." Age didn't seem to be a factor for those who were well trained and loved their work.

Not long after I became VP of inflight, it became apparent that we would have to make a major shift in the way that we boarded our entrees for meal flights. The present system was to prepare them just before flight-time and transfer the meals in what we called "hot-food-coffins" to the aircraft. They were then held at serving temperature until meal time.

The International carriers were using a system the caterers called "chill-pack." The food was cooked, chilled down and boarded in a near frozen state. It would then be reheated before serving. Several of the foreign airlines said they were having a great deal of success with the frozen entrees the flight attendants "re-constituted" in a "high-heat" oven in the aircraft galley. I liked the idea. Pat Glowe did some studies and the taste tests were favorable. I wanted to talk to someone who was using the exact oven that the staff had recommended. That would be Qantas Airlines and I could see it on an aircraft in Honolulu.

It was time to see how our Vancouver service was being handled out of Honolulu, so my son, Randy, and I went for a weekend jaunt. We flew from Los Angeles to Honolulu, with plenty of time to catch the flight from Honolulu to Vancouver. We would overnight in Vancouver and then take Canadian Pacific to Los Angeles; their food service was reported to be superior to ours on this route and I wanted to see it for myself.

When we arrived in Honolulu, I found that the Qantas Boeing 747 I planned to check out was already boarding the passengers for departure to Sydney, Australia. I gave the gate agent my card and asked if I could talk to the flight attendant supervisor on board. I asked young Randy to wait by the gate.

The Qantas supervisor was most accommodating and we went down the elevator to the lower galley of the aircraft where he showed me how the ovens operated. He said the flight group really liked the system. Looking at his watch, he said: "Wow! I hope they haven't closed the doors." We got in the elevator - it didn't start. He told me to jump up and down. There was barely room for the two of us to stand let alone "jump." The elevator began moving and I got to the door just as it was being closed. Because of my last minute request, this flight attendant had not advised anyone where he was going and the other attendant at the door thought I was a passenger.

After deplaning, I asked Randy if he was worried. He wasn't, he thought it would be a great adventure to get back home alone. The bottom line is that we bought the ovens and converted all aircraft. We were one of the first domestic lines to use this particular oven. It was, and still is, a very successful system.

We had handled Japan Air Lines food service out of our flight kitchen in Anchorage. It was a good fifty-percent of our revenue. Shortly after JAL insisted that we enlarge our facility to accommodate more 747's, they decided to build their own kitchen. We sold the extra vehicles and carts, but it left us "holding the bag" on the excess space.

One day a load of tourist-class passengers on a JAL 747 got food poisoning en route from Anchorage to Europe. Many of the people were hospitalized on arrival. They traced it to a breakfast boarded by their Anchorage flight kitchen. It came out later that a cook's helper had an open and infected wound that had contaminated the hot food in the tourist section. It was being covered by world-wide news.

Japan Air Lines quickly closed their entire Anchorage kitchen. We got a call from Tokyo asking us to do their meals. We declined for very valid reasons, one of them being that we'd sold all our 747 "rolling stock." They called again and offered to let us use theirs. At the time, the cause of their contamination was not yet known - or at least, not public. They had a lot of flights that made fuel stops at Anchorage and they were getting panicky.

We had begun working on an emergency plan to give assistance, when we received a telephone call from Tokyo: "No problem, we now open kitchen." We called our flight kitchen manager, Ken Downs, in Anchorage and he said the JAL manager in Anchorage had just committed "hari-kari." Ken said: "If we ever have a similar situation, I hope you don't expect the same action from me."

As the story unfolded, Ken Downs learned that they knew exactly what the problem had been, but closed their kitchen to "save face." Their manager's action took care of "face" and they were rolling within hours.

The only time I ever ran into a potential sanitation problem was at Guadalajara, Mexico. We had been granted permission to start serving this large city from Los Angeles and there wasn't a flight kitchen big enough to handle our needs. After two exploratory trips there on Mexicana Airlines, I had agreed to work with a man, Luis Limberopolis, who wanted to build a new flight kitchen at the airport. He presently owned a large restaurant in town and a small fly-specked catering operation at the field which handled a scanty food service for Texas International Airlines. His present facility at the airport could not be expanded, so we had to obtain a larger area in a more remote building.

Marriott had an executive chef named Hermann Duringer who helped us in food design and quality control. I asked Hermann if he would work with me on this project; that is, if I could get permission from the Marriott Headquarters. All were in agreement.

Hermann had owned a restaurant in Mexico and spoke fluent Spanish. He arrived a week before our inaugural flight. Pat Glowe, Dale Crogan and Ken Norton, all members of the inflight food team were with him. The job was to get the supplies arranged and train the people who would pack the food and equipment. Hermann would train the chef. I arrived four days before the first flight. For two days, we went through a complete mockup of our service. It was a disaster! Two days to go and the new walk-in refrigerator was not installed. Hermann suggested we "double pack" the food out of Los Angeles until we could get the kitchen running properly. We would board all equipment and supplies in Guadalajara. One chef and two of his helpers had quit, or Chef Duringer had chased them off - I could never get a straight story on this.

The morning of the first flight, our inflight team was in the kitchen at 6:00 a.m. We left that night at 9:00 p.m. It was to be like that for the next week. I would spend most of the mornings working as a kitchen helper and the afternoons arguing with the Mexican authorities about the delivery and installation of our kitchen equipment. I learned more about the operation of a flight kitchen in that week than I'd learned in my whole career. The only thing that kept Hermann Duringer with us was the late night poker game with Pat Glowe and her team. Fortunately, or by plan, Hermann won most of the pots.

Guadalajara finally settled down and became a routine kitchen. From this experience came a great respect for those airlines that had to open kitchens in foreign locations where sanitation was a potential problem.

Art Kelly scheduled a board of director's meeting in Mexico City in October, 1974. He asked three of Western's corporate officers to serve on a committee to see that it came together properly. There would be a lot of public contact between members of our board and local dignitaries at several large affairs and the affair would last three days. Ray Silvius, VP public relations; Bill Balfour, VP sales and service planning, and I were the three selected. Art had said he wanted the officers to have more contact with the members of the board and this was one way to accomplish this.

Each of the committee was assigned specific duties. One of mine was to get everyone and their luggage through Mexican Customs and properly ensconced in the Americana Hotel. Everyone's luggage arrived, except that of the wife of our major stockholder, Kirk Kerkorian. I located the bags in Los Angeles and told Kirk that I'd have them at the hotel by that night, even if I had to charter a plane. He said he'd expected nothing less. The bags came in on the next flight and we had them in the room by dinner. She'd left them sitting at the terminal entrance and they weren't tagged. After that brief fright, the rest of my "official" duties ran smoothly. My "unofficial" tasks did not fare as well.

Kirk Kerkorian had invited Cary Grant, the movie actor, to serve on the board of directors. I had met him before in Los Angeles; however, it was on this trip to Mexico that we got well acquainted. The first morning was a tour of certain key spots in the city. In those days, I always carried my camera. Knowing that several of the ladies would want their pictures taken with Cary Grant, I asked him if he felt comfortable with this. Cary responded,

"Delighted, Larry, and I trust you to 'wipe' any with double-chins;" meaning, lose those that did not do justice to his profile.

Our first stop was at the Statue of the Angel on the Reforma. With all the steps leading up to the angel, it was a natural for picture taking. I put a new roll of film in the camera. After many pictures were taken of Cary with wives of the members of the board and other Mexican officials, I became concerned that I hadn't yet come to the end of the film. I checked and found that I had not loaded the film properly and it was not winding on the spool. I'd lost thirty-six shots. To say that I was the most unpopular soul on the tour would be a gross understatement. Cary Grant was great; he said to get them back together at the next stop and he would make sure I regained my professional status. I'd taken thousands of pictures with that camera and had never run into this problem before.

The only difficulty I had was with the wife of a top executive from Mexico. At a garden party, I had taken three pictures of her while she was near, or beside, Cary. When the pictures were developed, all three were "double-chin-shots." She hounded me for the better part of a year to send the pictures. All I could say was that they didn't come out. She'd respond, "I know you've got them; all the others received theirs" - and she kept calling. I never carried my camera again on a company trip.

Cary Grant was very popular with the children in Mexico. We'd walk down the street and they'd cluster around him. Since he hadn't been in movies for years, I couldn't figure out why the little ones were so attentive. One of the Mexican members said it was because they could only afford to attend a "peso teatro" where they showed only the old movies; therefore, Cary was a "current" star. Of course, he never lost that "stardom." To this day, some of my grandchildren's favorite video rentals are the old Cary Grant movies.

We had one free evening. A large room had been set aside as the "hospitality suite." The board members and their wives had all scattered to various restaurants. Cary didn't feel like going out so he came up to the hospitality suite and visited with a few of us who had decided to have dinner at the hotel. Pretty soon he went over to a grand piano in the corner and started to play. I didn't realize he played the piano. He'd put a toothpick in his mouth and was doing a great imitation of Hoagy Carmichael. This went on for a half an hour. Finally, our hunger got the best of us. We six went down to a late dinner and left Cary alone in the room. I mentioned this to someone later and she said, "You mean you had a chance to spend the whole evening alone with Cary Grant and you walked out on him?" Guess I didn't think about it at the time; I was hungry and he wasn't.

One day, Cary Grant called with a request. He said: "Larry, would you send me some of those baggage identification tags to put on my luggage." I said I'd be happy to and reminded him that I'd recently sent some. "I got those," he responded, "but I need more. People keep taking them off my luggage. Why, just the other day at Heathrow, in London, a girl took one off the handle while the bag was at my side. I said: 'Here, what are you doing?' She walked away with the tag saying that I could get more. What am I to do?" I said we would put a code on the bag tag instead of his name and then they'd stay put. He said he'd think about it, but the requests for more tags kept coming in. When he first began calling me, the secretary would announce that there was someone on the phone imitating Cary Grant. Once, a secretary refused to put him through until he said who "he really was." Cary would just laugh and would never take umbrage at such behavior.

The last time we were to see Cary Grant was when I was CEO and we made an attempt to have him do a TV commercial for Western. We were trying to get people who had never done a commercial. He declined. He said, "If I ever decided to do a commercial, it would be for Western; however, I have avoided them all my life and I don't want to end my career by being seen in advertisements."

I really admired Cary's position. Having been privileged to this conversation, I was appalled when, after his death, they began using his image from film clips to "sandwich" on TV commercials. Every time I saw it on television I would cringe. He was a fine man, and Margie and I felt honored to have been acquainted with him.

Margie and I became acquainted with another person of early movie fame, George Montgomery.

In the late summer of 1974, our president, Art Kelly asked me, as well as Bert Lynn, VP advertising, who in Salt Lake City would make a good contribution to Western's board of directors. Art said it would be nice if we could find someone from the Mormon Church. He recalled the time that President George Albert Smith had served on the board. We both responded that Victor L. Brown would be outstanding. This was for two reasons; first, he was the Presiding Bishop of The Church of Jesus Christ of Latter-day Saints; second, prior to being called to this position, he had spent his career with United Airlines and understood the rudiments of our business.

Art made an appointment with the First Presidency and the three of us flew up to see them. We met with President Spencer W. Kimball and his counselors, N. Eldon Tanner and Marion G. Romney. They thought this appointment to Western's board would please "Vic" and they would make a few adjustments to eliminate any conflict of interest.

Bishop Brown was unable to attend the gathering in Mexico City during October of 1974. It was too short notice for him to adjust his busy calendar. His first meeting was on January 27, 1975. Cary Grant had asked the proper way to address Victor and was told, "Bishop Brown." He couldn't quite get this together, so he greeted him as "Vic, your eminence."

Bishop Brown was to be one of the two most valuable outside board members that Western had during its last ten years of troubles, woes and victories; Jerry Grinstein being the other. He received the highest of respect from his peers and the employees.

As a key member of the executive committee, Victor was the catalyst for many board decisions that were made to lead Western from the edge of bankruptcy to its ultimate success. He would be far too humble to ever admit the quiet power he interjected into the process of governance at Western Airlines.

Over a period of twenty years, Victor L. Brown became my counselor and advocate. He guided me into paths I did not always choose to travel, but, in his gentle way, would convince me that I had a duty to perform. Through the process of time and trials, our friendship grew. "Vic" passed away in 1996 after a long illness. He was a great mentor to me and became a very close friend.

At Western Airlines, in 1979, Bob Leinster decided to retire as VP ground services. Several times I have mentioned Bob as he was a very dear friend, as well as a close business associate. We remained in contact with one another until his death from complications of Alzheimer's disease in 1993.

On October 9, 1979, I was promoted to VP ground and inflight services, absorbing all of Leinster's responsibilities. I continued reporting to Richard P. Ensign, senior VP marketing. For the first time Western had a department that combined all areas of customer service systems and procedures and related training under one department head. I had every function in the way of customer contact from the time the passenger made a reservation, checked in, flew to his destination and claimed his baggage.

Jack Slichter was still responsible for the administration of all the field operations. My job would have been an impossible task had I not had a good rapport with Slichter. We trusted one another and he knew I would do nothing to undermine his authority in the field. Nevertheless, this new organization continued to be awkward in that the flight attendant base managers reported to Slichter's regional VPs, but we worked that out.

While I found Jack to be very cooperative, if kept informed, others in the corporate marketing group still did not make an effort to see that the new "field/staff" relationships were solidified. While the organization had its flaws, it was workable. The difficulty between Jack Slichter and Bill Balfour had not in any way diminished. Dick Ensign tried to ameliorate the problems, but Dom Renda took Slichter's side and Art Kelly took Balfour's. Dick Ensign was caught on the horns of a political dilemma that was to be resolved only when the ax fell on most of the hierarchy of the marketing division.

While I had the inflight service responsibilities, I went through two bouts with duodenal ulcers. I believe the first was from the previously mentioned period of pressure when we had to cut our inflight budget in an attempt to offset the rising costs of labor, fuel and equipment. The second round of ulcers came from the emotional pressure that began on the morning of October 31, 1979. Around 4:30 a.m., I was called by our dispatch department and advised that Flight 2605, a DC-10, had crashed on landing at Mexico City Airport. There were a few survivors, but this had not yet been sorted out in Mexico.

I rushed to the airport command center where they were organizing a flight down to Mexico City for the group that would handle things at that end. Jack Slichter and I divided the responsibilities of our area and he took the flight to MEX. I set up a mini-command center in the Los Angeles reservations office, where we had the best access to communications. In addition, this was out of the main stream of the daily operations.

During the next seventy-two hours, I was to get an aggregate of about eight hours sleep. This did not bother me as much as the emotional tension that permeated everything we were doing during that critical period. I was thankful Jack had volunteered to do the job in Mexico. It included the identification of the dead. I don't know that I could have lived through that one. I was much better suited for the work at my end.

Of the seventy people that were killed, thirteen were employees - eight of them being our flight attendants. The normal compliment on the DC-10 was eight to ten attendants, depending on the load. Eight attendants were working the flight down and two were "deadheading" to work the heavy return trip. Two flight attendants escaped with relatively minor physical injuries. The attendants were based in Los Angeles and most of them were relatively junior employees who had been recruited from Southern California. It was unusual to find a group on one flight that grew up so close to one another.

The deceased had graduated from schools in Artesia, Downey, Canoga Park, Gardena, City of Industry, Hacienda Heights, and two in Long Beach. That put a critical load on our Los Angeles Base Manager, Darleen Harris. She wanted her group to handle the contact with the parents, which pleased me no end. The flight attendant supervisors, and other senior flight personnel who volunteered to help, were by far the best group to interface with the parents in their grief. I asked that one be assigned to each family who then became their primary source of contact, whether day or night. Darleen had an unbelievable amount of energy and we kept worrying that she would fold, but she didn't. Her most difficult chore was to fly to Mexico and identify the remains of the eight deceased flight attendants.

I was in the flight lounge as much as possible to visit with anyone who needed to talk about the accident. The first three nights were spent with the attendants who were taking Flight 2605 to Mexico. This group seemed to need the most help. I made many calls to each of the parents of the deceased and, prior to the funerals, personally visited with each of them. Working with the families of deceased children, when I was a Bishop of the Scottsdale Ward, gave me some feeling for what we had to accomplish. During this period I often thanked the Lord for all my ecclesiastical training.

"Grief control" is necessary and must be carefully applied. I brought in two psychologists who were noted in this field, Dan Johnson and Margaret Barbeau, to assist us with the parents and the other flight attendants - especially those crew members who had been classmates with the deceased and had become close friends. Following is a quote from the November 19, 1979 issue of TIME magazine:

> Johnson and Barbeau are working with Western Air Lines flight attendants in the wake of the Mexico City crash last month. It marks the first time that grief counseling has been requested by an airline. Says Western VP Larry Lee: "We had a very heavy grief situation. Many had just graduated after seven weeks of training with some of the victims. They become so close in these classes."
>
> Johnson and Barbeau met the relatives and colleagues of the victims. They also gave a quick course in grief counseling to the senior employees, each of whom was assigned to help the family of one of the victims deal with their grief. The problem in the past, says Johnson, is that when the executives are responsible for coping with the grief of employees, they become so involved and work so hard that they develop the same symptoms as the grief victims themselves.

In the last sentence, Dr. Johnson had just described me; ergo, ulcers.

We only had one problem with a mother, one who wanted to view the remains of her daughter. I was well acquainted with the flight attendant's uncle who was General Manager of the Airport Marriott Hotel. He called his sister and pleaded with her not to view the remains. Getting nowhere with her, he called and asked if I'd intervene; he felt the viewing would "push her over the edge." She was scheduled to be at the mortuary in Arcadia in an hour. I called the mortician and asked him to stall until we could get there. Luckily, I caught Darleen Harris and we drove across town without the usual traffic.

When we arrived, the mother seemed to have her "feet in cement" on this issue. While Darleen had made the identification in Mexico, she could not recall the exact condition of the remains. I went in to the mortician and asked how she looked. He said he would not recommend a viewing.

It finally came down to one expressed need from the flight attendant's mother; she wanted to be sure that it was her daughter. Darleen said she knew the girl very well and would go look and make sure it was her. She did this and returned with the confirmation. The mother asked how she looked. Darleen said: "She is beautiful. She just looks like she's had a very bad sunburn. She died instantly from the heat but she is not burned in the way you would normally think of it." That finally satisfied the mother and we parted company. After the funeral, her mother came up to me and said: "I just wanted to hold her in my arms one more time." My ulcer grew another inch.

Margie and I attended every funeral in Los Angeles and, on November 14th, we held a special memorial service for all the deceased employees. That seemed to bring this episode to a close. However, as I am writing this, I am looking at the faces of these eight wonderful flight attendants and realize how much they became a part of my life.

Words cannot describe how fervently I prayed that we would not have another major accident before my retirement. That event took a lot out of me. The only thing that preserved my sanity was having a professional group of senior flight personnel who knew how to work with people when they were suffering.

I caught the usual flak from the operating group for "wasting money to bring in the shrinks." However, from this foundation, we got a better foothold on an employee "help" program that ultimately became one of the best and most cost effective in the industry.

Chapter 6

OF BULLETIN BOARDS
AND BLOODBATHS

The years in the middle to late '70's were very traumatic for the air-line industry. In 1975, noises were being made about "deregulating" the airlines. Art Kelly, then chairman of the board and CEO, was dead set against deregulation. Of all the airlines, we were the most vocal. He prepared a folder of material for each of the officers, one that could be used with our various contacts to thwart the efforts of the present administration. Consider this statement of Chairman Kelly; it appeared in the 1976 Western Airlines Annual Report:

> For nearly four decades, the air transportation system in the U.S. has grown and developed under regulation by the Civil Aeronautics Board that determines which carriers provide service over which routes and oversees the level of fares and rates. Although this system is admittedly not perfect, it has nevertheless given the American public the finest air transportation in the world - both in terms of price and service for the consumer - and it has encouraged economic viability for the airlines in producing that service.
>
> The past two years have seen a number of deregulation proposals come forth. These are based on the premise that the public would get better service at less cost if the airlines were given greater freedom to enter and exit markets of their choice and

given greater flexibility in setting their own fares. We strongly support free enterprise, but we also maintain that particularly in the area of route authority and pricing, air transportation should be regarded and regulated as a public utility. If a maximum number of communities are to continue to receive good passenger, mail and cargo service by air, at reasonable fares and rates, the present regulatory system must be preserved.

The erosion of such a federal regulatory pattern by irresponsible changes under the guise of public interest will lead only to a deterioration of the world's best transportation network with little or no permanent reduction in fares.

We recognize that some limited procedural changes may be constructive, but this can be accomplished by the Civil Aeronautics Board pursuant to provisions of the Federal Aviation Act now in effect. Accordingly, we believe it unwise and unnecessary to enact any of the pending deregulation proposals.

Art Kelly was accurate in his predictions. However, at that time most of the other airlines saw this as a chance for expansion; especially in the western part of the United States. There were three realistic ways to combat the effects of this "octopus" that was about to be unleashed by a Congress who had closed its ears to reason. One was to reduce the domestic operation to those "city pairs" that provided the largest traffic potential, while seeking to expand the part of our business that would remain regulated – the foreign markets. A second was to quickly realign our markets and control the feed before others could occupy our historical territory. The third was to merge with another carrier and thereby improve the economies of scale. Kelly and Renda chose the third.

There was to be additional fallout from the Deregulation Act; the Airline Industrial Relations Conference was abolished. It was said to have been an "anti-trust" organization, or something to that effect. We had so carefully structured this association to fight the accelerated bargaining from the unions that had placed the salaries of the airline industry in the category of being the most inflationary in the country.

I had enjoyed helping to develop AIRCON and felt the concept was strong. Looking back, I see its demise made little impact; deregulation turned the burner up on bargaining and the threat of bankruptcy kept most of the unions in line. Those that didn't see the light would meet the fate of Braniff, Continental and Eastern.

In late May of 1978, I was asked to join with my counterpart from Continental Airlines and meet at the Pacifica Hotel. A select team would develop a cost analysis of what the two airlines could do if merged. We were looking for the synergistic effects of combining our route structure and equipment. I brought along Carlos Hernandez and Diane Fuller to run the computer model which would give us the best prediction of cost. Our contracts were similar.

Maury Myers, who later became president of Aloha Airlines and then America West, was one of the key players from Continental. We were able to show an approximate ten percent improvement in productivity by merging the two carriers. On the first of June, Western and Continental announced their intention to merge. Then, in September, we filed for approval from the Civil Aeronautics Board. Both of our boards of directors had approved the merger. With all the signs now pointing to a "deregulated" industry, we felt sure we would receive approval.

On October 24, 1978 the Airline Deregulation Act was signed into effect. It would phase out the CAB's regulatory authority over routes by 1981 and fare regulation would end a year later. With that, the will of Congress was clearly expressed. Nevertheless, the CAB exercised its fading muscle to kill the Western/Continental merger; on July 21, 1979 they denied our application. The vote was three against and one for. Looking back, it's hard to believe how three people could do so much to foul up a significant part of our industry. Congress had put the rope around our neck while allowing a lame-duck bureaucracy to start a fire under our feet. The fact that Western, as a separate entity, would die was inevitable. How much we would suffer during our demise was the only question left unanswered.

Western had no concrete plan in place for this turn of events. The only thing left to do was re-approach the merger with Continental one year later. This was being done with apparent success and the Civil Aeronautics Board was to rule on it, but they never got a chance to proceed as Frank Lorenzo of Texas International Airlines made an offer to buy controlling interest in Continental. Their stockholders bought his plan over ours and the rest is history. I'm sure that the Continental board and many of these shareholders wish they'd supported Western. Today, my thousand shares of Continental stock are not worth the paper on which they're printed. The Western shareholder fared much better.

With the second attempt to merge at an end, the top management went to the "first option," which was to downsize the domestic system and increase our international flying.

We were primarily a north/south configured carrier - from Anchorage to Mexico City. The feeling was that we should control the western USA markets to Mexico with as many Mexican destinations as possible. We were chosen to be the official U.S. Airline to the Mexico Olympics. Western Airlines was well thought of by the Mexican Government as we employed only those who were citizens of Mexico residing in that country. There was not one "gringo" living in Mexico. However, the Mexican Government supported a National Airline, Mexicana. Their cost structure was much lower than ours and their price setting policies prevailed. We knew we had to have both a business and leisure market presence in that country.

Renda felt we needed to begin some service to Europe. One of the cities targeted was London, England. We'd take it any way we could get it. "Any way" was from Anchorage, Alaska, and later on, from Denver, Colorado. We were awarded authority to service London through the Gatwick Airport. Gatwick, at that time, was a new model of an old U.S. "non-sked" terminal. While it was served by several U.S. airlines, it did not run in the same league with Heathrow, the real International Airport and the one almost every business person preferred.

Gatwick is located in a beautiful part of the countryside, but required a long train ride to get into downtown London. That was the main ingredient that cut down on the number of business passengers through Gatwick. As a transfer point to Europe, or other destinations, it had a very limited offering. If you had to move over to Heathrow to get a connection, it was one and a half hours by bus. All of this portended more of the same type of low tourist fares and packaged deals that were bleeding us in the domestic service. Dominic P. Renda was now the president and chief executive officer of

Western. He made the decision to proceed with an expedited entry into this market. It was expedited because we were awarded the route, but only given a few months to get service underway or we'd lose it.

Jack Slichter was appointed the team leader to determine if we could get an operation in place within the appointed time. I was asked to evaluate the airport, inflight and reservations functions. The reservations operation would be the pacing ingredient. Tony Colletti, from maintenance, was sent with the team to analyze the needs of the operations division, as they would have to be contracted out. After a long week of meetings, we reported that it could be done in time. We would need to "jury-rig" some of the activities.

Since this was Dom Renda's pet project, it was well to have Jack Slichter as the project director to make sure we met our deadlines. Jack was an excellent communicator, had the CEO's confidence, and was a superb planner. Delta Air Lines had been granted permission to serve Gatwick a few years earlier. Their local managers said it was impossible to get an operation started in less than one year. We had three months. October 28, 1980, when our first flight landed, many Delta employees were lined up at the window of the concourse cheering as the wheels of the DC-10 touched down. They seemed sincerely happy that we had accomplished the impossible. Too bad it was such a waste of time. It produced a huge "start-up" cost with little return on the investment.

During these three months of preparation, I spend about half my time in England. When there, I stayed at the Portman Hotel in London and it began feeling like home to me. My expense account was quadruple any other period I had spent with Western; staying in London was expensive. Every step of progress had to be hand walked to the finish line, and then you weren't sure it was a goal you'd really crossed. Getting telephone service was next to impossible. Delta was most helpful in introducing me to the "shakers and movers" at the telephone company and, after many long lunches, things began to fall into place.

I brought over a small "start-up" team and they were outstanding. When it looked like it wasn't going to come together, they'd convince me that everything would fall into place at the last minute. It did, just as they predicted. They were great troopers and worked around the clock. These were the real heroes of the airline industry who never failed to produce the desired results.

This "fast-start-up" experience gave me confidence that one could accomplish the impossible; that is, if it was properly organized and you had the right people in place. This threshold of confidence would be of great benefit to me a few years later when I had the responsibility of developing the "Western Airlines hub" in Salt Lake City.

As I stated, the London operation proved to be a financial disaster. Western had no feed in Alaska and not enough local traffic to fill a flight. It was a shortcut to Hawaii, a very favored destination for the British. However, the only way you could market the Hawaiian product was through the "packaged" tour business. Their higher commissions cut the low fares even lower. There was no way we could be successful with this operation.

Denver to Gatwick made more sense, but it required Western to establish a "mini-hub" in Denver. But, a hub there of any size could not be sustained by just London. United, Continental and Frontier had "locks" on Denver and the competition was really tough. Denver to London could be a seasonal operation at best. We had too many of these "seasonal operations" already. Western's London operation was doomed from the day it started.

Following deregulation, there was one event that slowed the incursion of our competitors who were poised to pour over our historic "Western" territory. The Air Controllers went on an illegal strike and President Ronald Reagan fired them all and started training new ones. To manage the now restricted air-space, the government established a "slot" system that would only allow so many takeoffs per hour from any airport. At some of the larger cities, these "slot-times" were awarded by lottery. This created chaos in the scheduling departments of the various airlines, but it did slow down the over-capacity that was developing with the "start-up carriers."

I often wonder what life would have been like had Reagan not fired the controllers. I think we would have seen more bankruptcies among the older carriers. As I think about it, there may not have been more of them, just earlier occurrences. For example, Western would never have made it if, at that time, Southwest had been turned loose to fly when and where they desired.

Through all this, the overall business of running the airline proceeded with its other challenges. Along with Western's lack of a long range plan came the challenge of showing the public what we were. Were we an international carrier? A north-south specialist from Anchorage to Mexico City? An airlines specializing in leisure travel? We needed to quit fragmenting our message. Happily Art Kelly and Dom Renda appointed a "design committee" that reported directly to them. It was their job to clear anything that would impact the outward "image" of Western Airlines. This included all uniforms, aircraft interior designs, seat materials, exterior paint jobs, ticket counters, signage and VIP lounges. I sat on the committee as I had the responsibility for most of these. Bert Lynn played a large roll on this committee.

The selection of uniforms offered many interesting experiences as we would receive design presentations from the leading fashion designers; among them were Bill Blass, Edith Head and Ralph Lauren. The unions had provisions in their contracts to allow their input into the design of these uniforms. We successfully engaged the assistance of their appointed committees to make our final selections.

Western had ordered several of the new Boeing 767's, and we were among those with the earliest delivery dates. Topper Van Every and his staff did some unique design work on the 767 galleys. Boeing profited from Topper's interaction. Even though we failed to take delivery of the 767, this became a choice learning experience for our staff. Today, when I am traveling on this aircraft, I see many of the design features that were innovations from Topper and his group.

The reason we failed to take delivery of the 767 is that it was to be one of my tasks as CEO to swap our delivery positions on that aircraft for some 737-300's. We just couldn't finance the 767 package. It was a hard decision for me as I really liked the aircraft and felt it was a key for the success of the Salt Lake City hub. In addition, at that time it was the ideal aircraft to replace the McDonald Douglas DC-10's.

The fortunes of Western Airlines began to wane during the "watch" of Dom Renda, and he came under a great deal of criticism from some of the members of Western's board of directors. The feeling was that he had no definitive plan for the deregulated environment and the international program was a bottomless money pit. Even more devastating, the employees turned against him. There was a universal lack of confidence expressed by all the unions that Western did not have the type of entrepreneurial leadership required for the current deregulated marketplace. This problem was exacerbated by a widening chasm in communication between Renda and Kelly. Western's board of directors finally took the only course of action they saw available to them.

On, or about, October 1, 1981, at a special late-night meeting of Western's board, they dismissed both Dom Renda and Art Kelly and appointed Robert Kinsey as acting CEO. The search firm of Spencer Stuart was hired to locate a new CEO for Western. The board had set a few parameters that the firm must follow. They could interview whomever they wanted from inside the company; however the person must be under fifty-five years of age. Only a few were selected who were presently officers and within the age requirements. I was among them.

Bob Kinsey had called me to his office and said to give it "my best shot" as I was his choice for the job. He may have done the same thing with the others. He was a wily person. Nevertheless, on October 1st, Margie wrote in her journal that I did not want the job and that I was going around muttering something about the "Peter Principle."

It was apparent from the tone of the interviews that the feeling was to hire someone new from the outside. The unions were openly pushing for this and the pilots expressed the desire to get someone who had not even been associated with the industry. "New blood" was the phrase.

Before the "head hunters" could complete their job, Art Kelly introduced the members of the board to a plan that was proposed by a man named Neil Bergt. He was the owner and operator of a small Alaskan flight operation and was proposing a merger between his airline, Western and Wein Alaska Airlines, which was primarily owned by Household Finance. I never could figure out what the board saw in this financial scheme, but Neil Bergt sold himself to them and was hired as the new chairman and chief executive officer and president of Western Airlines, Inc. My records indicate this happened on December 8, 1981.

Kinsey, who was acquired in the merger with Pacific Northern Airlines, and had been in the position of "acting-CEO," stayed on in a supporting role and felt right at home as the Alaskans started to arrive.

It took one meeting to tell who had the real brains of the new outfit; they resided in an engineer named Frank Moolin. He was Bergt's right arm. He had an impressive background. His greatest accomplishment was his work on the Alaska Pipeline. When the "big three," Bechtel, Fluor and Alyeska, were floundering in this major project, they brought in Moolin. They were over budget and behind schedule. Frank took the title of "project director" and oversaw the completion of the pipeline, which he brought in on schedule. Frank then went to work for Neil Bergt and helped him amass a fortune as the "North Slope" of Alaska continued to roll forward. I'll not attempt to further extol the virtues of Moolin; suffice it to say, he was one of the most brilliant and best-organized men with whom I have had the pleasure to associate.

Bergt felt he had to come out with an immediate action that would hit the employees of Western between the eyes with a two by four. It would have to be something that would appeal to the unions and yet set a stage to show them he did not arrive for "business as usual."

A few days after Neil G. Bergt's arrival, the following communication was sent and posted throughout the Western Airlines system:

TELETYPE TO ALL LOCATIONS - FOR BULLETIN BOARD POSTING

December 10, 1981 To All Employees:

As the first step in Western's emerging Survival Plan, Neil G. Bergt, chairman and chief executive officer, has announced the elimination of 12 company officer positions, effective today. They are:

> Executive VP and chief operating officer;
>
> Executive VP - marketing;
>
> Senior VP - field marketing;
>
> VP - advertising and sales promotion;
>
> The four field divisions will be combined into two;
>
> VP - procurement
>
> Assistant VP - corporate law and assistant secretary;

Assistant VP - consumer affairs;

Assistant VP - schedule planning;

Assistant VP - properties and facilities;

VP - Los Angeles

Although the position of executive VP and chief operating officer has been eliminated, Robert O. Kinsey will continue to work with Mr. Bergt in an advisory capacity during the formulation of the company's Survival Plan.

(Bert D. Lynn, VP - advertising and sales promotion, and Harry L. White, VP - Southern division, were scheduled to retire on December 31. Their positions will not be filled.)

Sales and service functions, which had been combined under marketing, will become separate divisions, each reporting directly to the chief executive officer.

Willis R. Balfour will be VP - sales. Reporting to him will be David Holt, VP - passenger sales; Paul Harding, VP - Southern sales division (which now encompasses the central division); John Morris , VP -Northern sales division (which now encompasses the Eastern division); and Howard Culver, formerly assistant VP - regulatory law, who has been named VP - sales development and who will be responsible for scheduling, pricing, forecasting and route planning.

Larry Lee will be VP - service. He will be responsible for all inflight service, reservations, passenger service, cargo service and consumer affairs.

Also reporting to the chief executive officer will be Donald K. Hall, senior VP, general counsel and secretary; A. Colletti, VP - maintenance and engineering; R. G. Leith, VP - finance; F. E. Luhm, VP - data processing and communications; W. E. Newell, VP - flight operations; Ray Silvius, VP - corporate affairs; and D. W. Vena, VP - personnel relations.

Although changes of this nature are always difficult and particularly when the affected individuals have provided long and dedicated service to the company, the streamlining of Western Airlines is absolutely essential to its survival, said Mr. Bergt.

Public Relations, LAXGO

Bergt put Frank Moolin in charge of the processing of these people. The manner in which the management work force was cut and processed was the most impersonal bloodbath ever to occur in the airline industry.

The immediate elimination of two-thirds of the officers was done with a "meat ax." Officers were looking out their windows and seeing their name plates being removed from parking places before they were even told they were fired.

The second step was an order to reduce one-third of all management positions. Moolin had a system for doing this that was structured by grades so a department director could not just downgrade everyone and squeeze a group out from the bottom. It was to be accomplished so that the corporate management salary base would be cut by one-third. A deadline was set for this event, and those of us who remained as officers were putting in sixteen hour days, seven days a week to accomplish the task.

All the head-count adjustments and pay reductions in the management area were preamble to Bergt and Moolin asking for a temporary pay reduction from the unions. They had to show their muscle and this was the chosen arena because of the unions who felt Western was "top-heavy" with management. This was an erroneous perception as we compared favorably with other airlines our size. In fact, our ratio of management employees to rank and file was more in favor of the employee groups than most airlines at that time. The whole perception problem began when Dom Renda and Art Kelly approved the ten regional VPs. While these were not "Corporate Officers," they appeared in the annual report as such and therefore gave the impression of a "top-heavy" management at Western Airlines.

Making a major cut in the administrative group accomplished another goal of Bergt and Moolin. One of their objectives was to rid the company of those they felt had let Western get into such a sad financial condition.

Supposedly, to make up for the "shortfall" in management, Bergt announced all the remaining management staff would work ten-hour days, six days a week. For some, that was a joke as many of us had been working twelve-hour days for the past year to try to tighten every cost center we had under our jurisdiction.

This strategy seemed to have worked for the new CEO as the unions granted the temporary ten-percent pay reduction. It was not a sufficient amount and was not for a long enough period to escape the inevitable cash drain. The new management was pledging everything we owned to the bankers for loans to just keep us flying. But still there was no concrete plan in place as to what could be done to turn the company into a profitable entity. Had Moolin lived longer, he may have come up with the mental muscle to make things work better for Bergt.

Frank Moolin had cancer and it had been in remission three times. He was fading, but you'd never know it to watch him work. There were a few periods when he had to go back to Seattle to get medical attention. I could see what life was going to be like without his guidance, and it looked very bleak. Nevertheless, we moved on while doing the best with what direction we were given.

Neil Bergt was building a multi-million dollar home in Rancho Santa Fe, near San Diego. He had a private jet and his pilots would fly him back and forth to the LAX airport. When he spent the night in Los Angeles, the jet would be parked in back of the Western Airlines hangars. Neil also had a large home in Anchorage, Alaska. His permanent residence was to remain in Alaska, even with the mansion in Rancho Santa Fe. I was told the reason was that Alaska is a tax-free State and he did not want to have any financial ties with California. Therefore, Neil did not take a salary while he was at Western. Of course, he let it be widely known to all employees that he was working without pay as a show of his sincere interest in the financial preservation of the company. What this really amounted to was what one board member would later categorize as the "self-preservation of the financial stability of one, Neil Bergt."

Rather than a salary, Neil opted for three-quarters of a million low-price options on Western stock and an unlimited expense account. Because of his private jet, his expenses were running more than Kelly and Renda's salaries combined. However, I feel sure that during the time he spent at Western, he and Frank lost many opportunities to make a great deal of money on the Alaska North Slope operation. He claimed this was happening and I tend to agree with him as he had a nice setup in Alaska that needed their attention.

Of course, as so often occurs with this sort of thing, the employees at large were unaware of what was being spent by Bergt, therefore, the praise for his benevolence continued to roll on.

Now, back to Frank Moolin, I believe Neil wanted to make him the president and chief operations officer, but Frank wouldn't take it on account of his failing health. However, Moolin did unofficially fill that role when he was able to be at our headquarters. He was publicly very polite, one might even say, solicitous to Neil. I don't know how it was in private. They had almost a father and son relationship.

I did not agree with many of things Neil did, but there were limited options for those few of the old Western group who remained. You followed orders, or quickly explained why you felt they were wrong, and then you either followed orders, or you quit; there was no middle ground. Too few of us were left who knew how to keep the ship afloat to make a quick exit, so that option was out. I made good use of the open door policy, especially with Moolin, to let them know when they were not tracking right. Frank listened; Neil didn't.

Bergt and Moolin would have a weekly meeting with the officers and key directors. Most often, Moolin ran the meeting with Bergt in attendance. He called it the LIAHO meeting; an acronym for Let It All Hang Out. If you had any problems that were not aired in this meeting, or any suggestions not made that would enhance the profit line, then you probably wouldn't be around to attend the next session. I noticed when Frank was there, the meeting would flow smoothly and people would open up. When Bergt ran it, there was too much silence. He did not have the knack of soliciting participation, but he sure had a handle on how to shut it off. If you "opened up," without Frank Moolin to referee, it could very well be your job.

The year 1982 was a pivotal year for Western Airlines and, therefore, I am going to go into much more detail concerning what was happening. I'll use dates where appropriate to give you a feel for the timing of certain events.

You will see many quotes from my personal journals as they best reflect the details and emotional traumas of that period.

Having resigned myself to the fact that I was not going to be a "long-timer" on this management team, I did not bother to keep my mouth shut. Margie was encouraging me to do so until February the eighth, when I would turn fifty-five. That was the magic date, along with my over thirty years of service, to be able to draw early retirement. While that would barely be enough to sustain us, I knew there were more lucrative possibilities out there than here at Western and I was looking forward to testing the market. We just felt it foolish to throw away this small cushion unnecessarily as Margie would get fifty-percent of it when I died. The way I was working, that date with death would not be far off.

As long as I stayed in close touch with Moolin, things seemed to be all right. He did caution me not to "take on" Neil in front of the others. For Moolin's sake, I didn't. There were a few exceptions. One occurred in the LIAHO meeting the week before Christmas. Christmas Eve was on a Saturday and, as I mentioned earlier, we worked all Saturdays. At the close of the meeting, as Neil was dismissing the group, Moolin leaned over to him and whispered something. Neil then said: "Oh yes, we are not going to work this next Saturday." I couldn't hold it back, I bellowed out: "Oh Neil, you're all heart." Moolin gave me one of his stern looks and Neil responded: "Well, it is Christmas!" That was the end of that, but I sure enjoyed the rest of that day.

Arthur F. Kelly, the recently retired chairman, had been asked by Neil to join in these LIAHO meetings and re-occupy his old office in the building. He was to serve as an unofficial consultant to Bergt. Recall, it was Kelly who introduced Bergt to Western's board; at least that is what he claimed. Kelly did not sit at the big table in the meeting room; rather, he sat on the couch right behind me. We all seemed to have our unofficial seats.

The only time I really felt I'd gone too far with Neil was during a meeting where one of the items on the agenda was to discuss discount fares. Bergt felt we were too deeply discounting our product to the travel wholesalers and wanted this stopped immediately. This was in Bill Balfour's arena and Bill came to my office seeking advice on how to handle the situation. I told Bill that I understood his dilemma; however, I knew he wouldn't be around long if he didn't do as Neil asked. I advised him to agree, and then make the best effort he could to carry out the orders while preserving some sense of compatibility with the travel community. Bill said it couldn't be done. We were about to go into the LIAHO meeting and I could see Bill was not going to back off.

When the "discount fare" subject came up on the agenda, Bergt asked if the agreements had been cancelled. Bill responded with an argument. Bergt asked again if they'd been cancelled, per his orders. More arguments from Bill. Bergt pointed his finger at Bill and shouted that he expected Balfour to cancel them and wanted it done immediately. Bill, with a frustrated look, said: "What reason can I give?" There was a deadly hush in the room. I couldn't stand this any longer. I pointed to Bergt and said: "Just tell them this son-of-a-bitch ordered you to do it." Behind me, I heard Art Kelly let out a groan. There was no other sound. Bergt looked at me for a moment and then, turning to Balfour, said: "Yeh, you tell them just that!" The meeting ended and Art Kelly was sure I had also come to the end of my rope.

I don't think anyone in that room had ever heard me use a cuss word. I did not consciously resort to that kind of language. I mention this to show the level of frustration I had reached at Western. Balfour, who was heading up all marketing activities, was not long for his job. By then, I had most of Jack Slichter's old responsibilities, plus the staff group in the General Office. I reported directly to Neil Bergt. Neil had not filled Dick Ensign's old job of senior VP marketing and he was running a fairly flat organization. This was to change rather quickly.

Chapter 7

CIRCLING THE WAGONS
IN SALT LAKE CITY

O ne day Bergt and Moolin called a meeting of the staff and introduced us to Joe Lorenzo, newly hired senior VP of marketing for
Western. Joe was recruited away from Frontier Airlines, headquartered in Denver. My journal indicates this was January 18, 1982. Within
a week, another meeting was called and Lorenzo made a presentation that
showed Salt Lake City could be used as a "hub," much the same way Frontier
had been doing in Denver.

For anyone reading this who does not understand the "hub concept,"
I'll explain. Delta Air Lines had been using Atlanta in this manner for years.
Since deregulation, United "hubbed" Chicago; American, Dallas; and other
cities would follow. The objective is to have your aircraft over-nighting away
from the hub and bring them together at one time, much like a funnel. Then,
when the people have redistributed themselves, the aircraft leave to the various points of your system. The latter is much like scattering pellets out of a
shotgun. They then gather passengers at that point and the "funneling" and
"shotgun" process is repeated as many times as possible during the day .

This all sounds simple, doesn't it? Well, it isn't. Scheduling the aircraft,
crews and maintenance is a headache. Also, the strain it puts on the hub to
have enough flights on the ground at one time to make this work can be a
nightmare and requires a heavy investment in "start-up costs" at the hub. This
point, the "start-up" cost, is the crux of what I am about to relate.

Before making this presentation to the staff, Joe Lorenzo had come to me, explained what he was going to propose, and asked if I would work with him to head up the project for the operating group. I said I would as there was little to lose at this point and I too felt Salt Lake City would work as a hub. But others believed we could never compete with the airlines that were doing much the same thing out of the neighboring city to the east, Denver.

From January 18 to Feb 3, 1982, Joe and I met and laid out plans for the hub. I kept assuring him we could do it. Without the ground services being in place, there was no possible way this strategy could work.

Neil and Moolin gave the go-ahead to start work on the hub. I was asked to inform the key people in Salt Lake City of our intent. On Tuesday, January 26, 1982, I visited with Governor Scott Matheson in Salt Lake City and briefed him on our general plan for Utah. He said this would be the biggest thing to hit Salt Lake City since the covered wagons. I told him this was not to be immediately released to the press and I'd keep him informed of our schedule; he would be the first to know the timing and scope of our proposed route realignment around the SLC "hub."

While in Salt Lake City that day, I met with Bishop Victor L. Brown. He was just recovering from a gall bladder operation, but he looked great. He was very excited at the news. I told him we were looking at around eighty flights a day. Currently there were twenty-four flights a day operating out of SLC.

This week marked Frank Moolin's return from Seattle where he had been receiving more treatments for his cancer. I was really pulling for him to maintain his health as he was still the only rudder I saw steering this crazy ship. Bergt remained very dependent upon his judgments.

One day I sensed there was a change in the urgency of the route realignment. No one had backed off the hub concept, but there were other concerns. I felt it might have something to do with the board of director's meeting that was to be held on Friday, January 29th. I don't know what was discussed at that meeting, but I saw Dom Renda following the meeting. He congratulated me and said, "I would have given you more." I was sure he was speaking of "responsibility" as there were no raises being given, only pay cuts. I had no clue as to what was being discussed. I did have an uneasy feeling that there were still concerns at some level with regard to the "hub" in SLC.

I worked all day Saturday, but for some reason I could not get the events of Friday off my mind. I felt something was taking a wrong turn and I needed to talk. At 9:00 p.m. Saturday night, I called Frank Moolin at his apartment in the Marina City Club and asked if I could meet with him first thing Monday Morning. He said, "Let's do it tomorrow morning in my office."

Moolin and I met at 8:30 a.m. and I quickly outlined my concerns. We needed to get on with this project as we were running out of options at Western and had to move quickly. He seemed reluctant to discuss the speed of this plan, but he asked where I saw myself in the picture. I told him I would bring it on line for him, but he would have to keep order at home. I asked only one thing and that was to be given the title of "project director, Salt Lake City hub." I reminded him that this was the title he had assumed when he took over the faltering Alaska Pipeline project and saw to its completion in 1977. I told Frank it would be necessary to have that title so I could cross all divisional lines to get things moving and keep them on track.

Frank agreed with everything I had to say and indicated his confidence in me and that he had just been waiting for me to signal I was ready to stick around to get the job done. He added that he wanted to promote me to senior VP. I told him I did not need this. He said I did as it would be his signal to others in the company and to the community at large that "I was the man." He said I should sit on this for a few days and he would get things in gear.

Within this time frame, Lorenzo bounded into my office and said he had just fired Bill Balfour and asked if I would take over Bill's marketing responsibilities, along with my own. The answer was, no! He said he must shed these day-to-day burdens in order to focus on the "hub." I told him I would have exactly the same problem if I was going to fire-up the ground operation at the hub.

On Monday, it was announced that we would not be moving as swiftly as Lorenzo wanted. Joe almost quit when his proposed schedule was turned down. There was well-placed fear that the disruption of the schedule would hurt our cash flow and that was all we had to live on.

I was informed that sometime this week, the first week of February, we would see what recommendations the outside consultants had given to Neil Bergt and Frank Moolin for a new organization of the company's top management. I received this report on Tuesday. I'm sure this information tied to Renda's comment last Friday. Joe Lorenzo came to me and said he thought they were looking at me for the senior VP operations; a spot on the chart that had all of the ground service, flight and maintenance operations reporting to that position. He said the problem they were having is whether or not I was willing to stay with Western. I realized that this was a legitimate concern.

On Wednesday, February 3rd, 1982, Moolin called me to his office and said they were going ahead with my suggestions and that I would be project director of the Salt Lake City hub. He insisted I be promoted to senior VP for the reasons he had outlined in our meeting on Sunday. I was instructed to get a press release prepared announcing my appointment.

On the same day, Lorenzo was in my office with this story. He had just concluded a meeting with Bergt and Moolin on the "hub" start-up cost, which Lorenzo estimated to be twenty-five million dollars. Lorenzo was told that was out of the question and he was sent back to the drawing board. He paced around my office stating that they were "sand-bagging" and must have some way of raising that much money for this project. I could only respond that I had little knowledge of the current cash reserves; however, he'd better listen to Frank Moolin.

The next morning Lorenzo met with them again and explained why they must have the money. He then told Moolin and Bergt he felt we could do the hub for ten million. They told him he couldn't have one million. With that, Joe told them they could forget the "hub."

A few minutes after this meeting, an out-of-breath Joe Lorenzo charged into my office and stated he had just quit. He'd been told to immediately exit the property. Lorenzo's next to final words with me were: "Larry, you can do this hub in Salt Lake City. You have what it takes to get it going and I swear it will work, but you can't do it without the cash." His last words were: "How do I get to Denver? They told me to turn in my badge and my annual travel card." I said he could keep his pass and use it for the next month to get relocated. With that, he was out of the office and disappeared from Western as quickly and noisily as he had arrived.

While I didn't appreciate the way Lorenzo had handled the situation with Balfour, he was a brilliant person in his field. Neil Bergt later agreed with me on this, but added; "Yeh, if you could lock him in a room and just pass notes back and forth under the door, he might have worked out!"

Lorenzo had hardly left my office when Moolin called and asked me to join him in Bergt's office. When I got there, Craig Benedetti, one of the new lieutenants in marketing, was sitting at one end of Neil's desk and Moolin was in the middle. Frank waved me into the chair at the other end. Bergt stated that he had just fired Joe Lorenzo and asked if I would take over the marketing functions. I told him that this would not be wise if we were going ahead with the "hub." He then turned to Benedetti and said, "Then you take it." This seemed to be a rather flippant way of filling the marketing slot; however, hindsight might indicate that Moolin and Bergt had already discussed this and felt I should have first chance. Moolin knew why I would not volunteer to do this. He and I had already had a few discussions on the company organization.

When Bergt made the Benedetti statement, Moolin said, "Larry would you go to your office and draw up what you feel is the proper organization for the company and come up to discuss it with me before lunch?"

With that, the meeting ended and I started drawing my chart - one I had already drawn in my mind a dozen times. I took it up to Moolin within the hour and he studied it carefully before asking a few questions. The chart showed three key senior VPs reporting to Neil Bergt; one over operations, one having all the field activity, and one with the central marketing functions. The other two top officers for legal and finance would report directly to Bergt. The proposed "troika" would require the least amount of shuffling at this time. Western could not stand any major reorganization in the middle of such a cash crunch.

Frank Moolin had mentioned to me that Neil was committed to hiring someone from outside the company to be the permanent individual in the marketing spot and Benedetti was a temporary assignment in that role - he was not made a senior VP. We discussed this a bit more and Frank said he would consider what I had proposed and, in the meantime, they'd get the announcement out on Benedetti.

So, here we were with the Salt Lake hub apparently out the window for lack of ready cash, diminishing credibility with the travel agency and whole-sale community, and no operating plan.

I decided to have another private meeting with Moolin and see where he stood on the Salt Lake City project. We needed a plan, one that would give some glimmer of hope, and one with enough dynamics to involve the whole system. The more I thought about this, the more I was convinced we must proceed at full speed; even though Joe Lorenzo was not there to handle the scheduling and marketing side of implementation.

The following morning we met; Moolin did not look well and I got right to the point. I told him that I felt we must find some way to accomplish the "hub" with the resources we had and that I felt the Western team would pull together whatever was needed to make sure it happened. I explained I was worried about the cash flow during the period when we started the "hub" and made an immediate readjustment in the system-wide flying. I explained to Frank that he would have to look at cash flow and reserves to make sure we didn't die just before the new system got up and running. We would bring it on-line quickly and, in some areas, on a shoe string. However, I promised that it would be done safely.

Moolin had listened to this without a word. He then said that was what he had hoped I'd say and to get on with it. He said he wanted me to begin running the LIAHO meetings with a report on the progress from each division of the company.

The following day, with Moolin's approval, I promoted Charles "Topper" Van Every to VP airport services and Harold Achtziger to VP airport operations. Topper would handle the planning and Harold the execution of these plans. I set the target date to begin the "hub" on May 1, 1982; the date of our summer schedule change. This gave us less than three months to get it all off the ground. This project would take a lot of miracles to accomplish and I believed in miracles.

One of my first actions was to fly to Salt Lake City and hold a press conference and meet privately with some of the key media folks. On February 12, 1982 we made the public announcement that Salt Lake City was to be our new "hub." This was received as big news for the city. I used a phrase that caught the imagination of the media. I told them that Western was going to "circle their wagons" in SLC to fight off the incursion of other carriers that were bleeding Western Airlines by their invasion into our historic territory. The banner line in the newspaper was, "Western Circles its Wagons in Salt

Lake City." The "circle" concept worked well with the "hub and spoke" explanation of what we were doing.

I also met with Bishop Victor Brown and President Monson to outline what I perceived to be the impact of the "hub" on the LDS Church headquarters. Tom Monson was very pleased. Victor Brown told President Monson that he classified this move as the most significant thing to happen to Utah since the coming of the railroad. As I look back, I can agree with that statement.

It was at this time that I met Carolyn Hyde, Bishop Brown's Secretary. Over the next few years she proved invaluable by putting me in touch with Victor; no matter where in the world he was traveling. She became one of our best friends and continued to work for Bishop Brown up until the time he retired from Church service.

Having press conferences was a totally new experience for me. In one media blurb from Salt Lake City, I mentioned the inadequacies of the Denver International Airport and the mayor of Denver called me to chew me out. I said I wasn't bad mouthing Denver; I was just reciting the facts of their operation and comparing it to Salt Lake City. One reason I had to make these comparisons was that other airline heads were saying SLC was not a good place for a hub. They were telling the press that there was too much fog and snow at the Salt Lake Airport. They were also saying the city was too small to support a hub. The CEO of United Airlines saw Salt Lake City as nothing more than a spoke off their Denver hub.

One of the first priorities was to establish credibility with the Airport Manager, Paul Gaines, and key members of the Airport Commission: Kem Gardner, Alan Blodgett and Joe Rosenblatt. I spent as much time as possible orienting Mayor Ted Wilson and Governor Matheson on the concepts of our proposed hub and the positive economic impact I saw it would bring to the Wasatch front and the State of Utah

These folks were very supportive and they all proceeded to demonstrate their faith in the future of the hub with the local media. We needed the understanding and support of these individuals and agencies in order to obtain immediate backing to expand our gates and facilities at the airport. We required an additional concourse and expansion of every facility we had in Salt Lake City. It had to all be funded by the City as we didn't have a dime to spend on anything other than our own increase in ground and passenger-handling facilities. We also needed to rework Concourse "C" and obtain the exclusive rights to all the spare gates on Concourse "B."

Bob Crandall, CEO of American Airlines, was one of the individuals making negative remarks that were quoted by the local press. He supposedly said it takes three years to establish a "hub" city and Western couldn't do this in just a few months. There was no doubt in my mind that he was correct, when taking into consideration all the changes that needed to be made in "fine tuning" a hub. However, we had to realign the system by that spring in order to capture the maximum traffic in the summer of 1982. There could be no orderly progression and "slow turning of a battleship." That was where we had an advantage over American Airlines. Crandall said it took them three years to organize the Dallas, Texas "hub." They were big, we were small. We could profit from some of their mistakes and turn the ship more quickly.

All this chatter from other airlines reminded me of the comments of the Delta Air Lines managers in England when Western Airlines was getting organized to operate into Gatwick Airport. We proved them wrong then and would again.

I really didn't pay that much attention to what others were saying about our chances for success with the SLC "hub" as it was that or nothing. We were bleeding to death the way we were presently operating and this was our last hope. With success, it would serve as a foundation for other changes that could follow. It would have to be the banner to which the employees of Western could rally, there was no other way. I don't know of an employee in any department who felt we could keep going the way we were. We were being squeezed from every side and had no battle plan; only weak tactical means of handling the day-to-day skirmishes as the big battle was being lost in the debris of the newly deregulated industry.

We began the work on the hub by stripping every piece of equipment we could from our existing cities. There was a bit of screaming that we were running the overall operation into the ground by doing this, but my experience in Western's service division taught me that we were at our best when we were lean. Harold Achtziger was put in charge of getting the physical equipment phase accomplished and, with the assistance of Topper Van Every's game plan book, worked well with the field managers.

As stated, the agreed upon startup date was May 1st, 1982, and it was fast approaching. As the senior VP of passenger services, as well as director for the Salt Lake City hub, I was hopping back and forth between our corporate headquarters in Los Angeles and Salt Lake City. However, as the weeks progressed I found myself spending more and more time up north.

Brent Buma, regional sales Manager was based in Salt Lake City with his offices in the Kennecott Building. He had a conference room and it became my headquarters.

Neil Bergt and Frank Moolin, gave me free reign to get the operation realigned. There was no problem as long as I stayed within my budget; one of my staff said, "What budget?" We really didn't have anything to work with except the resources we already had within the system.

Over the years I had learned that I could depend on Charles "Topper" Van Every to see the big picture and devise the most efficient ways to weave a pattern through the corporate maze without becoming entangled in the political webs of the old-style system. He told things as they were and stepped on many toes in the process. Later on, George Kamats, an executive whom Bergt brought in to oversee the operations division, told Neil and others that Topper was one of the most valuable executives at Western's headquarters and that he was one of the best administrative people he had ever known. He was seeing in Topper what I had known and depended on for many years.

Van Every had what he referred to as "bubble charts" strung all over the walls of his office. They represented his own version of a PERT (Program Evaluation and Review Technique) chart, and he had every move planned for the personnel and equipment changes required by Western to meet the May 1st deadline of the route realignment. Since any one change in such a critical path could impact many areas, it was his map of "cause and effect" that kept things on track. When May 1st rolled around, I saw many people taking bows for what Topper had accomplished. Unfortunately, Topper was not one to play the politics of the situation and aggrandize himself by these successes; he was too busy getting on to the next challenge. I say, unfortunately, as this very trait would cause his downfall immediately after my retirement.

We ran into a severe hitch in our plans for the "hub" in early March of '82. The route realignment depended on our being granted "landing-slots" at key eastern cities that coincided with the new schedules in and out of the hub. These slots were allocated by the Federal Government as they were still getting their house in order from the disaster of President Reagan's firing of all the Air Traffic Controllers.

On March 11, 1982, I noted this condition in my personal journal:

Got word from Washington FAA today that didn't sound good for the hub in SLC. Our team will go back to DCA next Monday and see if we can trade slots for some good cities. If not, I'll be going to SLC to tell them the hub deal is off.

The team called on Monday and reported they were not making any progress. That evening, Neil Bergt said, "Well Larry, there goes your hub." New York City was one of the key elements in this "swap meet." I got a call the next morning that the group in Washington had a breakthrough and had obtained two slots to JFK, one to Houston and other things were looking good.

That evening I took off for Salt Lake City and met with the airport manager, Paul Gaines, and brought him up to date. He agreed to sit tight on the scheduling information until Friday, at which time we would call a press conference. On Thursday, I met with the Mayor, Ted Wilson, Governor Matheson, and Fred Ball, the president of the Chamber of Commerce. The objective was to brief them separately on the status of the "hub" and to give them a preview of the schedule we proposed. I told them I had set up a full-blown press conference the next day and solicited their support.

Ray Silvius, VP public relations, and his assistant, Linda Dozier, were not in favor of the press conference as we'd already received a great deal of media coverage in SLC on the hub. I felt they were wrong, but held my breath on Friday to see how much interest there would be by the local media. We scheduled the conference in the Horizon Room at the airport and it was covered by three TV stations, three newspapers and five radio stations.

Public relations called to say they were amazed at the coverage and we made the first page in the evening newspaper. What our PR folks did not realize was that we had been building up an atmosphere of suspense behind the scene and it played out well.

April 12, 1982, we met with about sixty bankers who gathered at the Los Angeles Airport Sheraton LaReina Hotel. The agenda was to give them the word on our finances and an update on the hub; Neil Bergt, when introducing me, said: "I have this recurring dream that awakens me about 3:00 a.m. in a sweat. The dream is that it is May 1st and nothing is happening with the route realignment." He then said, "I want you to meet the man I will be getting after if that dream comes true." I gave them a progress report. During the question and answer period, a banker said: "It's interesting that the man whom Neil picked to get the job done is the only one with gray hair - did that happen before Neil arrived, or after?" The bankers were well aware of Bergt's reputation.

On May 1, 1982, the Salt Lake City hub got underway with hardly a hitch. I was afraid our crew-schedulers might have left a few unmanned aircraft around the system, but there wasn't a glitch anywhere. This was the most massive change ever to take place in Western Airlines; therefore, it was only proper that Bergt and Moolin were on edge. I have to say, they stayed out of my hair and let me do what had to be done. I don't think either of them expected it to come off as easily as it did. All the credit goes to my great staff and the vital cooperation from field management and other divisions of the company.

Sunday, May 2nd, I went to the airport to check on the operation and found our Salt Lake City board member, Bishop Victor Brown, walking around the terminal checking it out. We walked together for a while and he seemed well pleased. Having previously informed him that I would not consider the position of president and COO under Neil Bergt, he asked me if I would take it on a short-term basis while they looked for a permanent president. I said, "It is not possible, don't count on this." He asked me not to do anything without speaking with him first. I promised to keep him informed.

That Monday, I got lots of kudos from Bergt, Moolin and others at headquarters. It was nice to hear, but I knew we still had a long way to go. On Tuesday, I held my first meeting of the "operations group." We would meet daily to fine-tune the hub. The group included the top representatives from every department of the company.

The meeting on the second day went well and the pattern was in place, so I headed up to SLC. Bergt was coming in to see the hub in operation and I wanted to be on hand to watch the proceedings. By now I realized that we would need someone from my staff in SLC on a full-time basis for the next 30 to 60 days. I decided Harold Achtziger, VP airport operations, should move up with his family until things were running more smoothly. School was about out and we would take care of his expenses. Topper Van Every could run the staff from Los Angeles headquarters. I would continue to coordinate the activities of my division and oversee the system through the operations committee meetings. This seemed to fit as all the focus of the company was on the fine tuning of the Salt Lake City hub.

For some reason I felt it was time to prepare a letter of resignation. To preserve the confidentiality I had my wife type my letter. I didn't feel I would stay beyond the summer and wanted to be able to give a thirty-day notice so there would be time for me to work with the Salt Lake City movers and shakers to assure them this had nothing to do with the future of their "hub." I placed it in the desk for the right timing. This act was also motivated by the fact that my stomach had been giving every sign that I had another ulcer.

When I called my doctor, Webster Marxer, he insisted I come in the next day for an upper G.I. I did so and it was no surprise that I had a large ulcer at the opening of the duodenum - it was about the size of a quarter. He said it was not too deep at the moment and I would have to totally eliminate aspirin. Because of my headache and neck spasms I ate aspirin like popcorn. On returning to work I heard Neil Bergt say he was going to have five offices built across from his on the fourth floor. They would all have glass fronts and face his office. I moved my letter of resignation to the front of the top drawer.

On May 12, 1982 we got the sad news that Braniff Airlines had declared bankruptcy. While they went into Chapter Eleven, I knew they were much like Western Airlines, deeply in debt, with almost all their assets pledged to the lenders. I could not see how they were going to be able to reorganize and begin flying again. This had a very sobering effect on both management and employees throughout the industry. All the airlines began scrambling to pick up the pieces that Braniff had dropped, such as landing slots. While we were among those at the feeding trough, we had stretched our aircraft hours and crew-time to the limit. There was very little slack for added service after the hub got going.

On May 15th I made an entry in my journal, "Day 158 since Neil Bergt arrived - seems like two years." I also noted that my new medication was not working well and I was suffering with constant headaches. Things were running well at the hub, and we were able to squeeze in some flights from SLC to Dallas to replace those dropped by Braniff. We also grabbed their gates in SLC for expansion. They were not ideal, but would work until a new concourse was built. I returned to Los Angeles on the weekend to run Monday's LIAHO (Let It All Hang Out) meeting. Recall, this was Moolin's idea to get people used to my command. This used to be the weekly Corporate Staff Meeting, but as mentioned earlier, Moolin changed the tenor and format of the historic staff to be more like he had used when he worked on the Alaska Pipeline. If anyone did not divulge a problem in this meeting and he found out about it, they would be spending the afternoon watching their name being removed from their preferred parking space.

While I was conducting my meeting on Monday, May 17th, Neil Bergt's secretary slipped me a note indicating Neil wanted me to join him for lunch. When the staff meeting ended, I went to my desk and put my letter of resignation in my pocket. I felt this might be the opportunity I had been looking for. That night, I made this entry in my personal journal:

Neil and I left in his Rolls Royce for his private club in Westwood. We chatted about family stuff on the way. Over lunch he asked me many things about the overall operation of the company and had some questions about specific people. Then, at the appropriate time, I asked him if he'd made his selection for president of Western. He said, 'No - I've interviewed two nice guys, but nice guys don't make good presidents.' I told him to get on with it. He said he and Frank had thoughts of me but weren't sure of a couple of things; one of them being that I was one of the good old boys and maybe not capable of handling the big picture. I told him he might be right and to get on with his recruiting. He said, 'not so fast; we felt that way at first but now we have seen what you can do and you've moved to the top of the list.' I said that would be a mistake and then divulged my health problems and slipped him my letter of resignation, he read it and threw it back at me; said that the health problem needed more explanation. I went into detail. He asked when I would have a final readout. I told him I'd have it in two weeks. He said for me to call him as he wanted to know the verdict; that he wouldn't fill the job until he'd heard from me. We had a good two-hour chat. I was very relaxed and I told him that in worst case I would stay long enough to make sure things were in good order.

The following day, Frank Moolin chewed me out because I had given Neil my letter of resignation. I told him the whole story of what I'd said to Neil and he felt much better about it. Neil was probably ticked-off and had left out the part about my having an ulcer, etc.

Victor Brown came back from one of the board of directors meetings and said they had unanimously endorsed the merger between Wein Airlines and Western. I could not see what that was going to do for us, but Bergt was pushing it. Seemed to me the board was grasping at straws at this point.

Web Marxer was not only my personal physician, he was a good friend. I went in to see him on June 8th and explained that I had given Neil Bergt a report on my health. He said the recent tests indicated that I was progressing well, but he strongly advised that I not take the pressure of the presidency with someone like Bergt at the head of the company. I guess I knew this, but I wanted his opinion.

I met with Bergt that afternoon and told him the doctor had given me a good review; however, I was not interested in the job of president and chief operating officer of Western Airlines. Neil then told me he was very worried about Moolin as he didn't know how much longer Frank could keep going. Frank was in isolation at the hospital in Seattle and they were giving him another dose of chemotherapy. Because of this, it sounded as though Neil wanted to move rapidly to get a president of Western in place. My timing was about right. I promised him I would help whomever he brought in to get up and running before I left at the end of August.

The month of June was filled with a great deal of traveling around the system, especially the "hot-spots" that were affecting the performance of the hub in SLC. This was good as I had neglected the field to get the hub going.

On June 15th, Art Kelly, the retired chairman of Western Airlines and currently Bergt's "ombudsman," asked me to join him for lunch at Hollywood

Park Race Track. Art was on their board of directors. The track was "off season" so we ate in the cafeteria. It was obvious what was going on; he was making one last attempt to influence me to take the job of president. I was very straightforward with Art and told him the whole story of my talks with Bergt and Moolin. I'm glad I did for it came out that Victor Brown had told him I was leaving as soon as the route realignment was completed. He asked if I would take over all the operations as an executive VP. I said I would give it consideration, but only to train someone else to be capable of becoming president. All of this conversation was in conjunction with his concern about not being able to find a suitable person outside the company.

Frank Moolin died June 29, 1982. What a loss of talent, especially for Western Airlines. I knew I would really miss him as we had developed a fine rapport and respect for one another. Ray Brown, one of Bergt's friends who was helping out in the maintenance division, called and said Neil was having a difficult time finding the right kind of talent he needed for the job of president and COO. That worried me as, without Moolin to guide him, I felt he would make a rash decision just to get the job filled and we'd wind up with a "ding-bat" as his heir apparent.

The first week of July was spent working with the Salt Lake City "Fathers," those who were key to whatever actions would be required for terminal and runway expansion at the Salt Lake International Airport; we needed to quickly accommodate more flights. The first was a high priority; we needed one more concourse. The runway could come later as we expanded to accommodate more "hub" flights. That meant a bond issue and I promised to help them sell it. After a few meetings with these men, it looked like a "done deal."

All this led up to an early July, 1982 meeting with the Mayor, Ted Wilson to get him to approve a two-million dollar program to get the engineering study completed for a new airport concourse. It looked like the overall cost for this would be between twenty and twenty-six million dollars. He quickly approved the cost and scheduled a press conference to announce the expansion. It was well attended and we got good coverage on the local channels.

Chapter 8

THE HARVARD MBA

On July 9th, 1982, Neil Bergt hired a person to fill the slot of president and chief operating officer. His name was Ned DeWitt and he had been the CEO at Five (or Six) Flags over Texas - a medium-size theme park operation. He reported for duty the day of the Shareholders' Meeting, Friday, July 23rd, and I met him for the first time that morning. Ned was a Harvard MBA; that always seemed to impress Neil.

After the meeting, I took a few calls of condolence that I didn't get the job. I continued to keep my mouth shut about the past events as I was pulling for the new man to be successful so I could shove-off with the company in good hands. Ned and I had a long meeting on that Monday and I probably shared more with him than was necessary - that is my nature. He commented, "I see you are a very forthright person." I responded: "What you see is what you get."

Back in April 29, 1982, Neil Bergt had hired a new chief financial officer named Andre Dimitriadis. He was formerly a financial officer with the small regional carrier, "Air Cal." He was a very dynamic individual. Some might say he was overly aggressive, but that seemed to suit Bergt's style. Andre was doing everything in his power to raise money, but he was pledging as collateral every resource we owned. Since the airline industry was deregulated, airlines of our size were considered very high risks and the lenders would require collateral at way over its current resale value.

At this time, Western Airlines had around fifty lenders in our line of credit. Dimitriadis wanted to have a big finance meeting in Salt Lake City to show them what was happening within the City, the airport and the realignment of Western's system. He wanted me to set it up locally and get all the right people to participate as speakers, etc. The meeting was scheduled in Salt Lake City on July 29, 1982. Bergt insisted that Ned and I fly up to SLC with him on his private jet.

We had a good attendance at the meeting. The spouses had been invited and we toured them around the area. The weather cooperated and the city was at its finest. The meeting was held at the Hotel Utah and Victor Brown, who was not only on our board of directors, but also served as the key member of the Hotel Utah board, made sure all accommodations and meals were excellent. I gave a general overview of the SLC hub and the route realignment; and I was surprised at how much these bankers were in tune with what was happening, even though the majority of them had never been to Salt Lake City before this meeting. Mayor Ted Wilson, and Governor Scott Matheson were very helpful with this endeavor.

The meeting was somewhat successful; however I could see "foreclosure" in the eyes of the lenders. Several of them wanted Western to be dead and gone and our aircraft, loading gates, landing slots, etc. used by others in the industry to which they had individually loaned more than they had to Western. Republic Airlines was a case in point; they stood to gain a great deal from Western's demise.

Ray Silvius and I were the last of the "old-time corporate officers" remaining with Western. Ray was VP public affairs. Bob Heath and I were meeting with Ned DeWitt on August 9th to plan for the next staff meeting. During this session, Ned told me he had let Ray Silvius go. He said his style would not work for him.

By the end of the day, Ray was gone. What really gnawed at me about this episode were the comments DeWitt made about Ray. He said: "I don't need someone in charge of PR who sits in his office in his rocker with his little red wagon." Silvius' first job as a young boy was delivering papers for the Arizona Republic. He pulled the newspapers around in that red wagon and it held a special place in his personal history. Ray also had a very bad back. He kept a rocking chair in his office and, when his back really got bad - usually about six or seven in the evening, sitting in that chair would help him get relief. I had never been in his office when he was using it, but the sight of it seemed to bother DeWitt. Personally, I think he just wanted to shed some old blood to make a power statement.

A few days later, the 13th of August, my old friend, Herb Jungemann, got the ax. He was the reservations manager in Denver. That day I made a note in my journal, "Staying around Western is about as much fun as spending a year in Auschwitz watching your friends drop off one by one."

These people were well respected by the employees and other middle-managers. It was "strike one" for Ned DeWitt. "Strike two" came in about the same time-frame when he decided to raise the service charges on the employee passes. The employees had taken a ten-percent pay cut and I told Ned this was not a good time to get into their pocket books. He didn't listen, so I talked to Don Vena, VP human resources, and told Don he'd better get to DeWitt as messing with the pass policy was like messing with Mother Nature. Again, DeWitt ignored the advice. Within a few days of the announcement there was a hue and cry throughout the system with Ned back-tracking as fast as possible. He said, "The order had been misunderstood," or words to that effect, which made Don Vena of Human Resources look foolish.

As was mentioned earlier, Neil Bergt had eliminated two-thirds of Western's corporate officers when he arrived. Then, there was the slow departure of some of the others for one reason or another. After the initial blood-letting, I would send him a page that contained the pictures of the former key executives with a note, "then there were six." This went on until there were only two us left from the original officer group; Ray Silvius and I remained.

When Ray was fired, I sent the usual picture page to Neil with a note, "Then there was one!" I guess I finally hit Bergt's hot button. Neil called me to his office and asked why I kept "bugging" him like this, all the while flapping the page at me. I told him that I was afraid he might lose track. He then related something rather interesting. He said, "There is only one reason you are still here and that is because I found out you were the only officer who had the moxie to go back to school to get your MBA so you could function at a higher level." He said this as though I'd kept my Master's Degree a deep-dark secret which he'd ferreted out during his investigations.

This was interesting in that I was never quite sure why I had spent two and a half years working so hard to gain this "sheepskin," except for the reason I had outlined earlier; which was "to think within the vocabulary of the employees with graduate degrees." I have often considered what Neil Bergt said that day about my education. There was always a question in my mind as to why Neil had kept me on when he could have said, "I got rid of all of them." That condition would have been more representative of his "kick-butt" style.

One August 20, 1982 I gave Bergt another letter of resignation. My date of departure was to be September 20th. Bergt asked me to keep this quiet until he had spoken to some of the board members. I then received a request from Bergt, and others, to stay on until next spring to help make sure the Salt Lake City hub operation would make it through the first winter. It was a legitimate request and I said I'd give it some thought.

Western's new president, Ned DeWitt, wanted to visit our larger locations and have employee meetings so they could become better acquainted with him. He asked me to accompany him on the trip. We began with meetings in San Francisco on August 23, 1982, and went from there to Salt Lake City; finishing up with meetings in Denver on Wednesday. They went rather well, but the employees were still not sure about their new leader.

"Strike three" for DeWitt occurred in early September. Neil, Ned and I had been invited to attend the Famsborough Air Show in England. I declined, but Neil and Ned accepted. When the employees heard DeWitt had accompanied Bergt on this trip, right at a critical time in the affairs of Western Airlines, they felt betrayed.

In my estimation, Ned was not going to cut it. After Ned and Neil returned, I had a long talk with Bergt and, based on his remarks, he too was having some unsettled feelings regarding Ned. I did not share with him the employee reaction as it might have sounded like "sour grapes."

On September 2, 1982 I told Bergt the organizational setup I had drawn for Frank Moolin would not work under Ned DeWitt. I also informed him that I would honor his, and certain members of the board's request to stay until next spring, but only if I could move to Salt Lake City and oversee the hub from that location. I would report only to Neil and would do my best to make sure the hub got through the winter. This was all subject to his staying with the company. He told me that he was thinking of leaving if the CAB did not approve his dual relationship with Western Airlines and his company, A.I.A. Bergt did not like my leaving for SLC, but wanted a commitment that I would stay with the hub operation until June 1, 1983. I promised I would, if he stayed put as I would not remain if the company was left in the hands of DeWitt.

I set a goal to be out of our house in Palos Verdes and into a rental in Salt Lake City by the third week of October. This would give me a chance to get established before the heavy winter weather. De-icing the aircraft in SLC was one of my biggest worries. We'd been working on a plan all summer, but equipment was slow to arrive and there were so many different factors involved that had not yet been resolved. I thanked the Lord we had some very capable maintenance personnel in SLC to handle this. I had also been working with our flight team on a plan to "seed" the fog and clear landing space for our "hubbing" flights. SLC had perfect weather conditions for this type of "seeding." Captain Duane, "Dewey," Gerrard was handling this and was very confident of its success.

On September 8th we had what could have been a setback. I attended the meeting of the Airport Commission in SLC and at the end of the meeting, Paul Gaines, Salt Lake Airport Director, announced his resignation. He had been offered the top job in Houston, Texas and it was at a salary the City could not match. This was a good step for him, but he and his first assistant, Lou Miller, had been my leading advocates in getting the airport expansion underway. I immediately went to work with the "politicos" to get Gaines' lieutenant, Louis Miller, assigned to the post. Miller was well versed in the operation of the hub and its airport needs for expansion. I met with the Mayor, Ted Wilson, and let him know how key this appointment was to the success of the hub and that Lou had all the training needed to fill this important roll. Miller got the job and everything stayed right on track.

By mid-September, Ned DeWitt was "waffling" on my move to Salt Lake City. We talked again and he finally approved my press release. On September 22nd I was interviewed by the Business Editors of the Salt Lake newspapers. One of them talked about doing a Sunday section on Western Airlines, the hub and my move to SLC. I had an afternoon interview with Jack Ford at KSL and, as usual, most of it wound up on the cutting room floor. Western had three minutes on the evening news; that seems to be standard coverage for a business entity.

All this press on Western having a top executive in SLC was seen as a precursor of more massive moves of our Corporate Headquarters to Salt Lake City. Questions relating to this came out during the interview and also in calls to our public relations department. PR responded quickly and on September 23, 1982, the Deseret News had a picture of me and a story relating to my move. The article ended with this statement:

> With our increased flight schedules in Salt Lake City, there has been speculation that Western will move its headquarters there as well, DeWitt said. Our present plans and conditions call for the headquarters and staff-level functions to remain in Los Angeles, but we will continually strengthen our flight connecting center at Salt Lake City.

That seemed to calm things down with the employees in Los Angeles, those who were wondering if this was another wild idea in play. I had pointed out in the article that our payroll in Utah was now over $36,000,000 a year and growing; we currently had over fourteen-hundred employees in Salt Lake City. I also noted that we were producing over two-million dollars a day in traffic at the "hub."

On the 23rd of October we said goodbye to our home, our neighbors and Palos Verdes as we headed north in a well-packed car. I've never regretted the move from Palos Verdes. We had a wonderful twenty-year stint there; however, it had changed and it was now time to move on. We had rented a condominium in downtown Salt Lake City for the next fourteen months.

Topper Van Every called me in SLC in early November to talk about the problems at the top of Western's organization. That day I wrote in my journal, "Topper called and he has the blues. He says things are going from bad to worse topside. Neil wants out; Ned is ineffective; Kamats is doing his own thing and Don Vena's going to quit as soon as possible." Vena, our VP human resources, was well respected by the unions and I didn't want to see him leaving the company at this critical time.

Part of the problem top-side started when Neil Bergt hired George Kamats as senior VP operations, he brought him in at $140,000 a year which made Andre Dimitriadis angry. But then, I was learning it didn't take much to make Andre angry. Kamats came from Capital Airlines, part of the "non-sked" industry. He looked and acted like a clod, but I was told by outside sources not to let that fool you as he had a reputation of being a fairly sharp operator. Andre did not like Kamats, reputation or not. The issue of Kamats' salary had a very negative impact on several other key VP's who had taken salary cuts and had received no promotions or raises, Don Vena being one of these.

I was already aware that Vena was looking outside the company for employment. He called me on November 2nd to say he would probably leave. I encouraged him to give Western one more chance and go tell Bergt what he required in order to stay. He finally did and told Neil he needed the title of senior VP and a raise. Neil said: "That is out of the question." Just that fast, Vena was out the door. He had another job lined up that provided a more secure future and Western Airlines lost a top labor man. Bergt just couldn't see the value of this individual, as is so often the case with CEO's who think they can do a better job with union relations. WRONG!

On November 4th, Jerry Grinstein, a member of Western's board, called Vic Brown to say Neil Bergt really wanted to leave. I had lunch with the bishop the following day and he outlined the conversation he'd had with Jerry. Neil had talked to George Suddock, an old Alaska business friend of Neil's whom he had put on Western's board. George called Jerry Grinstein and said that Neil was losing a bundle staying on with Western and he wanted out right away. Jerry talked to Bergt. Neil told him just what I suspected he would say. He responded he had the management team in place and Ned DeWitt could take over. Jerry disagreed and said Ned was not ready. All this was relayed to me by Victor Brown, and the conclusion that Vic relayed was that Neil re-committed to stay in place until Ned was up to speed.

Bishop Brown had suggested that I talk to Grinstein and get to know him better, but did not indicate there was any urgency. He said Jerry would be in Salt Lake City on December 11, 1982 to go skiing at Park City and he wanted me to spend some time with him. I agreed to this, but was not sure of Vic's reason for the meeting.

Our earliest challenge of winter operations went better than expected in some respects and worse in others. The fog and deicing remained as our major concerns, but it all went smoothly. Fortunately the fog we had was cold enough that we could seed the clouds and open up a highway right over the runway. Captain Dewey Gerrard did a magnificent job of organizing the dry-ice seeding flights. This was performed by a contract service and they would seed just before the "hubbing" was to begin. The effects of this would usually last until we could get that bank of flights in and out.

It was strange to see this system in action. I drove to the airport one morning to watch the fog operation and I could hardly see the road in front of me. All of a sudden, I broke out of the fog and looked to my right to see a perfectly open runway with fog on either side. It was like Cecil B. DeMille's depiction of Moses parting the waters of the Red Sea.

We had a special operations room that controlled the use of the gates during the "bank" of flights that constituted the "hub." I would wind up in this area during any snow storm or fog operation. It was here you could really get a taste of what was transpiring with the overall traffic. Later on, a tower was built to house this crew so they would have a more visual contact with the aircraft. The employees didn't mind my hanging around through any crisis so long as I kept my mouth shut and stayed out of their way.

I enjoyed the rapport I had with the group who worked in flight operations. They closely coordinated their actions with our dispatch department in Los Angeles and, between the two areas, kept things humming along. One night I was out to a special recognition dinner and the weather had really turned sour. When we had a break I called the "Ops" number and asked how things were going. The person answering said: "Who's this?" I said: "Larry Lee." He said: "Everything is fine, just get off the line." By that response I knew I was accepted as "one of the guys."

The only time I had a problem in the operations center was during the Christmas holidays. We'd had a morning snow on December 28th and flight 260, a DC-10 loaded with passengers for Chicago, was delayed an additional forty-five minutes because of a breakdown in communications. Captain Ralph Baxter, whom I had known for several decades, got me on the radio from his cockpit and royally chewed me out. It was transmitted over the

P.A. System and heard all over the operations room. I kept my cool, but the employees could see I was pretty ticked off.

The next day I went back to the field and met Baxter's incoming flight from Chicago. I spent an hour talking to him and then another touring him through the operations department. The complexity of the process was an eye-opener to him. I think it accomplished two things. The word quickly got around that this was not a normal station, and, the other was, "don't chew out Larry Lee unless you want to spend two hours getting a lecture after your incoming flight." These pilots were great guys, but they tended to see only their end of the world. I never blamed them as they had enough to worry about. I drove Captain Baxter to his hotel and we parted friends once more.

We were so short of tugs and carts that the baggage delivery system was suffering, especially in the winter when some flights were delayed. Once I spent the whole evening shift riding a baggage tug with an employee who was the loudest mouth in the group and always seemed to have answers management could not come up with. All of his palaver boiled down to: "We have too few carts and tugs."

After this experience I quickly ordered some tugs from a local vendor, one who promised prompt delivery. Harold Achtziger rounded up every other spare cart he could find and we set up a shop to repair them as fast as they would fall apart. The guys in finance started their usual yammering about my not going through the proper budget channels, and I told them to shut up or they would not have the cash flow to have any budget. That ended the chit chat.

An event occurred on December 7, 1982 that upset me - why do such things seem to occur on Pearl Harbor Day? After our morning staff meeting in Los Angeles, Ned DeWitt said he wanted to see me privately. The purpose of the meeting was to tell me that he had gotten 5,000 shares of stock options for me. I did not thank him nor make any comments. I just left his office. I had already received word from Dimitriadis as to what each of the key officers had received; I had been given the least. I could see why Bergt was not interested in doling out anything to me when he felt I might be leaving. What I could not understand was the board of directors approving this after members appealed to me to stay on until the hub in SLC was secure. You give share options as a carrot and for performance - they missed on both counts.

Ned DeWitt had received 250,000 shares and Neil Bergt received 800,000 shares. George Kamats, who had nothing to do with putting the Salt Lake hub together, received 50,000 shares. I could understand the award to Kamats as it was given as a carrot, an enticement, if you will, to stick around awhile.

It wasn't that I was looking for a reward for my performance during the past year, it was just the fact that the board of directors failed in an opportunity to say thanks. The giving of the shares would not have modified my decision to stay or to leave, but an appropriate number would have assured my staying on until things were more secure. Andre Dimitriadis had asked me how I felt about this situation and I told him that I was going to send a letter to Bergt that I was refusing the shares. Andre cautioned me to do this in person.

On Monday, December 13th, I called Neil Bergt at 8:00 a.m. to discuss the 5,000 share stock option. Nancy, his secretary, said he would return my call as soon as possible. He called me at 9:55 a.m., five minutes before going into the board of director's meeting in Los Angeles. Therefore, he wanted a quick conversation. I wasn't about to grant his wish.

I asked Bergt the question: "Am I a winner?" He said: "What's that mean?" I replied: "When you came into the company a year ago your first words to the staff were, "I am a winner." I then repeated my question: "Am I a winner or a loser? I committed to do a job for you and I did it. Why then would you 'dump' on me with this insulting stock option?" He said: "Ned put it together; I only saw it before it went to the board. You want to talk to Ned about it?" I told Neil I did not - that I wanted to talk to him about it. I said: "If those 5,000 shares reflect the job you think I did for you this past year, just tell me." He rejoined that he would talk to Ned and ended by saying: "Thanks for making my day." I signed off by saying that I thought I knew who my friends were; I just wanted to identify my enemies.

As it turned out this became one of the best things that could have happened to me. Ned DeWitt had become very unpopular with Western's employees and this word was now filtering to the board, probably by way of the pilots. Someone had made copies of the minutes of the special meeting of the compensation committee of the board of directors, which was held on November 29th and it had been posted on most of the bulletin boards.

Therefore, the employees were well aware of the list of 13 names that starting with L. H. Lee's, 5,000 shares and building to Ned DeWitt and Bergt with their 250,000 and 800,000 share options.

To make matters worse, the chairman of the compensation committee had written in the aforementioned letter the following statement: "The purpose of the meeting was to consider and act upon a recommendation that stock options be granted to company officers under the 1982 Executive Stock Option and Stock Appreciation Right Plan. The recommendation was made in light of the need to provide some additional or alternate form of compensation to the officers who generally are under-paid and have experienced severe pay cuts. Members of the committee expressed the belief that grants of options would be beneficial to the morale of those who had sacrificed so much. Some of the names on the list were circled with the comment: "What did they sacrifice?"

The employees, realizing my role in restructuring the route system of the company, felt this was indeed an insult to me and didn't hesitate in letting their feelings be known. I just responded that I was happy not to be in a prominent position on a list of that sort.

On Wednesday, December 15th, Victor Brown spent an hour filling me in on the board meeting. He said they had spent two hours without Neil or Ned discussing Ned's presence in the company. The feeling was unanimous that his personality was not what was wanted. While I noted this in my journal, I could not repeat it to anyone because I was not even sure Neil knew the depth of the board's concern. While I had done my utmost to make sure our team came through with the route realignment, it was obvious the company still did not have what it takes at the top to continue in business much longer.

Victor Brown left me that day with what was becoming a continuing plea, "Hang in there, my friend. Don't leave me now." He knew the internal struggle I was having as I wanted out, but not at any price; the Western employees deserved better than they were getting.

Vic Brown was still asking that I meet with Jerry Grinstein. As I said earlier, I did not see the purpose and Vic could not explain it other than he thought the two of us would hit it off well. I had met Jerry at several of the board functions and was impressed with the way he related to people. His demeanor was very relaxed and I told Victor I would be happy to show him around SLC and visit about anything he wanted to discuss.

Grinstein and his children finally came to town over the Christmas Holidays to ski at Park City. Jerry was divorced from his first wife. On December 21st, I met with Jerry and Victor Brown. We three lunched at The Roof Restaurant of Hotel Utah and, after a short visit to the offices of the Presiding Bishop, I took Jerry to the airport to see Manny Floor's setup in Airport Park. I wanted him to be aware of the growth that had been proposed in the SLC area. Grinstein seemed interested in what he saw. While we were driving, he asked my impression of George Kamats and Bob Heath. Bishop Brown had told me confidentially that DeWitt would be leaving.

I was impressed with Jerry as a person, although it bothered me that he did not have any questions about the long-range plans for Western - he was just interested in my views of our current leadership. However, I realized it was the management area that was uppermost in his mind at this time as he had been told Bergt wanted out and his replacement, Ned DeWitt, was leaving at the board's request. Why talk of long-range plans when there is no leader in place?

Grinstein did not question me on my status, for which I was grateful. I had an input that they were talking to a man named Howard Putnam to take over as CEO; however, this was a rumor and I later learned Howard was not interested in the job. Nevertheless, that rumor had sent a shudder through me as it was Putnam who had the "watch" at Braniff Airlines when it went into bankruptcy. I was waiting for Jerry to bring it up, but I don't think he knew enough about me to share anything at this time. I delivered him to his destination still wondering why Vic Brown had encouraged me to spend time with him.

The next day, December 22nd, I met with Elder Gordon B. Hinckley, Elder Ezra Taft Benson and Elder Howard W. Hunter of the LDS Church. They were all members of the Church finance committee. Also in attendance were Alan Blodgett and John Hunter from the Church and two members of Citibank who had been invited to sit in. The Church had asked Roy Simmons, chairman of Zions Bank to attend. The meeting was to take twenty minutes and it ran for an hour and a half. There were lots of questions. Andre Dimitriadis had put together a nice investment package for them and he presented it very well. It would be a thirty-million dollar loan secured by equipment. The loan could be convertible into WAL stock that would give them a twenty-one percent ownership in the company.

Our finance department was interested in a solid investor, such as the LDS Church, who had a vested interest in the success of the hub in SLC. It was obvious the Church was concerned about the type of publicity that could flow from this transaction. Roy Simmons later confirmed this. I was skeptical from the beginning as it would be an unusual position for the Church to take; they were cutting loose of major investments in private enterprise and I would have been surprised if they were to change directions. Andre Dimitriadis felt there was a very good reason for them to be interested, but he did not know the background of their investment policies.

This had all started when Alan Blodgett, an important member of both the Airport Commission and the LDS Church financial group, called to see if I would set up a meeting with his team and our chief financial officer. I was edgy about what was going to happen as I needed Alan Blodgett to remain enthusiastic about our plans to expand the SLC Airport. The whole Airport Commission looked to him for financial analysis. The meetings with Blodgett and his staff went well, and it was Bishop Victor Brown who got this meeting scheduled with the LDS Church Finance Committee.

A few days after the meeting with President Hinckley and the others, Alan Blodgett called and asked if I could stop by his office for a short meeting. I responded right away. There were just the two of us in the meeting and, after the normal chit-chat, Alan said: "Larry, you are an active member of The Church of Jesus Christ of Latter-day Saints and my question is this: If you were in my shoes would you make this loan to Western Airlines?" I had to be very careful with the answer as he wore not only the LDS Church hat, but that of the airport authority. I responded by telling him that I would not make the loan if I were in his position.

It was really not right for Alan to put me on the spot, but I knew enough about the way the LDS Church invested to know that they did not take risks anywhere near this magnitude and they would not deviate from this policy at this time. I then stated that I felt confident that the hub in Salt Lake City would be successful and, if it were, we would be in a much stronger position to restructure the current financing of the company. I went on to outline what this would mean to the City and the State and for the LDS Church. I summed it up by saying I felt it was a prudent risk; but, not for the Church. Alan then said he was confident I would respond as I did and that he agreed. It was obvious he had already decided to decline the deal. I think he was just doing an integrity check on me.

Within a couple of weeks of this meeting, Blodgett notified Dimitriadis they would not be able to accept the offer. I think Victor may have been as disappointed as Andre. He had excused himself from all meetings for fear of conflict of interest.

As it turned out, this would have been a grand investment for the LDS Church. In three and a half years the value of their money would have increased five times the original investment.

The best job of "white washing" one can give to the year 1982 at Western Airlines is contained in the Annual Report for that year. It was to be the last publication from Western issued by Neil Bergt. I'll share it as a summary of that year:

LETTER TO SHAREHOLDERS

The 1982 report does not tell the story that all of us at Western wanted to bring to you; however, it does bring a story of progress and accomplishments.

The fact that Western reported a loss of $44 million for 1982, its third consecutive year of losses, is a major disappointment even though these results are a substantial improvement over 1981's loss of $73.4 million. Early in the year, we had projected a profit by the third quarter - which we achieved.

The improved performance is more satisfying, however, when viewed in light of the changes and growth that took place at Western during 1982. Never in its long history has Western done so much growing in terms of flying and cities served. This was made possible by increasing the utilization of all available resources - men, women, machines and facilities. In human terms that meant sacrifice and determination on the part of all Western employees.

Western's Salt Lake City hub, which was put into operation on May 1, represented the greatest single achievement of 1982. Overnight your airline grew from a daily level of 29 flights at Salt Lake City to 59 flights (which increased to 75 in September and will be at 100 by June of this year). The hub provides convenient flight connections for approximately 300 city pairs daily.

The airline's critics broadcast far and wide that Salt Lake City would never work as a hub, that the local market was too small, the weather was too bad and whatever else they could find wrong. Most had never been to Salt Lake City, seen Western's modern facility there or known about the hometown status Salt Lake City bestows on this airline.

Western has proven them wrong as we knew we would - Utah has welcomed Western's expansion and supports the new travel and shipping services we have brought to the community. Today, local boardings represent 44 percent of our Salt Lake City business; much higher than the 30 percent experienced at other major carriers' hubs.

Weather has presented little problem to Western in Salt Lake City, but that is partially because we were prepared for most eventualities. All Western aircraft have been equipped with the most up-to-date low visibility landing systems available for each model. Moreover, at Salt Lake City we utilize a highly successful fog seeding operation. All of this means Western can operate in conditions some of our competitors can't.

Using the Salt Lake City hub, Western has expanded into 17 new markets west of the Mississippi, and we now offer more flights to more cities in the west than any other airline. To these new cities and the ones traditionally served by Western we bring the best possible connections to and from major eastern commercial and government centers - New York City, Chicago, Kansas City and all three Washington, D.C. area airports - plus Alaska, Hawaii and Mexico along with Western Canada.

The hub-and-spoke concept of operation gives an airline on-line feed opportunities that were not possible in the old linear route systems. In other words, when Western boards a passenger or shipment in one city, in many cases we now keep that business all the way to the destination, rather than turning it over to a competitor. This gives Western more control of its market. Western now has 58 percent of its domestic market availability in monopoly or one-other carrier markets. In April 1982, before the hub, that percentage of virtually exclusive markets stood at 21.

Western's operating costs in 1982 experienced a decline from the 1981 fourth quarter level of 8.13 cents per available seat mile to 6.99 cents for the fourth quarter of 1982. At the same time, however, Western experienced a decline in its yield - or average revenue per passenger mile - from 11.38 cents in the fourth quarter of 1981 to 10.02 cents for the final quarter of 1982. These yield declines cost us more in lost revenues than we were able to achieve in expense reductions. Had we been able to hold the 1981 yield levels, Western would have been profitable in 1982.

These conditions are the inevitable result of oversupply in a commodity market. In the airline industry, this has led to fare wars and emphasizes the necessity for an airline to continue reducing operating costs to live within this economic climate.

Mature airlines that have grown up in the regulated era during the last 40 to 50 years became unproductive in terms of labor efficiency and effective use of resources. In the past year, Western has worked diligently with the unions representing its labor force to reverse those trends which developed under the protection of regulation. We consider steps toward reversal as essential to Western's profitability in the future.

We expect that more low-cost operators may enter the marketplace as the economy improves, and we must be prepared to meet them head-on with cost efficiency in operations and superior services. Western is only one of many "mature" airlines in this squeeze.

Western has in operation one of the youngest aircraft fleets in the industry with an average aircraft age of 7.125 years, but even at that we have undertaken an appearance spruce up program which will be completed for most of the fleet by late spring. Aircraft interiors will be refurbished and those that need it will get an exterior paint job. At the same time all ground personnel who are in contact with the customer will graduate from newly developed training programs this spring, and we will implement the latest improvements in our automated reservations/passenger service system by June.

We call it the "new" Western, but as our advertising approach says "Western . . . We've Got A Name To Live Up To." We are doing everything in our power to keep Western on a course to full recovery and future growth. We appreciate your support and hope you will encourage your friends, relatives and neighbors to fly Western whenever possible.

Neil G. Bergt

Chairman of the Board and Chief Executive Officer, April 4, 1983

Chapter 9
TURBULENCE AT THE TOP

1983 began with little change in the chaos at Western Airlines. Example, I flew to Los Angeles on Monday, the 3rd of January to get queued up for the executive staff meeting that was now being run by the president, Ned DeWitt. I arrived at the General Office at 7:30 a.m. on Tuesday only to find the meeting had been cancelled and no reason was given. Ned DeWitt's car was gone, and I guessed that so was he.

George Kamats, senior VP of operations, didn't know what was happening and Neil Bergt wasn't taking calls. By noon I'd had enough of the place and caught a flight back to Salt Lake City.

The next day, January 5th, I got word that one of our key executives, Bob Heath, was leaving to work for the government in Alaska. Three key executives were out the door, President Ned DeWitt, Heath and Don Vena, VP, human resources.

On Friday, January 7th, Tony Favero, a retired VP maintenance, called and said he had talked with Fred Benninger, a member of our board, and Benninger had told him that he was unhappy with Bergt and wanted him "out." Tony finally got to the point of the call and said that he thought Bob Volk, another member of the board, would make a good president and CEO and wanted me to put him in touch with Victor Brown. He said Volk had already talked to Benninger and Grinstein. I called Victor to tell him about Tony's conversation, and Vic said he did not want to talk to him; Volk was up skiing in Park City. Vic said he would resign from the board if Volk got in power.

Bishop Brown called me again on Monday to say that everyone was unhappy with the way Neil Bergt was handling things and that Jerry Grinstein was heading for Alaska to see him.

Just when I thought things could not get worse, they did. On January 12th, word came out that the company had granted bonuses to nine of the officers. I noted in my journal that I figured that all hell would break loose, and it did. The head of Western Airlines' master executive council for the pilot union, Joel Jensen, called and asked if he could meet with me the following day. I suggested that we arrange a joint meeting with Victor Brown, if he was available and Joel asked if Duane Gerrard, the pilot base manager of SLC could attend. Bishop Brown was available and we met in his office.

The main thrust of the meeting seemed to be Captain Jensen's need to be sure that I understood the seriousness of what was happening with the morale of the company, especially among the pilots. Both Victor and I assured them that we were very much aware and that the board was doing everything possible to resolve the problems. Both Joel and Dewey asked why I didn't step in and take over, but I told them that I had to eliminate that as an option at this time.

It was obvious to me that neither my response nor Victor's did anything to encourage Captain Jensen. He indicated that the pilots, and, he sensed, others in the company had totally lost faith in the board and in the present leadership.

On Monday morning, January 17, 1983, Victor Brown called to say that Neil Bergt had agreed to leave the company and that the board of directors was setting up an emergency meeting for the next day.

Until this time, Victor had never mentioned the potential of declaring bankruptcy. Nevertheless, I knew he was extremely concerned that the resources of Western Airlines were dwindling rapidly, and that this condition could not continue much longer. I sensed the critical nature of this meeting and felt that several members of the board must be considering the possibility of bankruptcy, Bergt being one of them.

I suggested that, if this extreme measure became a decision of the board, Victor Brown push to have Jerry Grinstein put in as chairman of the board and CEO and have Andre Dimitriadis, who was now senior VP finance, put in the position of president and chief operating officer. What I was saying to Vic was: "Get a lawyer and a financial person in position to take the company into chapter eleven, if that is the only option." I reassured Vic that, from an operating standpoint, everything was functioning properly at the "hub" and we agreed Western's total future depended upon its success.

On Tuesday morning, January 18th, Art Kelly, former chairman of the board, called me. I could tell that he was on a "fishing expedition" to see if I knew what the emergency meeting was about. Topper Van Every called from Los Angeles to say the place was a "zoo"; Kamats fired Tony Colletti, VP maintenance and engineering, and two of his department directors . Kamats was bringing in VP maintenance from Capitol Airlines, his old employer; a man named Gordon Bethune. The word on Bethune was that he was a nice guy. He began work on January 20th.

One of the reasons I mention this is that Gordon Bethune didn't stay long with Western. I believe he felt that he was not going to be able to fulfill his dream of becoming a CEO while at this company. I say it is interesting because he ultimately became president and CEO of Continental Airlines and built it into an excellent service. Hindsight would say that Western had a replacement for Neil Bergt in hand and let the bird escape.

On Wednesday, January 19th, my journal reads: "I hear yesterday I came within one person's vote of being elected chairman of the board and chief executive officer of Western Airlines."

When Bishop Brown returned, he said they had presented Gerald Grinstein as CEO and Dimitriadis as president with me as vice chairman and a member of the board. The bankers would not buy it.

The board of directors then agreed that I be asked to take over as CEO but the lead lender from Citi Bank, Fred Bradley, said that would be all right under normal circumstances, but the other smaller lenders would not understand Neil Bergt's leaving at this critical time and unless Neil stayed for a while they would not give us a promised thirty million dollar line of credit. Victor said if Bergt decided to jump ship anyway, they were going to offer it to me. Neil finally agreed to stay long enough for the personnel selection committee of the board to find a new CEO from outside Western.

I asked Vic why the bankers and some of the board of directors balked at Grinstein for Chairman and CEO. It boiled down to the fact that Jerry did not have any corporate management experience that would be recognized by Wall Street. In addition, Andre, while showing a lot of creativity in the financial area, did not show the leadership characteristics that were needed at this time. Of course Victor could not suggest to the bankers that this was a "worst-case scenario" prior to declaring bankruptcy.

Victor Brown said they were increasing the efforts with their search for Neil's replacement. I told him I would ride it out unless Neil did something nutty. The rumor was all over the company that I was the new CEO, so someone must have leaked what was being considered by the board. My final journal entry for that day was: "Thank the Lord for saving me." There was no way that I wanted to get involved with trying to make any sense out of the mess that had been created at corporate headquarters.

It was increasingly obvious to me that Andre Dimitriadis was not seeing all the corners of the picture. I was beginning to comprehend that he was a very self-centered individual whose primary interest seemed to be his own aggrandizement. Unfortunately, Victor had made Andre aware that I had proposed that he take over as Western's president and chief operating officer, but he was not aware of the conditions under which I envisioned that happening. This was to "bite me" in tender places later in my career.

As for Jerry Grinstein, I had a good feeling about him and sensed that under any circumstances he should be made chairman of the board of Western. He seemed to be handling most of the board matters and should be given the recognition for his role.

Later, when examining the minutes of that emergency board meeting of January 18, 1983, I noted with interest how carefully the corporate secretary, Tom Greene, couched what transpired in that meeting. Following are the minutes of that over four-hour meeting.

A meeting of the board of directors of Western Air Lines, Inc. was held at the company's general offices in Los Angeles, California, beginning at 2:25 p.m., PST, on Tuesday, January 18, 1983, pursuant to telephonic notice to each of the directors.

The following directors were present:

> Neil G. Bergt
>
> Miguel M. Blasquez
>
> Victor L. Brown
>
> Gerald Grinstein
>
> Arthur F. Kelly
>
> Bert T. Kobayashi, Jr.
>
> George S. Suddock
>
> Roy G. Utter
>
> Robert H. Volk

Also present was Thomas J. Greene, vice president, general counsel and secretary.

Mr. Bergt presided and Mr. Greene kept the minutes.

Mr. Bergt began the meeting by stating his desire to update the board on recent events and to discuss future plan alternatives in light of deteriorating financial conditions. He described a concern expressed by some lenders regarding his remaining with Western or leaving, especially in light of the possibility of Alaska International Air entering the passenger market. Mr. Bergt stated that AIA does not intend to enter the passenger market.

In discussing the company, Mr. Bergt stated that essentially the airline industry had become a commodity business after deregulation, and even though Western had made substantial progress and become a low-cost carrier, overcapacity problems in the industry continued and competition dictated that an airline must "buy" traffic by offering deep discounts in today's market. Moreover, he stated that the market continues to deteriorate.

In that context, he indicated a need for the board to consider the future direction of the industry and the company's place within the industry. There followed a discussion among all directors of a variety of alternatives which the company might pursue, including the extreme measure of filing for *reorganization* along with less extreme alternatives. Various forms of retrenchment were discussed. Mr. Bergt expressed his opinion that a good possibility existed that none of the "mature" trunk carriers could survive as presently structured without the need for some form of *reorganization*. Some directors expressed confidence in the employees' ability to recognize the needs of the company and to do what is necessary to assure its survival. Other directors expressed a viewpoint that if filing for *reorganization* were to be seriously considered, it should be done at a point in time when the company has some cash and some flexibility.

At this point Mr. Andre Dimitriadis, senior vice president finance joined the meeting and at Mr. Bergt's request presented a brief summary of the financial condition of the company. He stated that problems with yield were continuing, and it now looked like the yield would average 9.75 for the first quarter of 1983, somewhat lower than the 9.9 level which had been hoped for. He stated that prospects looked good for gaining PBGC and IRS approval of the termination of the Pilots Fixed Pension Plan, and that he was also hopeful that the company's lenders would execute agreements for a new lending facility in the near future. With such measures in place, he expressed confidence that the company should improve. He emphasized, however, the need for a successful third quarter and for concessions from the company's labor unions.

At Mr. Bergt's request, Mr. Dimitriadis went on to summarize the status of negotiations with the various unions, particularly as some of them have been negatively impacted by the news of granting bonuses to certain of the company's executives since the first of the year. In particular, he reported that the Teamsters had tentatively agreed to a wage cut of 10%, but had withdrawn that agreement after learning of these bonuses. It was not clear whether or not other unions would similarly withdraw concessions which have been agreed upon.

A discussion resumed on various alternatives of future direction open to the company, including possibilities of grounding DC-10' s, of increasing 737 flying, of further emphasis on the Salt Lake City hub, and of an employee stock plan. Mr. Bergt indicated he would like a consensus of the board whether a contingency plan should be developed as a preface to a ***reorganization*** filing if it became necessary. Several directors expressed a preference, while wanting to explore all alternatives, to see how successful efforts could be to obtain concessions with respect to wages and productivity, and the possibility of a stock plan, before moving toward a ***reorganization*** filing.

A further discussion ensued regarding the executive bonuses and it was clearly the consensus of the board that the granting of such bonuses had been of doubtful wisdom. The directors discussed the practical difficulties inherent in trying to rescind or recover some or all of the bonuses, and it was the further consensus of the board to support Mr. Bergt in whatever action he determined was appropriate in dealing with that situation.

At Mr. Bergt's request, Mr. Robert Berghel of the law firm Fisher and Phillips joined the meeting at this point for a discussion with respect to the company's labor situation, particularly its efforts to obtain further productivity goals. Additionally, Mr. Berghel responded to several questions posed by directors regarding the status of labor agreements in a ***reorganization*** proceeding. After Mr. Berghel was excused, Mr. Craig Benedetti, vice president-marketing, joined the meeting and presented a report on marketing. He emphasized the problems with discounts and the corresponding problems created with yield.

Mr. Bergt then asked that the board ratify the appointment of Andre C. Dimitriadis as senior vice president-finance, effective December 15, 1982. Upon motion made and seconded, the board unanimously ratified such action.

Mr. Besomergt assured the board that management would continue to explore the various alternate plans available to it and would report to the board regularly on progress in this area. Several directors expressed concern about the departure of Messrs. Tony Colletti and Don Vena from their respective officer posts, and Mr. Bergt assured the board that those officers would be replaced by capable and competent people.

There was further a brief discussion regarding efforts to find a successor to Mr. Bergt. He indicated that several candidates were being considered and that he had asked Mr. Grinstein to act as chairman of an informal group of directors participating in that search. There being no further business to come before the meeting it was adjourned at 6:45 p.m."

(Emphasis on "reorganization," is mine.)

As so often happens, after a major skirmish, there was a lull and a breathing space wherein things seem to settle down. Dimitriadis called to say that Neil Bergt was in the saddle and we appeared to be back to square one, sans a few more top executives.

I noted in my journal that input from some key employees in various groups reflected feelings that they had been "done in by top management," but they seemed to understand there was nothing they could do about it that wouldn't hurt them in the end. It was as if everyone was just sitting back waiting for the next brouhaha to break loose.

Jerry Grinstein shifted into high gear and worked with a "head-hunting" firm to find a replacement for Bergt. The first real contender for the position was Tom Plaskett, senior VP marketing at American Airlines. Bishop Brown said they were homing in on one candidate, but he wouldn't tell me the name. I told him who it was and he was surprised. I related that our industry was noted for not keeping secrets. He said Plaskett was interested and wanted some time to consider it.

Plaskett would be an excellent selection and I let this be known. For some reason, Andre Dimitriadis did not like him. He notified Bergt he would quit if either Plaskett or Kamats was made president of Western. That probably got a yawn out of Neil. I had a hunch that this delay was mainly for the purpose of seeing what the alternatives were at American Airlines. Tom Plaskett wanted to fill the role of president and chief operating officer there which would queue him up behind Bob Crandall, who had not yet signaled who would be heir to his throne.

My feeling was Grinstein, et al., were really feeling confident that Plaskett would be the man. They began talks with him during the week beginning January 24th and this wooing continued until around the 23rd of February; at least that is when Victor Brown called to say Plaskett had turned down the job. So, the search went on.

On March 2nd, Bishop Brown called to ask what I thought of putting Dimitriadis in as the president and chief operating officer of Western. I told him that under present conditions it would be a disaster. He was on his way to LAX to another meeting of the board. It sounded as though things were getting into the panic stage.

The next day, Art Kelly called to say he had spent fifteen minutes at the board meeting presenting my name for CEO. He indicated that Neil Bergt was now receptive to this. I just listened and thanked him. Vic Brown called that afternoon to ask if I was interested and I told him I would only take it if it was the last resort and I would not stay longer than it would take to select and train a replacement; I told him I estimated that to be three years.

On March 16, 1983, I had lunch with Bishop Victor Brown and informed him I was not interested in the CEO position under any circumstances. I was hot under the collar, a condition Vic had not seen before, and I let him know that the board had jerked me around for three months with, "will you do this, or, will you consider that" and I was sick and tired of this treatment; ergo, count me out. I told him to inform the board that I would retire from Western on June 1st. He asked if I would consider anything that could tie me to SLC for a longer period. I responded: "Only with a three-year contract, but I'm tired of all these wishy-washy ideas that do not come to fruition." He said he understood and we parted good friends as usual.

In the midst of all this, Art Kelly flew to Salt Lake City to try to convince me to take the president and chief operating officer spot vacated by Ned DeWitt. He had no knowledge that I had already aborted a direct attempt by

Bergt to get me to consider this move. I let him know that this was not in the cards and he took the next flight back to Los Angeles.

On March 21st, Vic Brown arrived from a meeting of some the board members who had interviewed three candidates for CEO. He said the one in whom they were most interested was Martin Shagrue from Pan American Airlines. Marty was a good man. He originally came from the pilot group and made his way up at Pan Am through the personnel department handling labor relations. He was presently senior VP marketing there and, from what I understood, was a bit over his head in that capacity. However, he was a good administrator.

During the next few days Grinstein pushed hard to get him. I called Bishop Brown on the 25th and asked if they'd heard anything from Marty. He said Shagrue had asked for another twenty-four hours to consider the matter.

On Tuesday, March 29, 1983 I flew to LAX to attend the executive staff meeting. That night I wrote in my journal:

> This had to be the most depressing experience of my career! George Kamats certainly tried to manage the meeting, but he lacked any sense of direction and demonstrated the total absence of a corporate plan.

The lenders were up in the "Presidents Room" having lunch with Andre Dimitriadis. He was trying to get their agreement to let us draw on the thirty-million dollar line of credit. He was having a rough time convincing them, so he requested that Kamats and I join the luncheon so they could ask Kamats questions regarding the operation of the company. His answers were shallow. Andre looked like he was going to lose his lunch. I caught the next flight out of town. Andre's parting words were: "We can't get a new CEO without some money to allow him running room to get the company going and we can't get the money without some leadership ." Talk about a catch 22!

The next morning, March 30th, I called Andre to see what happened with the bankers. He said he got the deal completed and that it would allow us to put out some convertible subordinate debentures. The combination should be enough to see us over the rough spots until a new president could bring some order to the chaos. I asked him if this was enough to entice Marty

Shagrue to come to Western and he thought it might be. No such luck - Marty used the Western offer to cinch himself up another notch at Pan Am and that left us back at square one.

Victor Brown had shared with me some very confidential conversations that were going on at the board meetings and in private phone calls. The bishop was a very tight-lipped man, but he was also trying to keep me from jumping ship. He said the members of the board were getting extremely concerned with the financial condition of Western and several felt they were putting themselves in a dangerous position by not declaring bankruptcy to preserve what we could and try to reorganize under chapter eleven. Western's operating losses and interest expenses from 1980 through the first half of 1983 amounted to three hundred and eighty million dollars. At the end of 1982 our total assets were 808.6 million and current liabilities and long-term debt was 695.6 million. All of our flight equipment and spare engines were pledged as collateral for our debt. This painted a pretty grim picture.

We both had spoken of our concern that Western's situation was much more akin to Braniff's final days; that is, our resources had all been pledged to secure loans to the degree that we would not have the equipment nor the cash we needed to get back in the air following a declaration of bankruptcy, especially considering the amount of business we depended on from travel agents who would flee at any hint of the "B" word.

When Martin Shagrue turned down the position of CEO at Western, Victor called and asked if I could come to his office. It was Friday, April 1st - April Fools Day, but what was to transpire was no joke. When I arrived I could see he was extremely concerned about Western's situation. He said he had joined forces with a couple of the other board members to encourage the rest not to declare bankruptcy but he wasn't certain they could do it any longer. His banner line to those with whom he had spoken was: "Before we pull the chord, the employees of Western Airlines deserve one last chance to see what they are willing to do to rescue their company, and we will never identify what they are willing to do unless Western is organized under the leadership of someone they know and trust."

Then came the words I really didn't want to hear, but somehow knew I would: "Larry, you're the only one they'll trust and you've got to take the helm."

Bishop Brown was right and I knew this. I too felt the employees needed this last chance. The big question was, had the board waited too long? I told Victor we'd talk about this again on Monday and to sit tight until then.

Marjorie and I had planned to spend the weekend with her folks in Montclair, California. I decided there was no better place to think this over and make a decision. I spent Saturday and Sunday organizing my thoughts for what would have to be done.

By Monday I knew I had to give it a shot. I also knew I would need the full cooperation of Western's board. Bishop Brown and I met on Monday, April 4th and I told Vic I would take the job if I had one-hundred percent backing of the board and only then after I had spoken with key bankers and those who were working on a convertible bond issue with Dimitriadis. He assured me the board of directors would back me and that Neil Bergt had agreed to step down. Step down! - I almost laughed. Neil was ready to flee.

I told Vic to notify the members of the board of my initial position and to request a meeting of the executive committee of the board in San Francisco Friday, April 8th, to receive my answer and, if it was yes, discuss the conditions of my employment.

Andre Dimitriadis was immediately brought into the picture as I expected him to be on hand for some of the meetings with the financial group.

Before flying down to Los Angeles Tuesday morning, I had a basic plan in mind and decided to reduce it to a one-page hand written document that I could review verbally with the executive committee at the meeting. It also provided me with an outline of what I needed to relate to the lenders. With them I knew I had to toss in some meat as they had been seeing nothing but bones.

On Tuesday, April 5th, I walked into Neil Bergt's office and before I could say anything he said: "Well, I understand you finally agreed to take the job as president and COO." Before I could respond he added: "I know - I'll clean out my desk." I sat down and said: "Not so fast, you are half right. I may take the title of president and CEO, but not chairman of the board. If I do, I would like you to keep the chairman's title until the Stockholders' Meeting on May 12th."

That request caught him totally off guard and he asked my reasons. I said I had some other plans that I could not share at this time and asked him to stay put until after my meeting with the board of directors as I had not yet given them my final decision on taking the job of CEO. If I accepted the position, it was not to be announced until the following Monday. At least, that was the plan.

Bergt and I agreed that if I took the job he would be gone from the premises by Monday and his only contact relating to Western would be through me. We also agreed that if I took the post, he would resign from the board at the Stockholders' Meeting. He was very affable and talkative. As I left he offered his private jet and crew for my use this week. He also offered this advice: "Make sure you have a contract and you should not take less than one million shares of stock options - that may be all you get out of this risky job." Later, I was sorry I did not take his advice on the contract.

My first meeting was with Fred Bradley of Citi Bank. You may recall from a prior comment that he was our lead banker. We had lunch at the Regency Club in Westwood. The discussion went well and I felt I would receive his support in communications with the other lenders. I promised to meet with him again after making my final decision.

Dimitradis had me speak to some other bankers on Wednesday and brought me up to date on what he was doing with Drexel Burnham on a convertible stock issue. The board, on March 2, 1983, had approved a deal with Drexel to do this offering which was to raise between forty and fifty million dollars. The key man from their organization was a fellow named Ruben Shohet. He was located in San Francisco and Andre and I made plans to go see him on Thursday.

Thursday morning we used Bergt's Westwind jet, manned by his two private pilots, and flew to the San Francisco Airport. We parked by our hangar and had a car waiting to take us to Ruben's apartment. This had to be one of the strangest encounters I was to have. This man was a mine-field of innuendos of how their company operated and, without going into further detail, Shohet insinuated they would not work with us until they had their people on the property in management positions. They literally wanted to take over the management of Western before they would float the bonds. I was shocked by what I heard and Andre was backpeddling about his involvement with them. I could not believe Bergt had let him go this far with these bizarre people or that the board of directors would have approved this deal.

It was a further indication to me of how desperate they perceived Western's situation to be.

There was nothing to do at the moment but play along with the scenario until we could analyze other alternatives. This meeting almost caused me to back away from accepting the job. I had no idea whether or not their methods were within the normal framework of this type of venture, nor how legal they were. All I knew was that the whole deal didn't sound kosher to me. We returned to LAX in the Westwind that afternoon.

I flew back to SLC that evening to make sure Bishop Brown understood my concerns. I had the backing of everyone with whom I had visited, but things were worse than even Victor had imagined. He was not up to speed on all that was happening with Drexel Burnham. I advised him that, in my estimation, Bergt had allowed Andre to go beyond that which I felt was prudent.

Friday morning, April 8th, I was back in Los Angeles for a few more meetings and then flew to San Francisco to attend the evening gathering with the executive staff of Western Airlines board of directors. Victor Brown had assured me they had the power to make a deal. Tom Greene of our legal division was in attendance as corporate secretary and Gerald Grinstein ran the meeting. My situation was the only matter of business, so Jerry turned the meeting over to me to discuss my plans.

The task was made simple by my one-page sheet of goals. I stated what had to be done in each area and then opened for questions. Fred Benninger was first out of the gate with a statement and a question: "I agree with everything you've said, the problem is who are we going to get to do it?" I was wondering just where Benninger stood on my appointment. He had been pushing for his old friend from Flying Tiger, "Pinky the pilot," to come on board. Victor had been in an interview with him and classified the man as incapable of grasping what it would take to get a turn-around.

Benninger and I had crossed swords before; it was when Kerkorian had control of Western Airlines. Benninger was Kirk's right-hand man and during that era was vice-chairman of Western Airlines. Fred was sharp, but he felt he knew everything there was to know about labor relations and he nearly scuttled a critical pilot negotiation for which I was responsible as VP of industrial relations.

The bottom line was that I knew Benninger didn't feel I had the guts to do what needed to be done. Therefore, I was prepared for any confrontation. When Benninger made his comment, I turned to him and said: "Fred, I am going to accomplish these things and if you don't feel you can back me in this then you should get off the board!" Benninger rolled his cigar in his mouth for a moment and then said: "Okay, if you're up to it, do it." That ended round one. I looked around the table and asked for other questions; there were none.

It was then time to present my conditions of employment. That too was hand-written on a simple sheet of lined yellow paper.

> Pay me the same salary they had paid to Ned DeWitt as president and COO; $240,000 a year. I will reduce this by forty percent until we become profitable. In addition, turn over to me the 250,000 stock options that had been awarded to Ned Dewitt.

> Reinstate my Executive Pension Plan, the supplemental plan from which the board had disenfranchised me when I was a senior vice president.

> Provide a three-year contract.

I also stated that I expected them to pick up my housing expenses in Los Angeles and furnish me with a car.

It is customary to step outside while they discuss the matter of compensation; however, Grinstein said there was no need for that and asked if anyone had questions. There were no questions. I informed them they could go ahead with the tentative board meeting they planned for Monday, April 11th, and we agreed that, if my concluding meetings with the lenders were to my satisfaction, the announcement would be made following that meeting. There being no other business, the meeting of the executive committee was adjourned.

At this juncture it is not unusual for a few members of the board to offer their resignations. One of them surprised me. After the meeting, Jerry Grinstein said he thought it might be time for him to leave the board and get on with other things in his life. I said I had different thoughts and asked him to sit tight until I could get to Seattle to speak with him. He agreed to do so.

The weekend was spent in Salt Lake City preparing a plan for the coming week. There were three things I had to accomplish rather quickly. One was to speak to the employees in Salt Lake City and assure them of our commitment to the "hub." These meetings would also be the springboard to both stop and start rumors that could best flow from Salt Lake City across the system. I did not have the luxury of having employee meetings at each of the larger locations at this time and knew I could reach enough of our people at the Salt Lake City base to have the word spread.

Following are the relevant details of the actions that occurred on Monday:

Pursuant to the call of its chairman, a special meeting of the board of directors of Western Airlines, Inc. was held by telephone conference call beginning at 11:00 a.m., PST on Monday, April 11, 1983, under the provisions of Section 141(i) of the Delaware General Corporation Law.

Present by conference telephone call were the following directors:

Neil G. Bergt, Miguel M. Blasquez, Victor L. Brown, Walter J. Hickel, Arthur F. Kelly, Bert T. Kobayashi Jr., Arthur G. Linkletter, John G. McMillian, George S. Suddock, Roy G. Utter, Robert H. Volk

Also present was Thomas J. Greene, vice president, general counsel and secretary.

Mr. Bergt, chairman of the board, presided and Mr. Greene kept the minutes.

After briefly tracing the history of the search for a new president, Mr. Bergt asked Mr. Grinstein, the chairman of the informal search committee, to summarize the details of that search. Mr. Grinstein stated that after considering and interviewing several candidates, the committee strongly recommended the election of Lawrence H. Lee as president and chief executive officer, and as a member of the board of directors, and that the compensation committee determine a fair and reasonable compensation package. Mr. Grinstein went on to indicate the Mr. Bergt would remain as chairman for the time being, and that such realignment had the apparent support of Western's lenders and of the underwriters in the proposed public offering. After discussion, on motion made and seconded, the following resolutions were unanimously adopted:

RESOLVED, that effective immediately Lawrence H. Lee be and he is elected and appointed president and chief executive officer, at an annual salary to be determined by the compensation committee of this board, to serve until his successor is elected and has qualified;

RESOLVED FURTHER, that Lawrence H. Lee be and he is elected and appointed to the board of directors of this Corporation, to serve until the next annual meeting of shareholders;

There being no further business, the meeting was adjourned at 11:15 a.m.

It just takes fifteen minutes to change the leadership in a company, but it took me a week of wearisome travel and meetings to make up my mind that this shift in management would work to the advantage of Western.

One of the first items of business was to put out a message to all 10,000+ employees expressing my thanks for their support. I indicated that they knew me, or my reputation, and that I knew their capabilities and basic desire to have Western become a successful company. I expressed my wish to come out and meet with them, but first I must become acquainted with those who don't know me, our lenders, bankers, major investors, etc.

In that communication, I said: "No congratulations, please. Just send best wishes for our mutual success. When we move into the summer of '84, both healthy and cohesive, at that time let's congratulate one another."

Boeing Aircraft was a huge player in our future and I needed to visit with both the president and the chief financial officer to make sure they understood where we were going. The third goal was to have a visit with Jerry Grinstein and tell him of my plan for the selection of a chairman of the board. I figured we could take care of item two and three on the same day, so I called Jerry and requested he set up the meetings at Boeing. I also asked that he accompany me to these meetings. A breakfast for the two of us was scheduled at the Olympic Hotel during the week of April 11th. We would go from there to Boeing.

Gerald Grinstein was presently a partner in the law firm of Preston, Thorgrimson, Ellis, Holman and Fletcher in Seattle, Washington. He had been very active in the political arena in Washington, D.C. where he served as chief counsel for the U.S. Senate Commerce Committee between 1963 and 1967 and as counsel to its Merchant Marine and Transportation Sub-committees between 1958 and 1963. He was administrative assistant to Washington Senator Warren G. Magnuson from 1967 until 1969.

Grinstein's appointment to the board in 1977 was of interest. Dominic P. Renda, then president of Western Airlines, called Neil Stewart, our VP governmental affairs in Washington, and asked him to be thinking of someone from the Seattle area to replace Art Woodley, retired president of Pacific Northern Airlines, who had turned seventy and was going off the board. Neil Stewart had previously been sales manager for Western in Seattle for many years and knew the movers and shakers in that area. Neil told Renda that he had a name for him right then. Renda said: "I don't want it now, I just want you to be thinking of someone you'd like to recommend." Neil said that he had been aware of Woodley's retirement and had been thinking of this person for two years. He then mentioned the name of Gerald Grinstein. Stewart related that, after a short pause, Renda responded that it was an excellent suggestion and why hadn't he, Renda, thought of that.

I had known Neil Stewart and Melba, his wife, ever since I began working for Western in Salt Lake City. Neil knew both Washington State and Washington, D.C. better than anyone in the company. He later informed me of why he had suggested Grinstein and was so high on this man. He said Jerry was known as "the third Senator from Washington." He knew everyone who was worth knowing and was absolutely fearless in contacting these people across the country to ask their advice or assistance. He had a great sense of humor, Neil said, but along with that was a very fine intelligence. Neil saw him as a fast learner and an excellent arbitrator. I was counting on this input for what I was about to propose to Grinstein.

Over breakfast, I told Jerry I needed to have someone working close to me that I could trust, one who had not only a legal background but someone very familiar with the inner workings of Washington, D.C. I said: "You are aware that I left Neil Bergt in the slot as chairman of the board so I could fill that slot with someone else at the forthcoming shareholder's meeting." I went on to say: "Jerry, that someone is you." I think this truly caught him by surprise. He asked what it would entail. I said that I needed him one day a week in the Corporate Headquarters and that I would prefer that be Friday in case we needed to get together for anything special on Saturday; the other four days a week he'd spend at his law firm. He said he would have to discuss it with certain members of his firm to make sure there was no conflict of interest and that he'd let me know in a few days.

The primary purpose of this move (become chairman in April 1983) was to have Grinstein spend a day or so a week with me during the remainder of 1983 year so we could become better acquainted. This would give me time to measure his potential and give him time to see if he wanted to work with me. My instinct told me that he had all the qualifications to become a fine corporate executive, he just lacked experience - at least the type of experience that caught people's attention in the business world.

We finished breakfast (at the Olympic Hotel) and headed for Boeing for a round of meetings and lunch with the chief financial officer. We encountered no problem there, and I felt they accepted me in my new role.

Chapter 10

THE PARTNERSHIP PROGRAM

A few days later, Grinstein called to say he had cleared any obstacles with his firm and that he'd be happy to take the position of chairman of the board and, barring any emergencies at his law firm, would spend each Friday with me at our offices in Los Angeles. So began a wonderful relationship.

My next task was to hold a series of employee meetings in Western's crew lounge at Salt Lake International Airport. I scheduled the meetings between the banks of the hub and held them in the crew lounge so the pilots and flight attendants could come and go at will, or as needed.

Considering Western's financial condition, I knew there was little the unions could or would do in the next two months, so I structured the first part of my presentation to concentrate on a two month plan of getting us into the cash flow of the summer months. This was really a no-brainer, except it allowed me to speak to the employees about things they could individually accomplish during this period.

Second, I wanted to plant in their minds that there would be a "Partnership Program" which had to be ready by the time we started into the fall months, a plan that would take us into the summer of 1984.

Third was the statement on a five-year plan that must be carefully developed, one that would start from scratch as there was no real long-term survival plan in place for Western Airlines.

On April 21st I held day and evening meetings with the employees. One of the sessions was tape recorded so I have recently been able to review my message.

The three-step approach gave the employees and management their basic marching orders for planning and the time frames in which to accomplish what was necessary for Western's survival.

Interspersed with these planning comments were random thoughts on my position as CEO and other expectations. I gave them the guarantee that I would not leave until the job was done; that I was not an interim CEO; and, last, but certainly not least in the eyes of the employees, was the promise to recruit several people who would have the strength to develop a good marketing program and augment our operating plan. I told them it would be from this pool of talent that I would select my replacement when it came time for me to leave. I promised that never under my watch would there be a time when we did not have someone on the property capable of taking Western into the future.

To show how serious I was about the above mentioned promises to the employees on my future replacement, in the April 29, 1983 meeting of the board of directors the minutes of the meeting reflect this statement I made to them:

> [Lee] ". . . Described changes in titles and functions among the officers, [in the proposed company organization,] and expressed his projection that a new chief operating officer would be selected within one year, and a successor chief executive officer within three years."

A great deal of time during the next three weeks was spent reorganizing various departments of the company, mostly putting on Band-Aids until we could complete our outside search for a strong marketing individual and an equally well-qualified person to take my old job as head of the customer service division.

An example of this was forming a troika in marketing to handle the various sales activities without filling the top spot of senior VP marketing. I brought Brent Buma down from SLC to be VP field sales; promoted Jim

Watson to handle the agency and interline group, Bill Balfour's old job; and, Mark Dennett to be VP advertising and sales promotion. These three would temporarily report to me.

Art Kelly had been very close to Ray Silvius and I called Art to get his opinion on bringing Ray back to his old job as VP public relations. He advised against it as he had obtained a good position for him in an aerospace company. He also thought it might send a wrong signal to employees who were not familiar with the cavalier way in which Ray was ejected from Western.

It seemed that management was spending an inordinate amount of time working with the people from Drexel Burnham on their proposed debenture offering. Ruben Shohet was getting up my nose and I told Andre Dimitriadis I'd about had it with them.

Andre advised he had made contact with a couple of other financial houses to see if they were interested in doing an offering and he would let me know where we stood on this before taking any further action.

A few days later, Andre said E. F. Hutton was showing interest in doing a $65,000,000 offering and that they thought the timing was good to go to the street with this. I told Andre to shift into low-gear with Drexel Burnham until after the Stockholders' Meeting in Salt Lake City. This was uppermost in my mind at that moment.

On May 12, 1983, I participated in my first Stockholders' Meeting as CEO. It went smooth as glass. Neil Bergt bowed out as planned and Gerald Grinstein was installed as chairman of the board. Marjorie wrote in her journal that I was "poised, in command, dignified, effective, terrific and handsome." She also wrote that I'd answered all the questions with clarity and sincerity. She always made me sound better than I was, but it was nice to have such a supportive wife. When I retired, Western Airlines board of directors gave her a plaque that read: "Without your support, where would we be?" She was and is such a great lady!

Of the 13,000,000 shares of Western Airlines stock, 77.7 % of it was represented at this meeting. It was gratifying to see that in the counting of shares voted for my being a member of their board, I received more votes than any other member of the board. Even though it was a small margin it made me feel good, the new kid on the block, etc. The other "new kid" was Andre

Dimitriadis, newly appointed board member; he received the least number of votes.

If you have read this far, you may have noted several key events in my career where I related how I knew the Lord was there to guide me when the going got tough. I had great faith the Lord's help was always available to me and that I would be guided through the rocks and shoals. I want you to know this was never truer than during this particular time at Western Airlines when the going was not only very tough, but our options were very few. I asked for the Lord's help daily and felt myself inspired to work beyond my normal capacity. However, I did have a concern for my health.

The day after the Stockholders Meeting, I asked Victor Brown if he would give me a blessing to sustain me through this period with good health. He called his friend, Elder James E. Faust of the Quorum of the Twelve Apostles, and he said to come right over. Victor asked Elder Faust to give me the blessing. Elder Faust gave me some wonderful assurances. After this, I had total faith I could do what was necessary without incurring additional ulcers that had plagued me through these many years.

By the first of June 1983, we had shed ourselves of Drexel Burnham and Ruben Shohet and his minions were off the property. Dimitriadis had been working with E. F. Hutton in doing $65,000,000 in 10 3/4% senior secured trust notes due in 1998. With this package we had to have approved 3,240,000 shares of common stock and warrants to purchase an additional 9,000,000 shares.

I traveled to New York and spent several days working with E. F. Hutton's team, those who would be selling this issue. I also had to meet with both of the national rating agencies to have the "issue" rated.

One of the people Drexel Burnham had brought in to "oversee" the management of Western Airlines was a man named Don L. Beck. Don was known to me as he grew up in the service arena of Continental Airlines. He had retired as the president of Air Micronesia, a subsidiary of Continental. Beck expressed an interest in going to work for Western and, after several interviews and checks with others; I brought him in as senior VP of our service division. Topper Van Every, Harold Achtziger and several others in that area reported to him. I took Don to New York with me to show we were bringing in some well-known talent to our top management.

When I returned from New York City on June 3rd, 1983 it appeared we had the package put together and approved by the senior management of Hutton. By this time, we had selected Harry T. Chandis to fill the other top spot of senior VP marketing. He started with Western on June 6th. Chandis had spent many years with American Airlines and then moved to Allegheny Airlines, which became US Air, at that time a highly profitable hub-oriented airline. He had been head of marketing and scheduling for US Air, which made him a very high-profile individual for us to have on the team and he was well known in the aviation circles on the east coast.

Most recently, Harry had served as president of Texas International Airlines. Presidents didn't last long at T.I. and Harry held the record of lasting the longest to that date. Frank Lorenzo, the owner, fired more presidents than Steinbrenner did managers of the New York Yankees. Harry accompanied me to New York and Boston on June 8, 1983 so I could get him acquainted with those at Hutton.

This experience on Wall Street was totally new territory for me. It was a real education. Hutton had a team of men and women assigned to the project who were highly organized to script and sell this offering. I spent two days in their offices being briefed before we held meetings with potential buyers. One of the men on the team came out of the finance division of TWA and, when he had retired, Hutton hired him to work on "transportation packages." One day he and I were discussing our "deregulated industry." He said most of the older airlines would make progress slowly as they were realigning their operations. As an example of progress, he gave me a story that became one of my favorites; and, one that I often used when speaking to the employees.

Jack and Joe, brothers from New York, took annual trips to Alaska to fish. They liked to go back into isolated lakes with a 'bush pilot' in a float plane and fish a lake where they could be alone - far from the crowds of New York City.

This particular year a pilot dropped them off at the pier on a lake and said: 'I'll be back in one week to get you. Remember, there are a lot of fish in this lake, don't keep too many fish. This is a small lake and we can only carry so much weight out of here.'

'Yeh, yeh,' the two responded. 'We've fished the lake before.'

A week later the pilot landed on the lake and taxied up the pier; it was covered with fish. He said: 'We can't get out of here with all these fish - I told you not to keep so many!' The brothers replied: 'Well, last year the pilot was willing to try.'

Being one of the more competitive 'bush pilots' he finally said, 'Okay, load them up and let's go.'

The pilot taxied to the back of a cove, made a wide and fast circle and roared down the lake. He rose above the water and had just about cleared the tall trees, when a pontoon caught in one of them and down they went.

Joe came to and began shouting, 'Jack, Jack, are you okay?'

Jack said: 'I'm up in the branches, but I'm okay - where are we?'

Joe replied: 'I'm not quite sure, but I think we are about a hundred yards farther than we were last year.'

On several occasions, I used this story at employee meetings to stress the point that we may not always be successful in our endeavors, but we must have the attitude that we will try, if only to gain "another hundred yards."

We had two days of doing nothing but selling this issue. In the mornings we had several private meetings with buyers of major mutual funds. The small team that accompanied me consisted of one staff member from E. F. Hutton and Andre Dimitriadis, our CFO. Andre answered most of the financial questions while I fielded those relating to present and future goals. I also outlined the new management organization.

The afternoon of the first day marked a meeting with many buyers at the Waldorf Astoria Hotel. Hutton wanted me to handle some financial questions in this meeting to be sure the potential buyers would see I knew what was happening in the area of finance. Thank the Lord for my MBA degree. I conducted this session with a visual overview of where we had been in recent years and where we were now heading.

One thing that both pleased and surprised me occurred immediately after we adjourned from the question and answer period that followed my presentation. A man approached me and said: "I came here this afternoon for one reason and that was to look at you in person. We know more about you than you can imagine. We've just been waiting to see if you'd take the reins of the company. I bought several million of this offering this morning."

By the next day I was in Boston going through the same routine and the $65,000,000 offering was over-subscribed; we wound up selling $90,000,000.

The issue became effective June 15, 1983 and well exceeded what Drexel Burnham had alluded they would do; and, I might add, with a few week's work compared to the drawn-out and convoluted negotiations with Drexel. The bonus for me was working with highly efficient people at E. F. Hutton who knew exactly what had to be done and how we would do it. Even they were amazed that this issue was over-subscribed. They could have sold more, but we at Western felt that was as far as we could prudently go at this time.

This ninety million gave us the ability to restructure our loans and get rid of a lot of small lenders. It also gave us the running room to put together the basis for an eighteen-month plan to get us into the summer of 1984. As mentioned earlier, we called this plan, "the Western Partnership."

During June, '83, we had one other addition to our corporate officer staff, Robert L. Moore. We brought him in as VP market planning. Bob had an impressive background and Harry Chandis felt he was a key addition to the marketing efforts of Western. Moore began work on June 29th.

During the second half of 1983, I asked Jerry Grinstein to assist in identifying the technical details of an employee profit-sharing plan as a way to establish an award of Western's shares that would partially compensate employees for the sacrifices they would make if they accepted the "Partnership Plan." I also asked him to accompany me while making some contacts with the unions; one would be with the president of ALPA in Washington, D.C.

These union contacts were important to my long-range plans for Jerry. I could see our local union heads were beginning to trust him and this was a real breakthrough as two of them were not in harmony with my bringing him into the picture as chairman of the board. Before making that move public, I had met with the local and regional "honchos" from the key unions to explain that I had asked Grinstein to take this slot. The reactions of the union representatives varied, but one objection was stated by all: "He has no airline or other business experience outside of the political arena."

I never shared these conversations with Jerry as I had confidence they would see in him what I had seen. The Teamsters were so paranoid about this situation they put a provision in their "Partnership" document that if I left the company as CEO, their contract would be null and void. I figured this provision would go away within a couple of years.

One of the reasons I mention all this is that, when I asked Grinstein to assist in the development of the profit sharing and stock plan, Andre Dimitriadis was pushed out of shape. He felt this was a pure financial matter and should only involve him. I responded that I felt it was equally a labor relations and legal issue and that all actions would be closely coordinated with the finance group. I said it was really my project and having delegated some of the day-to-day events required to execute the plan did not restrict him from being in the loop. This did not placate him as he personally wanted to be seen as "the man" with the unions. His ego was getting in the way again.

Another reason I mention Dimitriadis' reaction is that I knew another shoe might soon drop that would really land on his toes. I did not see Andre being "heir apparent" to the office of CEO, or even the chief operating officer.

What the unions finally agreed upon was a salary reduction of ten percent for most workers, twelve and a half for management, and eighteen percent for pilots. In return for the wage and work rule concessions, we gave them a chunk of the company. We turned 7.8 million shares of Western common stock over to them. This amounted to roughly a thirty-two percent interest in the company. Grinstein and Tom Greene, Western's legal counsel, did a fine job of pulling together all the details of this stock award. It was no easy task to accomplish all of this in such a very limited time frame.

Along with the stock, the employees were offered a three-year profit-sharing program, allowing them to earn fifteen percent of the first $25 million of pretax profits and twenty percent of pretax profits that were in excess of $25 million. The unions representing the employees were also given the opportunity to select individuals to fill two of the seats on Western's twelve-member board of directors.

Selling this plan to the employees took a lot of travel and meetings on my part as the employees felt they had sacrificed enough in the past two years. During my meetings I got an added boost when Continental Airlines declared bankruptcy on September 24, 1983.

Continental's bankruptcy seemed to have a more sobering effect on the employees and their union representatives than had occurred when Braniff went under. I believe it was for two reasons; one, this was the second airline of our size to fold and, two, they were more oriented to the western part of the United States than was Braniff - Continental had been our corporate neighbor at Los Angeles International Airport for several decades. The Western "Partnership" was concluded in November, 1983, at which time the employees ratified the agreement between the five unions and the company.

A summary of my stewardship and activities during these past critical nine months is best expressed in my letter to the shareholders, as published in the "Western Airlines 1983 Annual Report."

CHAIRMAN'S LETTER

Fellow Shareholders:

While this 1983 Annual Report gives you a picture of yet another difficult year of change, it also describes a year which saw us achieve great strides in the second half of the year after a disappointing first half. We regard that second half progress as substantial and we intend to build on it in the coming years.

When I was elected president and chief executive officer on April 11 of 1983, our company was facing a number of serious problems. The company did not have a strong, unified senior management team in place. First quarter industry fare wars, together with an imposing near-term debt load, had us in an adverse financial position. Finally, our employee group was frustrated, given their efforts and sacrifices, at the lack of visible progress on the part of the company.

Solutions were required and the first priority in April 1983, as I saw it, was to assemble a strong, unified team. We did that.

Andre C. Dimitriadis, our senior VP finance and administration, was already with us and had earned respect and credibility with Western's employees while distinguishing himself in his dealings with the financial community.

We appointed Seth M. Oberg as senior VP operations. Already heading our flight operations department and having spent 26 years with Western, he was an obvious choice to assume responsibility for maintenance and engineering as well.

Don L. Beck, our senior VP service, brought to us over 25 years of airline industry experience, gained at the old Continental Airlines and as president and Director of Air Micronesia.

With the vital importance of marketing strategies in mind, we brought Harry T. Chandis to Western as senior VP marketing. After many years at American Airlines, he moved to what was then Allegheny Airlines and was the key figure in effecting a most successful marketing adaptation to deregulation, resulting in today's highly profitable US Air. Before joining Western, he served as president and general manager of Texas International.

Finally, Gerald Grinstein, former chairman of Western's board of directors, and involved in activities of the company's board since 1977, was elected president and chief operating officer on January 9, 1984.

As chairman and chief executive officer, I have the highest confidence in the senior management group we have assembled. It represents a strong blend of Western experience and new, fresh perspectives and accomplishments.

Western employees stepped forward from the time I took office to ask if they could help get Western back on track financially. The answer was that of course they could, but only after we had a management team they could rely on with confidence and a financial restructuring to give them time to help. Western's successful $90 million public offering, completed in June, and another for $65 million in November gave us the operating flexibility to effect some necessary changes.

Participation by employees required a complete program. Unlike some other carriers, Western's condition had precluded its people from receiving increased wages and benefits for some time. Our employees had already sacrificed. They deserved more than just the opportunity to give again. They were willing to accept an active ownership role in their company and the management team was committed to seeing they were involved.

The Western "Partnership," completed in November, was born out of cooperation and contribution by labor leaders, individual employees and management with the strong support from you, the shareholders, who approved the employee stock plan. Held up as a model of labor management teamwork, we see the "Partnership" as uniquely suited to Western.

Finally, we began the process of redirecting the company's efforts to make Western competitive and profitable in the marketplace. We made good progress. An operating profit of $2.8 million was recorded for the second half of 1983. This reflected significant improvement from the $16.8 million operating loss recorded for the same period in 1982, and it was the first time in five years that Western reported an operating profit in the second half of the year.

Our new marketing thrust has many facets, but its main effort is geared toward the frequent business traveler. With this market objective our first priority had to involve scheduling. While the Salt Lake City hub operation had been launched a year earlier, it needed further refinements. We strengthened this operation by adding new major business cities and refining schedules to attract the frequent business traveler. The number of connecting opportunities we offered our passengers was increased significantly. We seized the opportunity to capitalize on our position as the second largest carrier in Los Angeles by developing an international hub here in September. From the Los Angeles hub we could interconnect travelers moving between our domestic points and Mexico, Hawaii, Canada and Alaska. This enhanced our services system wide.

We have moved forward in the pricing area as well. Western had to establish more effective revenue and yield management systems if it was going to make any progress.

The steps we took, combined with the general economic recovery, resulted in significant yield, or average revenue per passenger mile, increases during the second half of 1983. While yield improvement must continue, we are pleased that Western has closed the gap from a position well below the industry average in yield to one even with the industry average.

To capitalize on our new marketing strategy, we chose the advertising agency of Doyle Dane Bernbach to deliver our new product message to our customers in an aggressive and stimulating manner.

All of these changes were accomplished almost entirely in the second half of 1983 and were designed to make Western a strong competitor in the face of a rapidly changing environment. This environment is illustrated most vividly by the phenomenon of Continental Airlines, which had represented about five percent of the U.S. major airlines domestic traffic, and filed for protection under the Bankruptcy Code in September 1983. Overnight this formidable competitor turned into a low-cost carrier and within weeks it was diverting traffic in many important markets in the West and Southwest. The emergence of several newer airlines, together with the new Continental and the new Braniff, ensure that Western and the rest of the established airlines will continue to face low cost competition.

Your management recognizes that, despite the accomplishments of late 1983, this company must continue its progress toward achieving the levels of efficiency achieved by the newer and the resurrected carriers. We view the Western "Partnership" as a foundation, and as concrete evidence that labor and management can work together toward mutual benefits. Such cooperation in reaching difficult decisions must continue in order for Western to return to profitability.

Western has staked out its territory. We are pleased with the early results of our new marketing efforts. While we are implementing additional cost efficiencies, we will remain aware of the continuing need to improve revenue performance and maintain a competitive posture.

You'll note that the remainder of this Annual Report to Shareholders is being presented to you in a somewhat different format. We have incorporated the company's Annual Report on Form 10-K, which is filed each year with the Securities and Exchange Commission in a prescribed form. It is more detailed than most traditional annual reports and we believe it will be preferred by most shareholders.

I hope that, as investors, you will take the opportunity to use Western's services whenever possible for your business or pleasure travel needs and urge your friends and associates to do the same. We appreciate your continued interest and support.

Lawrence H. Lee
Chairman and Chief Executive Officer

March 16, 1984

As you will note in the above title, I made a change in the executive office prior to the previously mentioned publication. I will outline the background of this change, but first allow me to set the scene.

Having completed the second step in our survival plan, it was now time to put together a longer-range strategy, hopefully one that would be in place for three to five years.

Following the approval of the "Partnership Program," I felt members of my senior staff might rest on their oars. I was right; everyone seemed to have gone back to a tactical mode with little consideration being given to a long-range approach for survival. Therefore, I notified the key players there would be a meeting at the Salt Lake City Marriot Hotel beginning Friday evening, November 18th, and that we would work there with only sleep breaks until we had the framework of a long-range plan in place.

This news was received with the anticipated grumbling, but it was the only way to get this group thinking "outside the box." I believe they really felt the Partnership Program was going to be all that was needed; or, all we would be able to get from the unions. Wrong!

During late 1983, Jerry was still working for his law firm and spending a day or two a week in Los Angeles with Western. So far, I sensed he liked what he was doing. During the first eight months he never protested if it was advantageous to have him spend an extra day at the corporate office.

The union representatives, especially those who at first had been reticent concerning his involvement, were becoming more accustomed to his presence. Now, he just needed time and a high profile project on which to focus, one that would put him into closer contact with the union hierarchy. The implementation activities of the forthcoming "survival plan" would afford Jerry that opportunity. The big question: "Was he ready to make Western his full-time employer?"

When the senior staff met in Salt Lake City, I outlined my goal for the workshop. We had the basic financial data we needed from Glen Stewart, one of our key officers in finance. It gave a rather bleak forecast if we did not reduce costs even more than we had done with the "Partnership." This came as no surprise and I had alerted the unions that what we had accomplished might not be enough for the long run.

We ended the discussions in Salt Lake City on Sunday afternoon with the basics of a plan. The team returned to Los Angeles with instructions to spend the next two weeks preparing what their individual divisions and departments would be doing to bring about the changes we would need to achieve this profit plan. They would have to meet the parameters that had been outlined in the workshop.

While I had regular meetings with the division heads during the next two weeks, I tried to play no other role with them than being a facilitator; this was done mostly where plans required a cross-over between the various departments. I wanted to see how far they felt they could go on their own; we could always rein it back, if necessary. They did a good job and, when we met around the first of December, each was prepared.

The final planning meeting was scheduled at the Sheraton Hotel across the street from our headquarters so no one would be distracted at the general offices. Before the second day ended, we had a sound approach and we had agreed to name it the "Competitive Action Program"; known from that time on as "CAP."

My intent to implement the Competitive Action Program was first announced to the board of directors in our meeting on December 15, 1983. I did not go into all the details, but did outline that CAP was designed to get us through the next three years; years that would not be very different from those we had recently experienced.

Realizing that it would be impossible to keep this from leaking, we scheduled a meeting with the local heads of each of the unions and briefed them on what we were undertaking. This was no great surprise to them; I believe they were in the same mood and mode as my staff - they just wanted more breathing room between the Western Partnership and "CAP." I told them that this was going to be a task in which we would jointly be engaged well into 1984 and we just wanted them apprised of what to expect during this period.

Jerry Grinstein had approached me in late August 1983, to say he was deeply in love with a wonderful woman named Lyn Tuttle, a resident of Seattle, Washington. They became engaged in early September, at which time he said he may have to abort any future plans I had in mind for him that would require a move to Los Angeles; he didn't feel Lyn would ever agree to the move. By then, I had talked to Jerry about my strategy for having him become my replacement. When he gave me this new information, I loosened the drag on the reel and let him have his run and counseled him to do the same with Lynnie.

In November, the Los Angeles Management Club asked me to be the feature speaker at their dinner at the Marriott Hotel on December 5, 1983. I requested that Grinstein be my co-speaker. I then asked Jerry to see if Lyn would accompany him as Margie would be with me at the head table. Lyn cooperated and Jerry gave a wonderful speech. It had to impress Lyn and I'm sure she saw the acceptance of Jerry in the enthusiasm of the group. I was hoping this would cinch my getting him to accept the proposal I was about to make.

Following our planning meetings in Salt Lake City and Los Angeles, I told Grinstein it was time he made a decision on his future with Western Airlines. I proposed to have him elected Western's president and to fill the vacant office of chief operating officer. All this would take place the first of the year, January 1984. I would take the title of chairman of the board and chief executive officer.

It had always been my policy to be completely open with Grinstein; therefore, I informed him of one condition associated with his taking this position. I said I was unwilling to take Western into bankruptcy and, if it became necessary, Jerry would have to do this and I would resign. I could not envision presiding over this event after putting in more than forty years with this fine company.

At this time I also informed Jerry there was a quid pro quo with this condition; that is, if we were successful I would step aside at the appropriate time to make sure he would get the majority of the credit for saving the company. I felt there was an eighty-percent probability we would be successful. I just had to make sure he understood and had agreed he would not jump ship if the employees did not do their part in helping to turn Western into a profitable airline.

Now, recall the "three-step program" I outlined as I took office on April 11, 1983; that is, (a) a plan for getting into the summer of 1983, (b) implementing a Partnership Program to move us into the summer of 1984, and last, (c) a five-year plan, now called "CAP," that would bring us back into a viable and financially secure airline. If anything, we were at this point ahead of schedule with the implementation of these plans.

Before accepting my proposal, Grinstein now had three considerations; obtaining a leave from his law firm, getting Lyn's agreement to move to Los Angeles and whether or not he would be willing to handle the leadership if bankruptcy were the only option. It didn't take long for him to get back to me and the news was good.

On January 9, 1984, Grinstein was elected Western's president and COO and I was elected chairman and CEO. This put Jerry in place to learn more about the day-to-day operation of the company. It would also put him within the spotlight with the unions during the next six months. My prediction was that, following this period, he would be seen by them as a replacement for me.

The minutes of the board meeting held on January 9, 1984, reflect the actions relating to this change in titles at the top:

> At this point Mr. Grinstein was excused from the meeting. Mr. Lee described to the board the initial development of a three-year Competitive Action Program, and a series of employee meetings which would be held in conjunction therewith. He reminded the board that at the time he became chief executive officer, he had highlighted the need for a meaningful management succession plan, and had indicated his intention to name a chief operating officer within one year. He stated he now wished to propose to the board that Mr. Grinstein be elected to the office of president and chief operating officer. Working with Mr. Lee and the senior officer team, Mr. Grinstein would quickly acquire experience in running the day-to-day operations of the company, and would then be well prepared to assume the role of chief executive officer at such time as Mr. Lee relinquished that office.

> Under such an arrangement, Mr. Lee indicated that the operations division under Mr. Oberg, the service division under Mr. Beck, the marketing division under Mr. Chandis and the corporate affairs functions under Mr. Van Every would report to Mr. Grinstein as chief operating officer. The finance and legal divisions, under Mr. Dimitriadis and Tom Greene, respectively, along with Mr. Grinstein, would then report to Mr. Lee as chairman and chief executive officer. Mr. Lee indicated he would propose a base salary of $240,000, the same base salary as his own, and indicated Mr. Grinstein would forego 12½ % of that salary during such period of time as the other officers continued under a 12½ % wage reduction.

I had informed Dimitriadis of this move in advance of the board meeting. As I anticipated, Andre was once again pushed out of shape - REALLY pushed out of shape! He felt he was the "heir apparent" to the office of the president. Unfortunately Victor Brown had made him aware I had recommended him as Western's president and COO, but that was before I took the reins and at the time the board of directors was weighing the possibility of declaring bankruptcy. As you may recall, I had recommended Grinstein as CEO and Andre as COO only if the board decided to declare bankruptcy. Under no other circumstance would I select Dimitriadis for the COO.

I would continue to use the best that Andre could offer in the financial and administrative area, but, as mentioned, the union heads were seeing the same thing I had observed in his behavior and they did not hesitate to make those feelings known to me.

We continued to assure the union officials that Dimitriadis was an excellent financial leader and we needed his creativity. They could not disagree with that. However, with this management change I knew he would now be a "short-timer." I also knew he aspired to "zap" me the first chance he got. During this particular board meeting he had that opportunity; he got me in my pension - a place that really smarts. I had to agree to delay the contractual arrangements of my pension, even though the board had twice affirmed I was to receive what Art Kelly, Dom Renda and other senior officers were getting; that is, 75% of their final pay with other "bells and whistles." This was all Dimitriadis' doing and I couldn't avoid the smirk on his face as this was discussed with the other members of the board.

The outcome is reflected in the minutes of the board meeting held on 1/9/84:

Mr. Lee then turned to the subject of his proposed employment agreement, which the board and compensation committee had discussed on several occasions in the past. He stated he was eager to avoid any misunderstanding, either among board members or the company's employees or shareholders, especially in light of the concepts embodied in the employee "Partnership" agreements. In that light, he traced the chronology of the development of the employment agreement, from April 1983, at which time he was elected president and chief executive officer and a compensation package was agreed to in principle, through August 1983, at which time the board had been advised that the compensation committee had settled upon the basic terms of such an agreement. He indicated that he had worked with Mr. Greene and outside counsel, as well as with Peat, Marwick, Mitchell & Co. in the preparation of a draft agreement, with particular attention being paid to any accounting impact. Notwithstanding the board's earlier agreement to include in such an agreement supplemental pension benefits which had formerly been available to senior officers of the company, there was a concern that even reduced supplemental pension benefits might create problems, [this input was from Dimitriadis] and accordingly Mr. Lee had determined to forego such supplemental pension benefits and had now arrived at a consensus on the terms of an employment agreement which in terms of compensation would be less than he was entitled to under the former senior officer supplemental plan and thus less than what had been agreed to in April and August of 1983. He described the basic terms of the agreement as follows:

The term of the agreement would be five years beginning April 11, 1983.

(a) Base compensation would be $240,000 year. [Less 12 ½ percent voluntary reduction.]

(b) Stock options would be as previously granted by the board of directors.

(c) Apartment rental would be provided at Los Angeles not to exceed $25,000 the first year, with such maximum [inflation] amount at 10% per year during the five-year term of the agreement. Mr. Lee would agree to maintain his residence within 15 minutes normal driving time of the airport in view of the critical problems facing the company.

A discussion followed, during which several directors expressed the belief that the board should recognize the commitment made earlier to Mr. Lee regarding supplemental pension benefits and should further recognize the desirability of reinstatement of such benefits in the future at such time as conditions may permit. [Emphasis added by LHL.]

The reason the board members could only allude to the future adjustment of my pension was that, according to Dimitriadis, any contractual commitment to this end would require a pre-funding of the plan. I later found out this was not exactly as Andre had outlined it to the board. Nevertheless, his "pre-funding" scenario appeared to require funds be pulled out of a locked-in pool of money Jerry and I would need to grant raises to key personnel and, since I didn't want to do this, Andre knew he had hoisted me on my own petard.

The only reason I am going to any length in mentioning the history of my pension is so you, my posterity, will understand why Margie and I did not live the life of most CEO's who had finished a successful career with a "Fortune 500 Company." Thanks to the Lord, we had sufficient for our needs and, until Delta went bankrupt, enough to provide occasional help to our grandchildren.

With the approval of Grinstein's full-time employment I had accomplished another of my goals, which was to create an orderly avenue for my departure from the company and leave it in competent hands. This had to be done in careful stages to preserve the image of management stability while, at the same time, effecting the changes at the top. Moving Grinstein into the spot of president and COO at this early date was a gamble; I could have been moving too fast. However, given Jerry's marriage to Lyn, it was a necessary risk as their move to Los Angeles at this time was essential to this plan of management progression.

Things went well with the publicity. The Wall Street Journal is the bellwether of how the "market" sees this type of change. An article in the Journal on January 11, 1984, a few days after the change at the top, blended the management change in with an announcement we made about swapping our orders for six Boeing 767's for eighteen 737-type aircraft. This was not planned as a strategy; it just worked out that way. In the third paragraph of this article they reported:

Western Air said its chairman and its president exchanged titles in a move designed to give Gerald Grinstein additional duties as chief operating officer. Lawrence H. Lee, formerly president, was named chairman in addition to his post as chief executive. Mr. Grinstein, who had been a part-time chairman, will serve as president on a full-time basis. Mr. Lee is 57 years old and Mr. Grinstein is 51.

Andre Dimitriadis was then given the attention he craved; he was interviewed on how the aircraft fleet modifications came about and how Western was going to pay for the aircraft. This was right up Andre's alley. The article then concluded with another blip on the top management.

The reassignment of Mr. Grinstein puts an executive in the position of chief operating office for the first time in a year. [Recall I took the title of president and CEO and left the COO position open.] As a long-time Western director and a Seattle attorney, Mr. Grinstein had been instrumental in hiring Neil G. Bergt as Western's chairman at the end of 1981; [not according to Art Kelly, who took the credit - or the blame.] Mr. Bergt, a former Alaska air-cargo executive, initiated a number of cost-cutting and marketing moves but was unsuccessful in slashing Western's enormous losses and resigned as chairman and president early last year. At that time Mr. Lee, a Western executive with a background in labor relations, was named president and chief executive and began a program of restructuring debt and winning wage concessions from an employees' group that is receiving a stock ownership position in the company.

For good reason, I had fear of what the press might say about the change in top titles. It could easily have been a sour grapes header like, "Western does not seem capable of keeping a stable work force in its top positions."

While we had played out the Boeing aircraft exchange as being a very positive part of our fleet planning, the bigger picture was that we could not finance the 767's and they didn't work well within our present needs at the

SLC hub. Had we just canceled the orders for the 767's, with no substitute aircraft, we could have faced cancellation penalties of somewhere between 50 and 60 million dollars.

The work that Andre Dimitriadis did on the Boeing project was very commendable. I told the Boeing executives I was sorry to give up on the 767's as I saw a need for their added capacity at a later date. For now, the excess capacity was not going over well with our analysts, even though our traffic and yield per passenger was on the rise. I saw no hope in financing the 767's, where there was some hope that we could finance the 737's.

The Wall Street Journal had already given Western considerable coverage on the Partnership Program and on October 7, 1983, published a quarter-page article featuring comments from Dimitriadis and from me relating to the fact that the unions were out seeking ratification of the plan. It was under the headline of "Western Airlines and Unions near Accord in Shadow of Ailing Industry." Grinstein is not mentioned in that article; I'm sure Dimitriadis, who led the financial discussion, made sure of that. While this earned him a picture next to me in the article, it didn't generate any new points for him at Western.

The New York Times gave what I considered to be the best account of this reorganization at the top and what had transpired at Western during the last nine months. In the "Times" dated Wednesday, January 11, 1984, under the heading of, "Western Air Shifts Top Management," they said:

> Western Airlines announced yesterday that its Chairman, Gerald Grinstein, had been named president and chief operating officer. Lawrence H. Lee, chief executive, takes on the additional duties of chairman.

> The airline, which is building up its hubs at Los Angeles and Salt Lake City, also said yesterday that it would purchase 18 additional twinjet 737's for about $378 million from the Boeing Commercial Airplane Company. The order replaces one for six 767's, which was valued at $240 million.

Mr. Grinstein's appointment as president, puts the 51-year old attorney into the company's management full time. He has been on the board since 1977.

Mr. Lee, 57, is leader of a new management team in place since last spring that is attempting to revive the airline. "I made an announcement when I took over in April that I would look over the team and wait until the first of the year to make a selection." Mr. Lee said, "Jerry has shown exactly what we wanted and now we need his talents full time. This puts him in a strong role for the future."

A stronger management has been one of Mr. Lee's major goals. The airline, buffeted by deregulation, suffered from a weak management structure, Mr. Lee said. "There was no management succession program in place," he said. "Merger with Continental was their first plan and their second plan was merger with Continental."

Mr. Lee is a 40-year employee who started as a baggage handler - "I was born at the airport," he said. He has taken on the labor unions in a non-confrontational manner and has instituted employee ownership and profit sharing in exchange for wage cuts.

He enjoys good rapport with the employees, who view him as one of their own. The "Partnership Program" worked out between management and workers becomes void if Mr. Lee resigns or is dismissed.

With these house-keeping items behind me, we were set to launch the final stage of Western's survival plan, the strategy that would carry us into a profitable future. I knew that this was going to be all or nothing at all. Either the employees were going to get behind this plan, the one we developed last December in Salt Lake City, or we would be hard pressed to go into the winter of 1984/85 without declaring bankruptcy.

With the restructuring of Western's debt, we stood a better chance of closing down and starting up again under chapter eleven. Continental had accomplished this, where, on the other hand, Braniff had failed. Jerry was now in position to handle a bankruptcy, if it was necessary. While it would be a hard fight, my belief was that the employees would back me in this final phase and see the vision of a much better way to operate without outsiders calling the shots.

The additional duties of being chairman of the board were miniscule and had no effect on my work schedule. The chairman does little except call the board meetings to order and preside over that event. Nevertheless, you have to have one in place. There is one other duty; he conducts the annual shareholder's meeting.

Chapter 11
THE COMPETITIVE
ACTION PROGRAM

The implementation of CAP got off to a slow start. We had agreed to open the company books to any representatives the unions would care to bring on the property. That caused the delay. My goal was to have this program completed and ratified by the end of the summer. As I said earlier, our financial outlook indicated we could not get into the summer of '85 without this plan in place. I was now wondering if we could get it done on time.

Grinstein was working with a couple of people he had contacted to make sure the changes we proposed to make to the "Western Partnership" would not cause any legal or unseen labor problems. We had to be careful to preserve what we had gained if the rank and file did not go along with our new proposals.

Opening the books was a major step forward in our relationship with the national headquarters of the three largest unions; the Airline Pilots Association, Airline Flight Attendants Association and the Teamsters. The other large group was represented by the Air Transport Employees, known as ATE. This union was mainly associated with Western, and the president was a hard-nosed guy named Jim Shields. Shields' whole existence as ATE's president depended on the viability of Western. He had little trust in anyone, especially if they were members of Western's management.

Jim Shields had come into the Western Partnership kicking and screaming, but he knew we could not survive without it. This new plan was a different story; he was dead set against it. I knew I'd have to bypass him and go directly to all the ground service employees. Nevertheless, I held off as long as possible. My instincts were telling me that if we could get the pilots union, ALPA, and the Teamsters Union onboard, we would have a much better chance with the flight attendants and the ground services people.

The Teamsters took a very professional approach to examining our books, as did the pilots. Our five unions represented over ninety percent of our employees. The fifth union had only a handful of people, the airline dispatchers. I knew they'd go along with the others. I met with some of the top people in the Western Conference of the Teamsters and got little reaction, which was typical of that group. Ray Benning, our company representative for the Teamsters, told me not to be concerned about this until after they had a chance to see what the others were willing to do. This was what concerned me; that is, the thought of each waiting out the other while we kept sucking cash from the company's coffers.

Mr. John G. McMillian had submitted his resignation to Western's board of directors effective January 9, 1984. I advised the board that the nominating committee should be looking for an outside director to fill this spot. In addition, we had promised two seats to represent the interests of the employee groups, pursuant to the provisions of the "Partnership" agreement." During the January board meeting, this was approved and we increased the size of the board of directors from twelve to fourteen.

Following one of my selling sessions with E. F. Hutton in Boston, Massachusetts, I had flown home on a TWA flight. I was able to get a last minute seat in first class and sat by a gregarious gentleman named Spencer Stuart. I recognized the name was the same as the "head-hunting" firm with which I had initially interviewed for CEO at Western, back before Neil Bergt came in. I asked if this was his business and he said he indeed was the founder of the firm of Spencer Stuart and Associates, although he had sold the firm and started an investment company.

The Western Airlines board of directors had historically been staffed with executives from different cities Western served; for example, Gerald Grinstein represented Seattle, Washington. In my mind, the best way to assemble a board is to put a "matrix plan" in place to identify board members for their ability to provide the best oversight to the various senior management functions of a company. The members should be top executives with proven history in certain fields; such as, finance, labor, human resources, operations, etc.

As an opening on the board became available, such as McMillian's resignation, I wanted to take advantage of the opportunity to fill it with a specific talent. Spencer Stuart fit that model as he was a leader in the field of human resources and understood the basics of good company organization, staffing and compensation. I suggested the nominating committee consider him.

At the board meeting held March, 9 1984, Spencer Stuart was elected to the Western Airlines board and I recommended he function on the nominations and the compensation committees. That was approved.

At this time we did not have an employee at our hub in Salt Lake City who could be a prominent representative of the company in community affairs and also serve as administrative head of the airport operation. I felt we needed a strong personality and someone with a good financial background, a combination that is difficult to find. Glen L. Stewart, who was presently vice president and controller, met these qualifications and had agreed to make this move. We took the necessary action at this meeting and changed his title to vice president and project director - Salt Lake City. We filled in behind him with Douglas B. Swets, who presently served as assistant vice president and treasurer.

The forecast for Western's passenger traffic was that it would be slightly down this January and February, as compared to those months in 1983; last year, there were massive promotional fares in place, fares that grossly eroded our yield. We were now seeing the yield change from being the lowest in the industry to being par with other carriers. While we projected a small loss for the first quarter, we were appreciably ahead of the first quarter of 1983.

Harry Chandis and Robert Moore were doing a fine job of marketing and scheduling our product. However, if we were going to show a decent turnaround in profits, we still had to reduce our cost per seat mile. We couldn't do anything more with fuel or debt service, so we had to keep moving forward with the unions to get them to accept the proposed Competitive Action Program.

From the time the basic framework of CAP had been worked out in December of ' 83, I had asked Jerry Grinstein to keep a high profile in the implementation effort with the local union leaders to make sure they were able to access the information they needed to satisfy their national leadership.

We had to assemble sufficient financial data to demonstrate to the union leadership that Western wasn't going to make it without their help. Jerry would have to draw on resources from Andre Dimitriadis' territory if he was to do this. I talked to Andre about this need and, judging from his reaction, I could see he was still having a problem with my decision to put Grinstein front stage center on this project. This sore was to fester the rest of that year.

Grinstein recommended we bring in some outside assistance to give additional counsel on labor matters and to review the financial assumptions we had made to promote CAP. Western had a good labor relations executive in place, but he was getting snowed under dealing with five unions at the same time.

With excellent contacts in Washington, Grinstein recruited several resources from the east coast. Wayne Horvitz, former head of the Federal Mediation and Reconciliation Service, and an acknowledged labor expert was engaged to help in this endeavor. We also brought in the Massachusetts firm of Temple, Barker and Sloane, which was widely recognized as having expertise in the transportation industry. They were reviewing all our economic assumptions and would be helping us prepare a video presentation to employees.

As usually happens when you bring in an outside firm like TB&S, they hype their agenda and, in our case, where we had asked them for a drink of water, they began giving us a hose in the face. They later persuaded Grinstein and our labor relations group that we needed two scenarios of CAP to present to the unions. This move slowed down the process of approval even more. Knowing the industry and watching the effects of the emerging low-cost carriers, I could see we had to have the economies of our originally designed CAP, and that it had to be in place before winter hit us in the pocketbook.

On March 6, 1984 we arranged our first major meeting with the collective unions and our consultants. While there was skepticism of the plan voiced by most of the union leadership, I received the feedback that they were impressed by the open attitudes shown at the meeting and they could see we had done our homework. One of the big factors for me was

Grinstein's presentation in the meeting. This was the first time they had collectively seen him in his recent management role. Jerry came off very confident and persuasive.

We concluded this session with an agreement to meet individually with the various leaders. These meetings were to take place toward the end of March and early April.

I asked Jerry to present the Competitive Action Program to the board at our March meeting. They unanimously adopted a resolution to support it; like, they had some other alternative. E. F. Hutton & Company was working with us on another offering. Grinstein would handle the financial folks in New York City on this offer. That gave him a chance to be seen by that important group. Jerry handled it with his usual aplomb; he was fearless in facing most challenges and was an excellent student. I was always surprised he got his degree in law at Harvard as he seemed more like a Harvard MBA in his capacity to learn and grasp financial and management problems.

Western had a need for additional small aircraft and Boeing approached us with a 737-200 they had available and ready to go - one where the order had been canceled by another carrier. We decided to buy it. What a great feeling that was to be in a position to purchase aircraft and not be selling them, as had been the case in former years when half of our 737-200's had been sold in order to show some profit.

Prior to the Annual Shareholders' Meeting, Roy Utter and George Suddock informed me they would not be standing for reelection at the forthcoming meeting. This would open the way to add an additional two union representatives to the board without increasing the size of the board to an uncomfortable number. When a board gets larger than 14 or 15 members, it is too cumbersome to work with and additional numbers add no strength. We currently had the commitment to install two union reps and I could foresee the request for two more as a condition imposed on us if the CAP was to be approved.

The thought of having four union representatives on the board did not cause me any concern. In fact, under our present condition and what I perceived it to be in the future, I felt it would strengthen our communications with each of the four large unions.

Our new management team was functioning well, with the exception of the continual "wall to wall" carping from Dimitriadis. His complaint to me about being "passed over" in favor of Grinstein was getting up my nose. He was also in a rage because Jerry was going directly to various members of his staff for information that Andre felt should be passed through him. Things were continuing to heat up between them. It was mostly Andre's problem and this was no time for that sort of difficulty.

I didn't detect as much compartmentalization at Western Airlines as there had been under Renda and Kelly. The SLC hub was such a dynamic part of our current operation that it tended to draw the company together; no one piece of the operation stood alone. Every change necessary for the growth of the hub involved some part of each department in the company.

How were we now being perceived by the rest of the industry and its analysts? The following article appeared in the March, 1984 issue of OAG Frequent Flier Magazine:

> Lawrence H. Lee had his job cut out for him when he became Western Airline's chief executive officer in April 1983. The company had lost $190 million since 1980, and its 10,500 employees had already suffered through a two year wage freeze. The unions were in no mood for further concessions. And Western's lenders were demanding a quick end to the red ink.
>
> Lee saw an answer to the carrier's woes in what he called the 'Western Partnership.' Under this program, the airline's unions agreed to a salary reduction: 10 percent for most workers, 12.5 percent for management, and 18 percent for pilots. In return for the wage concessions (which saved Western $42 million), Lee offered his employees a chunk of the company, turning over to them 7.8 million shares of Western common stock, amounting to roughly a 32 percent interest in the company.
>
> Along with the stock, Western employees were offered a three-year profit-sharing program, allowing them to earn 15 percent of the first $25 million of pretax profits and 20 percent of pretax

profits in excess of $25 million. Employees also won two seats on Western's twelve member board of directors.

What's so striking about the Western "Partnership" is that the program was negotiated before the much publicized problems at Eastern and Continental. Negotiations were characterized by cooperation rather than confrontation. Labor didn't threaten to strike, and management didn't threaten to file for bankruptcy.

'I think what made the difference,' says Lee, 'is that Western employees asked to become involved rather than management hammering at employees saying, 'you better do this or else.' I told employees, 'I don't expect you to tear up your union contracts or downgrade your union leadership. We're going to work with your union leaders on this.'

To be sure, both sides didn't always see eye to eye. Initially, labor insisted that employees should be able to vote their individual shares. But management was concerned that the possibility of a dilution of stock might trigger rejection of the plan by shareholders. The compromise: stock is kept in a blind trust and employees can vote only in limited situations. Another problem developed when labor's request for representation on Western's board was initially rejected by management. Once these differences were resolved, 89 percent of Western's shareholders approved the program last October, and all employee groups had ratified the plan by November 9, 1983.

'One reason we cooperated with management is because we were assured Lee was not trying to get unions off the property,' says Ray Benning, a Teamsters official. 'Mr. Lee is a very credible man, and management was very open with the financial records. If I felt Western didn't need the money from the employees, I would have been the first to say no. Looking back on it, though, it's my opinion that without the Partnership Program, Western Airlines would not have made it through this winter.'

Lee insists that the Western 'Partnership' has already had a significant impact on employee morale at Western. 'I think the way in which Western went about putting the Partnership together provided an initial boost to morale,' says Lee. 'It got people talking to one another. Now that these people have a meaningful piece of the action in the company, they're going to be more concerned in providing service, controlling costs, running a safe operation - all of the things that are necessary to make a good, strong, competitive airline.'

---DAM. (David Martindale)

So far as the airline industry media were concerned, this seems to encapsulate the general impression of where we stood at that moment. Little was being said about our work to complete the Competitive Action Program.

Harry Chandis, senior VP marketing, had been elected to the board of directors. At the board meeting that is held in conjunction with the annual Shareholders' Meeting, it is a practice to elect or re-elect the corporate officers of the company. At the meeting held May 10, 1984, I proposed to advance the titles of Chandis and Dimitriadis to executive vice president.

Prior to the meeting, I reviewed all of this with both of them in order to get a common understanding that this change would have little impact on their work load, but would have some increased responsibilities. I then advised we would be unable to give them a raise in salary at this time. Nevertheless, it would recognize their level of expertise and daily involvement in matters pertaining to highest priorities in running a profitable airline. I would propose an increase in their stock options. This went over like a pregnant pole vaulter.

They both deserved salary increases, but we just couldn't chance it at this time. In fact, I made certain my exact comments to the board of directors were inserted in the board minutes that day.

Mr. Lee then described to the board a proposal to promote Messrs. Chandis and Dimitriadis to the positions of executive vice presidents. There was some discussion regarding appropriate levels of compensations for such positions, and in that connection, Mr. Lee particularly requested that his following comments be included verbatim in the minutes of the meeting:

The most effective guarantee of a successful business enterprise has repeatedly been shown to be a dedicated and effective management team. One of my most significant objectives as CEO has been to develop such a team. The first major step was the selection of Jerry Grinstein as president and COO and now I would like to make a second major step toward establishment of such a team.

Today I am asking the board to promote Andre Dimitriadis and Harry Chandis to the positions of executive vice president finance and administration, and executive vice president marketing, respectively. They, along with Jerry Grinstein and I, will constitute the Western Airlines executive policy committee. Both will assume greater responsibilities in establishing, as well as implementing, corporate policy.

The promotion to these newly created positions warrants, in my view, for each of these men a substantial increase in compensation. I think, however, that any increase in compensation at this time for higher management officials, even though justified as incident to bona fide promotions, would be impolitic due to the wage reductions in effect under the Partnership Program and might make it more difficult to achieve the hoped for success of the Competitive Action Program.

I do, however, urge the compensation committee to review the appropriate compensation levels of these officers and to be prepared to make appropriate provisions for increases in compensation when the restrictions incident to the Partnership Program are no longer in effect and when the Company's Competitive Action Program has been implemented. Needless to say, the appropriate level of executive compensation is a significant element in any competitive plan, and I expect the Hay Associates Survey will indicate that for companies of this size and complexity the compensation level of such officers should be substantially higher.

The reason I wanted this inserted in the board minutes exactly as I had given it, is that the union representatives would have access to these minutes and I wanted to be sure they saw how seriously we were following our commitment to cost containment.

The annual Shareholders' Meeting, held in Salt Lake City, went very smoothly. There were no unexpected questions and the few we got were mostly related to the new aircraft orders. These were ably handled by Grinstein and Dimitriadis.

My remarks were a bit long, but we had a few things to crow about. The minutes of the meeting, as entered into the board minutes, summarized my comments as follows:

> Mr. Lee reported that 1983 was a year of significant positive change for Western. The company was able to report an operating profit of $2.8 million in the second half of 1983. This was the first time in five years that Western had an operating profit for the second half of the year, a substantial improvement over the 16.8 million operating loss reported for the same period of the previous year.

> Mr. Lee stated that that 1983 redirection of Western Airlines involved a number of factors. It was necessary to reconstruct a management team. The company's financial house had to be put in order. Marketing efforts needed focus and direction. He noted that positive results of marketing programs are now being seen, and the company has also succeeded in maintaining overall costs at or below last year's level. Management is operating under formal cost control guidelines. Western employees have taken a vital part in restructuring costs. The Western "Partnership" evolved and management-employee relations were improved.

> With all of this in place by the end of 1983, Western was able to address future aircraft needs. Agreement was reached for delivery of twenty-two Boeing 737 aircraft, replacing 767 aircraft which had been ordered. These aircraft will allow schedule frequency and bring maintenance and operating economy.

Mr. Lee pointed out that in the 1984 first quarter, Western set a new quarterly revenue record, and it is expected that April revenues will reach new highs. In spite of this, the company has not been able to optimize bottom line financial performance because of the new competitive environment in which it operates. Since deregulation, the western United States has been a magnet for upstart airlines and expansion of older lines. Western has staked out its territory. Its commitment is to serve the western United States, including Alaska and Hawaii, western Canada and Mexico. Western will maintain its commitment to quality service as a full-service airline.

Mr. Lee noted further that the company is determined to provide a competitive cost structure. Labor costs - wages, benefits and work rules - that represent one of the few controllable factors in airline expenses are being constantly addressed.

Mr. Lee concluded his remarks by noting that the company has established a much improved environment between labor and management. It has touched on the pioneering spirit which is at the core of everything Western Airlines has done and will do in the future.

Having this Shareholders' Meeting in Salt Lake City allowed us to have some of the city's movers and shakers join us for lunch. I had become acquainted with them at the time I was up there organizing and watching over the hub. This provided an excellent follow-up to previous conversations with them, many to elicit their individual support for the expansion of the hub.

Spencer Eccles had invited me to join the First Security Bank board in 1983. It was one of the most prestigious boards in Utah and I had accepted the invitation. During my time at the hub I had also gone onto the board of directors of the Chamber of Commerce. Bill Jones, chairman of Intermountain Health Care, and Don Cash, chairman of Questar, the gas company, had asked me to be on their boards, but I had to turn them down as I couldn't commit the time.

I had also been asked to go on the board of the Del Webb Corporation. I would have liked to have joined that board as they had a lot of interesting properties. Unfortunately, at the time they owned the Sahara Hotel in Las Vegas and some other gambling interests. I just couldn't see myself making much of a contribution in those areas, so I turned it down.

We had become one of the major employers in Utah and, at that time, the people of Salt Lake City were showing a supportive reaction to Western's presence. This would diminish after the merger with Delta Air Lines as Delta treated them as second-class citizens.

Delta's corporate management just didn't catch the vision of how to work the Utah territory. I often wondered if I had been in Salt Lake City during that period if things would have been different? I doubt it, as the CEO of Delta, Ron Allen, didn't want any input from ex-Western executives. He was a headstrong man with a goal of having the name of Western disappear as fast as possible.

On June 4, 1984 we convened a meeting of the board of directors to review our progress with the Competitive Action Program. The directors were getting weary of these monthly meetings and we barely scraped together a quorum. Vic Brown, Wally Hickel and Bob Volk were the only outside directors in attendance.

The sole purpose of the meeting was to go on record as having reviewed with the board the methodology we were using to proceed with the implementation of CAP. The presentation had already been made to key members of management and the unions. Grinstein was asked to describe the role of Temple, Barker and Sloane, the consulting firm that was working with us to assist in preparing the analysis and communications of the financial implications outlined in the parameters of CAP.

William Farrell, whom we had appointed as assistant treasurer, had worked with me on the original formation of CAP. He was an integral part of the team from the beginning and we asked him to lead off with an overview of CAP.

Bill described in detail the methodology used in preparing the program, and put particular emphasis on the planning process and economic assumptions we had utilized. Bill outlined how the "base case" models were formed by using both an assumption of "snapbacks" of employee wages at the end of the present wage-cut period, and alternatively, assumptions of no "snapbacks." We used three "base models;" most pessimistic, most optimistic, and most likely. A 65% probability factor was assigned to the "most optimistic" approach.

Then Don Kem, our senior director of economic planning, presented a summary of the company's yield performance versus the rest of the industry. While we had shown considerable progress since 1982, he stressed that yields had peaked and could not be relied upon to produce continued increases in revenues. Our assumption was that they would be flat over the next three years. This was due to the impact from the new carriers in the industry and the pricing pressures from their "low-cost" structure.

Darrel Danielson, assistant controller, presented a conclusion that the overall implications of such cases resulted in a bleak outlook for the future unless some fundamental changes are made in our cost structure - ergo, CAP.

Bill Farrell summarized with two alternative plans, designated CAP I and CAP II. Those plans anticipated profitable results if the basic assumptions proved accurate and certain cost reductions and efficiencies could be affected.

I then advised the board that all planning activities and labor negotiations presently ongoing in the company were being conducted against the background of the assumptions and conclusions contained in the CAP presentations.

Jerry Grinstein talked about the present status of negotiations with the various unions. In 1982, there had been an agreement signed between the company and pilots to mediate, and then arbitrate, twenty open issues in their contract. This process was nearly completed and the Air Line Pilots Association, (ALPA), would not consider anything further until this arbitration, or whatever, ended. That would be in about 30 days. The Teamsters were still indicating the demands were excessive and the other unions were sitting on their hands until ALPA did something. This meant very little was going to happen with the implementation during the month of July, 1984.

We had advised the labor groups that there was a deadline of July 15, by which time the company needed to know with some certainty whether its requests of the unions were capable of being achieved. After that date, the company's ability to accomplish several of the key elements of the Competitive Action Program would be severely limited, if not impossible.

This board of directors meeting convened at 9:30 a.m. and ended at 12:25 p.m. Grinstein did an excellent job with his presentation and, all in all, this was without a doubt one of the finest examples of good management planning in action a Western Airlines board would ever see, and it made me ill that so few showed up for the presentation. There was no way the missing board members could grasp the planning, organization and urgency of this meeting by reading the minutes. Nevertheless, I was satisfied that the presentation had now been completed with management, unions and the board - that covered all bases.

As we went into the summer of 1984, the yield flattened as was predicted, but traffic deteriorated faster than had been anticipated in the T.P.&.S. models. Continental Airlines had recovered more rapidly than anyone had forecast and, with their heavy presence in the West and their new low-cost structure, they were siphoning off both passenger and cargo revenue.

Our outlook for the CAP was now moving more toward the "pessimistic model" and, in the minds of our consultants, had a very low probability of acceptance by the unions.

We were projecting a loss of 14 million dollars in the second quarter. That was an improvement from the second quarter of 1983, but it also signaled a slowdown in our rate of progress. We were not seeing the normal surge in summer traffic. My personal opinion was that the increased traffic from the Summer Olympics did not materialize; in fact, I think the Olympics hurt us as people shied away from the Los Angeles area because of the forecast of mass Olympic congestion.

Following the Summer Olympics, it became clear that we at Western Airlines needed to move into high gear with the unions to obtain the further reductions in labor costs that had been requested. If the pilots agreed with our proposals for wage cutbacks and productivity improvements, we would have the lowest cost pilot agreement of any major carrier in the industry. We still felt confident that the Teamsters would fall in line. The ATE, which represented the passenger and cargo workers, and the AFA, representing the flight attendants, were still balking at doing anything.

My biggest problem was a strong feeling we would need even deeper cuts than we had proposed. On July 12th I told the board of directors:

Our recent meetings with the employees suggest that the company cannot accomplish everything it has asked the unions for, at least not by September the 1st by which date the company believes it needs to implement the Competitive Action Program. He stated that while many employees are individually willing to do virtually anything to ensure the company's survival, one of the legacies of past management/labor negotiations was a distrust of any management. Lee continued by stating that he felt management had used its absolute best efforts to achieve the needed concessions, and that since the chances of achieving the Competitive Action Program by September 1st appear minimal, and the cash situation appears to be worsening, there appears little alternative but to try for contracts which would result in even deeper cuts than called for under the Competitive Action Program. (The one we had been discussing was CAP II, which was being presented to the unions at this time.)

After much discussion among the board members, it was determined that inasmuch as the mid-July deadline was arriving and the company had not achieved the concessions it believed it needed, the plan known as Competitive Action Program II, which had been formulated by the outside consultants, was no longer viable and that fact would be announced to the unions on Monday, July 16th."

The company had promised to put a hold on consolidation of certain reservations offices and additional layoffs as a part of the CAP considerations. We now advised the ATE union we were moving ahead with these plans.

The original Competitive Action Program that we had felt was necessary to secure Western's future had been thought to be more than was required; this input coming from the consultants. I was never comfortable with CAP II, which watered down the original plan. It was just another level of pain and still didn't provide a cure for the problem.

The main reason I felt comfortable with our original plan was that it would give us the basis for an operation under bankruptcy. If you are going to put the ultimate plan for survival before the employees, it had better contain all the elements needed under bankruptcy conditions in case the union leadership convinced the rank and file to vote against it and it became necessary to pull the plug.

We now had the financial wherewithal to rise up from the ashes of bankruptcy much like Continental Airlines; where a year ago, with the financial mish-mash we were stuck with at that time, we would have wound up like Braniff Airlines - never to rise again as a viable entity. If required for survival, Western could now reorganize, implement CAP and be in the air with an employee program that the unions understood - even though they might not agree with it.

It is one of my viewpoints that "understanding" does not always produce "agreement." One thing I knew for sure, the employees did understand how CAP worked and you could bet, under the bankruptcy scenario, the majority of the employees would jump at the chance of operating under the "CAP." At present, their union leadership was saying it exceeded the long-term requirements of the company. I guess they thought we would continue to pay their salaries by borrowing other people's money. The bankruptcy word had not yet been used, but I could see it coming.

On July 29th we decided to have the board of directors authorize the executive committee of the board to be empowered to take all actions needed for and in behalf of the company; with the exception of declaring dividends or amending the by-laws of the corporation. It was unanimously approved. The move allowed us to speed up the period where fast decisions would be necessary and it would be hard to convene the whole board on short notice.

This seemed to be the best time to go out and meet with as many employees as I could. I set up a grueling schedule at all the key locations throughout the system. There were some days that began at 6:00 a.m. and ended at 10:00 p.m. San Francisco was one of those examples.

San Francisco had always been one of our most pro-union locations with very vocal employees. As they were also the most influential, we had to win them over. For example, the SFO flight attendant base was very senior and they flew a good cross-section of routes and aircraft. At the risk of repeating myself, during the time I was vice president of inflight service and felt there were problems of morale, or whatever, on the line, I could go to San Francisco and spend the day in the flight attendant lounge and, by the end of the day, I would usually know what had to be done to tune up many parts of the system. It was very important to get the employees in SFO onboard if the contract changes were to be ratified.

At an 8:00 a.m. CAP meeting in SFO, in a conference room at the Airport Hilton, we had in attendance most of the employees from the midnight shift and many that were just coming on duty; these were mostly the passenger and ground services personnel. Four mechanics who had stayed from the midnight shift joined us and sat in the back of the room. It was obvious they had knocked back a couple of heavers before entering the meeting as their negative retorts got louder and louder.

I wearied of their barbs and finally addressed them, saying: "You guys are licensed aircraft mechanics who do not have a problem getting another job. However, most of the folks here do not have a license and will have a tougher time getting comparable work." I then said, "We're all in this boat together and, if you don't like the direction I am going and want to get out, do so without kicking holes in the boat." There was a smattering of applause.

This slowed the mouthy foursome a bit, but they soon started up again. At that point, one of the passenger service personnel turned around and hollered, "You heard what Larry said, don't kick a hole in the boat on your way out." With that the applause grew and that phrase became a byword at subsequent meetings. The mechanics left early.

Another humorous event occurred in Los Angeles. I had scheduled a meeting in the large conference room at a hotel right across the street from our general offices and next to our revenue accounting building. There were several hundred people in attendance. A month or so earlier, I had reduced my salary to one dollar a month. I did this very quietly and the word had not leaked out from our payroll department.

This particular late-afternoon meeting just happened to be scheduled on payday. I had my paycheck in my pocket. After the deduction it amounted to a very few pennies. I made my presentation and opened the meeting for questions and answers. Mid-way through that part of the meeting, one of the ATE employees stood to be recognized. He said, "You don't have to worry about how to take care of your finances with your large salary." He was sitting near the front of the room and I said, "I would be happy to exchange paychecks with you." He took the bait and came to the microphone where I was standing. He had his paycheck in hand. By the time he got there, I had mine out and ready. I said, "Okay, let's switch." He grabbed mine and pulled his back. He looked at the figure and blurted out, "It's less than a dollar!" I asked for his check and he responded that it was no deal and returned to his seat.

This person's blurting out his revelation to the group and his reaction to the discovery really tickled the audience and there was a great deal of laughter and applause. It eased the rest of the meeting and the word immediately traveled throughout the system that I was working for a dollar a month. I had a feeling this was the right thing to do at this time and that it would somehow pay off. This was payday! I couldn't have set it up any better if the whole thing had been staged. Subterfuge on my part was not even a consideration as the whole audience witnessed the employee's double take, one that only a Jack Nicholson could have duplicated.

During the process of the many employee meetings I held during the last year, I acquired the acronym of "SST." That is the contraction of a "supersonic transport." I felt they were using it as an indication of how fast I was moving about the system. Years later, I was to learn from Lyn Grinstein it stood for "Sunday school teacher." I guess it was my "preacher" style. The word would go out that the SST was coming to town to hold another employee meeting. It could have been worse.

One evening toward the end of the CAP presentations, I was meeting with the reservation agents in Los Angeles and Jim Shields, the president of their union, ATE, showed up at the meeting. He didn't participate in the open part of the meeting, but toward the end he rose and said he would like to debate management on the issues that had been discussed. I said I'd be happy to see him right after we adjourned.

We were meeting in a training room at our headquarters. So Jim and I stepped into the manager's office and he got right to the point. He said he'd like to have an open debate on the merits of CAP at the larger locations on the system. As I recall, he suggested Los Angeles, San Francisco, Seattle, Salt Lake City and Denver. I told him, "You're on."

The next day I informed Jerry Grinstein that I had accepted a challenge from Jim Shields to have a debate with Jerry at our major locations on the merits of the company's plan. Jerry was not happy that I had done this to him. He felt I should handle debates. There were two reasons I wanted Jerry to be the man in the hot seat. First, he would be a new voice - I was just completing a tour of the system. Second, he was the one they would be working for if they did not accept CAP, for I would not preside over a bankruptcy and that is where we would be headed without this program in place during the winter of 1984/85.

Grinstein agreed and said he would like to take Mike Palumbo, vice president and treasurer, and Harold Achtziger, vice president airport operations, along with him.

When I called Jim Shields to notify him of possible dates for the debates, he asked whom I was bringing along. I said, "I'm not bringing anyone - Mr. Grinstein is representing the company in the debates." Shields was furious, as I knew he would be. He said, "I invited you to debate me." I reminded him that he had made no such request. He had just stated he wanted to have a debate. Shields said he would cancel the debate and I told him the employees were now aware of this event and he would wind up looking like he was afraid to proceed.

I knew what Jim desired; he wanted to try to blow my credibility with the employees. I didn't feel that was possible as he had no ammunition to do so, but this would have diverted the focus from the job of getting CAP approved. We didn't need that at this critical point. I had also realized what a great opportunity this was to have another voice with a tough, but realistic message, reach the rank and file of Western Airlines and Jerry was a perfect fit for this mission.

By early August, when there was no significant movement, it became obvious we had to select an attorney who specialized in bankruptcy law. I talked to Jerry and Tom Greene about this and Tom felt it might be premature. I reminded him how obstinate Jim Shields of the ATE and Susan Edwards Pace of the AFA could be in reaching an agreement. We then proceeded with the selection of an attorney.

We didn't want any record of a meeting with this man as the first interview would be just exploring the nature of our problem and what he had to offer. Jerry and I drove to his office in Beverly Hills for the visit. His firm looked and sounded like the right organization and we engaged the managing partner to commence looking at what needed to be done at Western in the eventuality a reorganization was necessary.

On August 17, 1984, we convened the executive committee of the board and reviewed the status of our work with the unions. I needed to inform them what Jerry and I were doing to prepare for bankruptcy, should the employees not see fit to ratify. We informed the others we were being more candid with the employees and that this word would surely get out to the travel agencies. Marketing had said that any admission of potential bankruptcy would provoke a loss of business from travel agents, possibly as much as a $20 to $25 million loss of revenues.

Considerable discussion followed relating to the loss of revenue. I stated that would be only "a hiccup" in the overall revenue/cost picture if we were to declare bankruptcy, which was inevitable without CAP.

The executive committee reached consensus that management should communicate with the Company's employees and convey the urgency of the situation, including the distinct possibility of bankruptcy proceedings among the severe consequences which might result without ratification. This cleared the air of any hindsight problem.

With this in place Jerry and I asked Tom Greene, Topper Van Every, VP corporate affairs, and William Farrell, assistant VP finance and treasurer, to be an ad hoc committee of three to work with the bankruptcy attorney to have whatever plans were needed made ready to implement should that severe step be required. I felt there was little chance of that occurring, but we would not have been doing our job if we had not prepared for this contingency.

This threesome was to accomplish their work without involving any other employee as I didn't want to chance information leaks that could be avoided. Recall that Western was 92% unionized and that included many of the secretaries. We had to be very careful not to even give the appearance that we might be preparing for reorganization under chapter eleven for as long as possible. Talking about the possibility of this happening was one thing, but the knowledge we were actually doing the planning for this event could have some negative consequences at this stage of our negotiations. For example, the union leadership might think we had decided to head in this direction regardless of what they did with CAP and they would pull their support in order to hold onto whatever they now had in the way of a contract to improve their bargaining position during the reorganization of the company.

Grinstein and Shields began their debates. Harold Achtziger called me after each meeting and reported they were going well. He was not participating, but was there as a resource for Jerry. He said Mike Palumbo was doing an excellent job and that Grinstein was picking up steam with each session. My pipeline to the field was also pumping in a good reaction. I think the timing of the "one-two" punch of Lee and Grinstein could not have been better.

Thanks to Jim Shields, these sessions could not be construed as being anti-union; or in any way breaching the Railway Labor Act. Rather, we were just showing our cooperation by meeting Shields' challenge to debate. Since some employees from other unions showed up at these sessions, we were getting the added bonus of introducing them to the most serious message they would receive in the next month. Jerry did an exceptional job, as I knew he would. Debates were right up his alley.

By mid-September, the Air Line Pilots Association had ratified their contract as well as the dispatchers, the smallest group, who were represented by the Transport Workers Union. The International Brotherhood of Teamsters, who represented the mechanics and related workers, finally ratified their agreement, but it caused a great deal of controversy as the ATE and AFA did not believe their productivity savings amounted to their fair share of the cuts. Because of this, the ATE failed to ratify. They agreed to resubmit the CAP proposal if we would hire their financial consultant and arbitrate the provisions on questions as to whether or not other labor contracts met the Competitive Action Program. We agreed and they resubmitted. It was subsequently ratified by the rank and file.

Susan Edwards Pace, presently the chairperson of the master executive council of AFA at Western Airlines, advised us that on her recommendation, ratification by the flight attendants had been suspended. She was hung up on the same matter as the ATE, this relating to IBT not having done their part. We had talked to her about the ATE problems and how they were being resolved, but that didn't faze her. Jim Shields, having lost his battle, was now leaning on Susan Pace to hold out to keep the pressure on Western to reconsider the whole program.

On September 12, 1984, I called together the union leaders of each of the five unions. We met in the "Charles Russell" conference room at headquarters. Jerry Grinstein and Tom Greene, VP legal, were in attendance, neither of them knowing what I had in mind.

Beginning with ALPA, I addressed each Western Airlines union head and asked if their CAP contract had been ratified. Each answered yes, until I got to Susan Edwards Pace. When I asked her this question, she began to give a speech about the Teamsters not doing their part. I politely, yet firmly, cut her off and again asked, "Has your contract been ratified?" She said "no." I then read them a letter I was submitting to the executive committee of the board of directors of Western Airlines. The meeting was then adjourned without further discussion and I returned to my office.

Following is the letter I read to the union leadership. I had prepared the letter ahead of time as I suspected Susan Edwards would pull this delay tactic:

September 12, 1984

Executive Committee Board of Directors Western Air Lines, Inc. Los Angeles, CA

Gentlemen:

As of September 12, 1984, we are at an impasse in our negotiations with the Association of Flight Attendants. Unless this condition is altered immediately, I am compelled to submit my resignation as chief executive officer and do so herewith, effective at 5:00 p.m., P.D.T., Friday, September 14, 1984. I ask that the executive committee act favorably on my resignation.

Let me review briefly the course of events that lead to the regrettable but unequivocal conclusion that without ratification from all five unions, I must resign.

When I agreed to become chief executive officer, Western was already in desperate shape:

- Four consecutive years of heavy losses.

- Short of cash.

- Damaged management creditability.

- Little employee participation and employee morale at an all-time low.

- A management team missing quality people.

- No plan to establish Western's profitable presence in the deregulated environment.

As you know, I acted immediately to remedy all of these conditions and implemented our Partnership Program, followed by development of the Competitive Action Program. The CAP required considerable additional sacrifices by employees and management to achieve the low cost structure necessary to compete in a marketplace which can only be described as chaotic when compared to the period of regulation.

Following a direction from the executive committee of the board, I sent written communications to all our employees and had direct meetings with large groups at our major locations in which we indicated that failure to ratify any contract almost certainly would result in the company having to face bankruptcy proceedings. I also advised them that I had notified the board that, since I did not return to preside over a bankruptcy, I would not remain as CEO if they failed to ratify. I also advised them there would be no further negotiation of these conditions because we were running out of time. I did not intend these statements as threats; I regarded them as candid statements of fact.

Since I have given the leaders of the AFA and their individual members the complete picture of Western's financial condition, and in spite of that knowledge they have failed to ratify the agreement, I must consider this action as a demonstration of their lack of trust in my leadership.

Therefore, I believe it is in the best interest of all concerned, consistent with my personal integrity and standards, and with the public statements I have made ever since I became CEO, that I tender my resignation in this form and at this time.

To the board and those who have supported my efforts to set Western on a solid track, I want to express my sincere appreciation.

Sincerely,

/s/ Lawrence H. Lee

That evening I convened the executive committee and read the letter to them. They prevailed upon me to reconsider. I would not. They then asked if I could delay this to give Susan Edwards sufficient time, should she chose to reconsider her position. I finally agreed to stay until 5:00 p.m. on the following Monday, September 17, 1984.

Shortly after I walked out of the meeting with the unions, Grinstein and Greene came into my office in a high state of frustration. I informed them that this was final as Western had no other option than to declare bankruptcy and the outside bankruptcy counsel had already been advised to be available, if needed, for the forthcoming board meeting. I informed them that the letter said it all and further conversation was a waste of time.

At an early stage in my life, I had taken a course at UC Berkeley relating to labor relations. One of my favorite stories that came out of that class was a tale related by the professor regarding the newspaper business. He had talked about what a tough union represented those doing the grunt work of getting out the news; the typesetters, machine operators, etc.

The good professor was making a point that management has a great advantage if the chief knows the property, its people, what they do, and understands the basic operating functions of the property over which he presides; if he doesn't, he loses his edge. He then related this story:

Negotiations at this newspaper had gone on for many months and all issues were resolved but one; the union wanted an additional nickel an hour.

There was a final meeting scheduled in the publisher's office. In that office was a window which overlooked the presses. The union head knew that at a certain time of day the presses were turned off for just a couple of minutes to make a certain change. Banking on the possibility that the publisher did not know this, he said: "If I pull down the shade on your window it means we are at an impasse and the presses will cease to operate. If I raise it again, the men will stay and the presses will roll."

The local union representative had timed the meeting to coincide with this daily event and one minute before the scheduled shut-down he asked the question, "Are we or are we not going to get that nickel an hour." The answer was "No." He then rose, walked to the window and lowered the shade. The noisy presses came to a stop. In that moment of silence, the two of them stood eye to eye and the publisher finally said, "Okay, you win, you can have the additional nickel." The union leader walked to the window, raised the shade and the presses spooled up again.

What does this have to do with my resignation? The answer, I knew the actions of my people. This is where someone like Jerry Grinstein, wonderful man that he is, could not have made such a daring move. Sure it was a gamble, but I was not flying blind. As I had said earlier in this book, I'd negotiated several contracts with Susan Edwards Pace and my experience was that she never knew when to quit negotiating. Something drastic had to occur, such as going out on strike, or she wouldn't move.

The reason I read the full letter of my resignation to all the unions was not for the benefit of those who had already done their job; I was turning up the highest burner under Susan that I could bring into play. The threat of our declaring bankruptcy was not enough for her. She needed to hear exactly what was going to be put out to every employee of the company if she did not finish her ratification immediately. Susan was a very bright lady and she knew the flight attendants were ready to ratify what had been proposed. She halted the count in order to turn up the heat under me and I'm sure she had no vision of what I was about to do.

All this reminded me of the movie, "Patton." George C. Scott, who was portraying General Patton, was in a tank battle with General Rommel's forces. He was watching the battle between the Americans and the Germans from a bluff and the American tank force was cleaning Rommel's clock. Seeing that success, he shouts: "Rommel, you SOB, I read your book."

Patton was an avid student of history and knew the tactical plans used by Rommel. I had read the Susan Edwards Pace book of negotiations. There wasn't a doubt in my mind as to what she would do.

The next day, September thirteenth, at our full board meeting, we took care of the usual business and when we got to the final agenda item of "new and unfinished business," I officially informed the full board of my decision to leave. This part of the proceeding is recorded in the board minutes of that day. I began with some general comments relating to my perception of current conditions. The minutes of that board meeting are recorded as follows:

> Mr. Lee stated his belief that everything in the company's future was essentially contingent upon securing ratification of the Competitive Action Program labor agreements, and while four of the five unions had indeed ratified, the AFA situation remained and was threatening the very future of the company.
>
> Because of the impasse which had been reached with AFA, Mr. Lee told the board he felt compelled to submit his resignation as chief executive officer, and in fact had done so the previous evening in a meeting of the board's executive committee. He read to the board the text of a letter he had submitted to the executive committee.
>
> [At this point the letter with the revised date of my resignation is inserted in the minutes. I knew some of the board members were squirming with the way this letter was written; especially the six "bullets." While it was not meant to bring back to life old memories, it was a reminder to them of how they had allowed Western to sink to such a terrible condition.]
>
> Mr. Tom Greene was then asked to read the resolution which had been adopted by the executive committee the previous evening:

WHEREAS, Lawrence H. Lee, in a letter dated September 12, 1984, has tendered his resignation as chief executive officer of this Corporation effective September 17, 1984; and

WHEREAS, Lawrence H. Lee has advised the executive committee that such action on his part results from failure to obtain from all of this Corporation's unions timely ratification of agreements reflecting the Corporation's Competitive Action Program; and

WHEREAS, in particular, the Association of Flight Attendants has failed to so ratify such an agreement, and as such, is the only one of the Corporation's five unions to fail to do so, with the result, however, that ratification by the remaining four unions may cease to be effective; and

WHEREAS, Lawrence H. Lee has publicly advised the unions and their members that failure to ratify such agreements so as to permit them to be effective as of September 1, 1984 would probably result in bankruptcy proceedings, and further advised them that he was unwilling to preside as chief executive officer in such a bankruptcy proceeding; and

WHEREAS, The executive committee of this board has prevailed upon Lawrence H. Lee to condition his resignation so as to allow him to withdraw such resignation if the Association of Flight Attendants ratifies such an agreement or reasonably satisfies the Corporation that ratification is immediately forthcoming, and will be effective as of September 17, 1984;

NOW THEREFORE, IT IS RESOLVED   that the resignation of Lawrence H. Lee as chief executive officer of this Corporation is accepted with great reluctance and regret by this Committee, effective Monday, September 17, 1984, only upon the express condition that such resignation be tendered with the following condition: that in the event by 5:00 p.m., P.D.T. on Monday, September 17, 1984, the Association of Flight Attendants has satisfactorily notified the Corporation of its ratification, or the imminence thereof, of an agreement reflecting the Corporation's Competitive Action Program goals, and thereby has become the fifth and final union to so ratify such an agreement with the Corporation, Mr. Lee's resignation as chief executive officer will be withdrawn. This Committee further expresses its belief and understanding that Mr. Lee has agreed to so condition his resignation; and

RESOLVED FURTHER that the president of this Corporation be and he is authorized and directed to take all reasonable steps prior to 5:00 p.m., P.D.T., on September 17, 1984, to secure such ratification by the Association of Flight Attendants.

After considerable discussion, it was unanimously agreed that this meeting of the board should be recessed and adjourned over until 5:00 p.m., P.D.T., on Monday, September 17, 1984, at which time the meeting would be reconvened by conference telephone call, and the board could take such further action as might be appropriate at that time. Accordingly, the meeting was so recessed at 11:50 a.m.

On Monday, I received the report that Susan Pace had called to say the CAP agreement had been ratified by the AFA. I then reconvened the board in the telephone conference that had been scheduled and assured them I was withdrawing my letter of resignation and we would get on with some important financial matters that were pending this full ratification.

That was the second letter of resignation I had submitted to Western. The first, given to Neil Bergt, was done with a serious desire to leave; this was not. Nevertheless, it was the only way to play out the hand. While it wasn't a bluff, some thought I must not be playing with a full deck as I would have left the company with nothing - which is usually the case when bankruptcy follows. Had Susan wanted to get rid of me, she certainly had her chance at that time. As I have said, while Ms. Pace and I didn't always agree with one another, there was a mutual respect and in this case she came through as I felt she would.

Peace settled over Western and I could sense everyone breathing a sigh of relief that the tussle was over. We now had a sound foundation in place to return to profitability and it had all been accomplished within eighteen months. Grueling months, they were; however, my goal of helping Grinstein get up to speed could not have been accomplished nearly so well at any other stage of our corporate existence. He performed admirably. With the exception of Jim Shields, I could see the union leadership now had confidence in Jerry; one must keep in mind Jim Shields did not trust anyone.

Susan Edwards Pace didn't show any signs of holding a grudge because of my actions against her. She was professional in that regard. We were to work well together from then on.

In the final analysis, the outside consultants offered little that proved of value. It came down to what had been originally proposed at the beginning of the year and required tougher decisions than they were recommending. Wayne Horvitz was the exception. He gave a good deal of high-quality counsel and advice in the area of labor relations and his voice was always respected by the union leadership.

At our most recent board meeting, Michael J. Palumbo had been elevated to the office of senior vice president finance and treasurer. This was done in hope of holding on to him until we had finished our financial deals that were in a holding pattern. He was excellent in the area of outside financing and had been the key in our work with E. F. Hutton. The problem was that he was seen by those on Wall Street as a valuable resource and the head-hunters were banging on his door.

The next board meeting was held on October 11, 1984 and it was at this gathering two new members joined Western Airlines board of directors. The Association of Flight Attendants had selected Susan Edwards Pace to represent them and the Air Transport Employees union was being represented by their president, James J. Shields. They were elected and appointed until the next Annual Meeting of the Shareholders. At this point they both joined the meeting and were welcomed by the others.

Neither ALPA nor the Teamsters had as yet appointed their representatives to fill the other two board seats. However, as Andre Dimitriadis was going to present the third quarter financial results, we had invited Marv Griswald, regional head of IBT, and John Donnelly, president of ALPA, to attend the meeting. We felt it was very important that each labor group be made aware of our current financial situation.

The core of Dimitriadis' presentation was concerning possible aircraft sales and purchases and the current labor arbitrations over CAP. He indicated that we would be unable to raise any money until the arbitration was over and the CAP concessions were firm. Andre felt we needed additional cash to hold us over until the benefits of CAP began to accumulate to Western.

During my meetings in the field with our employees, I picked up one thread of distrust that needed to be addressed at the board level. While the employees were willing to make sacrifices from their paychecks to save the company, they were unwilling to see a dime of this money wind up in the pockets of management. Among other things, the old barb of the officer's bonuses granted with board approval in January of 1983 was still festering.

Based on past performance, I could understand the employees concerns and I devised a way to handle the wage, salary and benefits program for management. At this meeting, I informed the board we had hired the firm of Ernst and Whinney to monitor the activities associated with management pay and benefits. Working with the finance division, they would establish a cost basis for the management group and that would represent a pool of money that would be frozen until such time as the unions once again received salary increases.

The caveat in all this was that the CEO could move that pot of money around in any way he or his division heads felt appropriate to recruit and maintain a viable work force. In addition, Western would have Ernst and Whinney perform a quarterly audit of that fund to make certain it was not being violated. They would report their findings to the board of directors after each audit.

By setting up management compensation in this manner, I could be assured there would be no more concern registered by the employees, or by their representatives, that they were "lining management's pockets with their pay cuts," while at the same time, giving the company the controls we needed to govern.

I knew this act was not sitting well with some of the members of our management team - some near the top. It appeared to them we were turning over the reins of governance to the unions. Their employment was too recent to see the quid pro quo that was necessary to overcome the bitter pills of the past.

If the current airline industry took this same approach they would have half the problems they are now facing in obtaining salary and benefit roll-backs from the rank and file of their employees. I have never seen a period of time when senior management has wallowed in so much greed while their companies are losing billions of dollars; and, with their shareholders suffering massive deterioration in their investments.

Increasing Mike Palumbo's stature in the company was not enough to keep him off Wall Street. He left to go do what he enjoyed the most - invest-ment banking. On November 13, 1984, we brought in a fine replacement for Palumbo's position, a man named Tom Roeck who had been with Global Marine for many years. Roeck was an ex-Marine officer and carried himself with that stature. My personal opinion was that he fit the position better than Palumbo and would be a natural replacement for Dimitriadis when he left. I would not have considered Palumbo for the chief financial officer. He had the experience and creativity, but not the personality needed for our company at this time.

Word had reached me that Andre Dimitriadis was looking elsewhere for employment. I could guess about when his resume went out. Andre had been trying to cut the legs out from under Grinstein and this situation was becoming quite apparent to others. Jerry wasn't helping resolve this problem - feisty fellow that he could be. It was something that had to be nipped in the bud. I called Andre into my office and explained to him that what he was doing had to stop immediately or I was going to fire him. Dimitriadis, in his spirited style, paced back and forth in my office telling me all the awful things Jerry was doing to undermine him. I patiently listened to his tirade and repeated my statement that he was out of here if his antics did not imme-diately cease. I believe his resume went out right after this encounter as he knew I would keep my word.

Our executive vice president marketing, Harry Chandis, had resigned to take a better paying job with an airline publishing firm back east. Harry was not happy with union members being on the board and, as I have already related, he felt we had given them more power than was necessary. This, and the fact he had not been given a raise when promoted, seemed to gnaw at him and I was not surprised to see him leave.

Harry was a very colorful human being and I had a good association with him and a lot of respect for his abilities; however, there was no way he was going to move up. He, like Dimitriadis, did not feel that he should have been bypassed when I elevated Grinstein to chief operating officer. I could not blame Chandis for feeling the way he did. As a former President of Continental Airlines he had already demonstrated he could perform in the role of an airline president; however, I knew he could never be seen as "the man" by our unions and, in that sense, he was right in believing that the unions had a great deal of power at Western. I knew their cooperation was our key to survival, not management standing alone; Harry was a loner.

Our search for a replacement for Harry Chandis was taking more time than usual as we had to have someone with a good knowledge of advertising, as well as general marketing. Mark Dennet, one of the creative individuals who had worked under Bert Lynn, VP advertising and sales promotion, had been holding things together since Bert retired. We really needed someone who could replace Harry White, retired VP field sales, and Bert Lynn. Grinstein was working with some headhunters on this recruiting effort.

Adam M. Aron, age 31, was our final selection for the marketing job. He joined us as vice president marketing programs. Adam was a very creative individual and one of the first things he directed us to do was change advertising agencies. This was done and Adam came out with a new approach to our advertising. He had the agency select some highly visible Hollywood types who had never before been in an advertisement for a company product.

The first of these new ads engaged the services of Fred Astaire and Gene Kelly. They had appeared together in several films and were naturals for this type of commercial. Margie and I went to the studio the day they shot the commercial and, after taking one look at Fred Astaire, I asked Adam Aron if he felt sure about this ad program as Mr. Astaire looked like he wouldn't live long enough to allow us to get the value out of our million-dollar expenditure. My fear subsided when the cameras began to roll and Astaire assumed his role. He came to life and was sharp as the proverbial tack.

There was a great friendship between Fred and Gene and you could see it in action as Kelly worked with this master of the dance. This was a memorable day for me. My father used to tell me so much about his work with Gene Kelly at MGM. He thought Kelly was one of the most caring among the Hollywood actors. I could see why dad felt this way when I observed the friendly manner Gene displayed in working with all those on the set.

The next commercial featured the two stars of "Star Trek," Nimoy and Shatner, and it was equally well received by the public. These were fresh and hit the heart of our territory. Nevertheless, this was not what Jerry and I wanted for the long run. We wanted to bring back the "Bird." Wally Bird, as he had been lovingly dubbed, was the long-time symbol of Western's better days. The employees had been after us for several years to reintroduce the Bird commercials - along with his well-known phrase, "Western Airlines, the O-o-o-nly Way to Fly!"

In October, 1984, Miguel Blasquez died. He was one of our longest serving members of the board, having served since 1973. Miguel was from Mexico City and had done a fine job of representing Western Airlines in Mexico.

Before the board meeting in late November, I was notified by ALPA that John A. (Pete) Kammermeyer, a Western Airlines captain, would be their representative on the board. Also, the Teamsters notified us that Dr. Charles Levinson, of Geneva, Switzerland, would represent them. They were elected to the board of directors on November 29, 1984. This increased the count of board members to fifteen, still a workable number. We were the only airline in the United States to have four union reps on their board.

The financing of aircraft, an event that had been on hold until CAP was approved, began to fall in place and we were even able to get General Electric to finance the first of three 737-300's we would be receiving in early 1985. This was a far cry from a year ago when the lenders would run at the mention of Western Airlines.

The November, 1984 meeting of the board of directors was the last for Andre Dimitriadis; he had found employment with a hospital firm. Within a year of Andre's arrival at that company, he was in trouble with the board of directors. Jim Jacobson, an acquaintance of mine, was on that board and said there were several members who wanted Dimitriadis removed from the company. Jim had been nominated as a committee of one to seek my advice. When he contacted me I asked him if one of their present needs was for some creative financing. He said yes and that this was a very high priority. I told him that Andre was his man and I recommended they hang on to him. They did for a period of time and then I lost track of his whereabouts.

All this work with CAP did not deter us from making other progress that was needed during 1984. Management moved aggressively to position Western to be the dominant full-service carrier of the western part of the United States by refining schedules and strengthening connecting operations at Salt Lake City and Los Angeles, the airline's primary hubs.

We were by far the largest airline operating at Salt Lake City, with over 70 percent of the airport's daily departures. You will recall the work we did with the City of Salt Lake and with the Airport Commission to finance and build another concourse for Western. That new concourse "D" opened in October 1984. Flights were now operating from 21 second-level boarding gates. We planned a further 29 percent increase in departures in April 1985 which would give Western 108 daily flights serving 38 nonstop destinations.

The Salt Lake City hub was operating smoothly, and it was an increasingly attractive alternative to Denver for passengers throughout the western United States.

Our marketing group had also boosted its schedule at Los Angeles International Airport. The airline was now operating the most daily departures from Los Angeles. With nonstop flights to 25 cities, Western also served more points nonstop from Los Angeles than any other airline. In addition, the Los Angeles operation was scheduled as a connecting gateway, with service to Canada, Hawaii and Mexico, which were all key pleasure travel destinations.

We were also taking action to gain a larger portion of the business travel market through improved schedules and service as well as a fleet-wide upgrade in the design and configuration of the aircraft interiors.

Our services were geared to the business traveler through advance seat assignment and roundtrip check-in. In addition, we enriched the Travel Pass II frequent flyer program in 1984 to maintain its competitive edge through a simple structure and fast rewards.

As mentioned, we began a longer-term program of redesigning the aircraft interiors. First class sections were available on all Western flights, and we were upgrading our coach sections throughout the fleet by adding newly designed seats to give passengers additional leg room without sacrificing capacity. Larger over-head bins were installed aboard 727 and 737 aircraft to accommodate demand for carry-on space. Grinstein was very much involved with the implementation of this program.

Topper Van Every was working hard on the aircraft interior program. He had been through this many times while working for me and knew his way around that part of our industry. He was also doing a fine job in coordinating it with our maintenance department.

Jerry Grinstein wanted to give our aircraft a face-lift, replacing the red, white and black paint scheme of the last 15 years with a simple, bright red Western "W" outlined in blue and white on a polished-aluminum fuselage. It was a good move as there is nothing like a new paint job on your aircraft to tell the world we're going to be around a while.

In 1984, Western Airlines turned the corner. The company reported its first full-year operating profit in five years as well as a fourth quarter operating profit of $6.9 million, Western's highest fourth quarter ever. Although the company still finished the year with a net loss, it was reduced by $25 million from 1983. Not counting an extraordinary gain in 1983, the net loss reduction was $67 million. At the same time, the company was positioned to return to full profitability in 1985.

The following key paragraph appeared in our 1984 Annual Report:

The successes of 1984 did not come about by chance. They are the result of strategies designed in the preceding year, and of management and labor reaching the understanding that both sides can cooperate in key areas to assure Western's future success.

It took a year and nine months, to get the company straightened out. When I accepted the position of chief executive officer, I said my job would be completed in three years; that included training my replacement within this period of time. We were right on schedule. I felt good about the team we had finally assembled and looked forward to the rewards of all this effort, a harvest I predicted Western would reap in 1985.

Chapter 12

THE ONLY WAY TO FLY

Jerry was building up steam as each month went by and was doing well with his added responsibilities. As I said earlier, he was an excellent student. I enjoyed our relationship and knew he respected me as his mentor. His wife, Lyn, was a great asset to him. She complimented his personality so well and Lyn was one of the few people I knew who could have a queenly presence about her and yet make everyone in the room feel at home. Another thing I appreciated so much about Lyn was the kindly way she treated my wife, Margie.

I had decided it was time to drop the mantel of CEO on Jerry, but also knew we needed a strong operation-oriented second in command. I told Jerry it was my intent to make this change in late January or early February of 1985. He would carry the title of chief executive officer and we would hire a president and chief operating officer to replace him in that position. I would remain as the chairman of the board until I felt it was time to begin withdrawing from full-time management. I had now been with Western Airlines over forty years and felt that was long enough.

In late 1984, Jerry and I began looking for an airline operations oriented individual who could move into the spot of president and chief operating officer. The firm of Spencer Stuart Associates was again assisting in this matter and it finally came down to one person that Jerry and I felt could take the spot. His name was Robin H. H. Wilson. He was currently the president of Long Island Railway. Of more importance, he had been with Trans World

Airways for seventeen years in a variety of positions and was senior vice president of operations when he left to join Long Island Railway four years ago. Wilson was also credited with accomplishing a major turnaround at that railway company while he was in charge.

Grinstein and I were in Washington to an industry meeting and asked Wilson to join us there for dinner. Everything went well that evening and we both gave him a "thumbs up." At the board meeting on January 22, 1985, he was elected president and COO and was also voted a member of the board. At that same meeting, Grinstein was elevated to the office of chief executive officer. I remained chairman of the board.

The board had to modify the bylaws of the Corporation in order to have a CEO without either president or chairman as part of his title. Our current organization was a bit unusual, but it was a necessary step in order for me to gain the approval from one of the unions to drop the title of CEO on Jerry; recall that the IBT agreement locked me into CEO for so long as the "Partnership Plan" was in place. Our modified agreement was that I would stay on as a full-time employee and be part of the "troika" at the top. That was no problem as this had been my plan for the near term and Jerry did not seem to be threatened by my staying in place for a while.

Spencer Stuart had been active in helping me recruit a board member who had been the CEO of a large Fortune Five Hundred company. Archie R. Boe had recently retired as president of Sears Roebuck Company. Prior to taking the top spot at Sears, he had been chairman and CEO of Allstate Insurance and was the key individual to build that company. Spence felt I should go to Chicago and speak with him about joining our board. I did so and things went well.

We also needed someone on the board who had a strong financial background, one who would be able to replace Benninger when he retired from the board. We had heard good things about Joseph T. Casey who then was executive vice president and chief financial officer at Litton Industries. Joe Casey had a reputation of being a down-to-earth, nuts and bolts financial person and I felt good about him from the moment we met.

Both of these gentlemen passed muster with the nominating committee and had accepted the responsibility of coming on Western's board. They were elected on January 22, 1985.

In the first two months of 1985, Western saw the full fruits of "The Partnership" and the "Competitive Action Plan." The employees and management were working together with the same goals in mind; which was to make a profit and improve the position of the shareholders who had suffered by both losses and dilution of their shares.

The best way to present this success is to repeat what was written to the shareholders for the first quarter of 1985.

Fellow Shareholders:

Western Airlines reported a record profit of $13.3 million, or 44 cents per share primary, in the first quarter ended March 31, 1985. This compares with a loss of $23 million, or 98 cents a share, in the first quarter last year.

First quarter operating profit totaled $23 million, compared with an operating loss of $12.9 million in 1984. First quarter net results include pre-tax gains from the disposition of assets of $3.9 million in 1985 and $3.2 million in 1984.

The $36 million turnaround in net income is the result of strong passenger demand and significant reduction in labor costs. This combination tells us that the strategy is working - that the company has an improved cost structure, route system and marketing program that position Western as the dominant airline of the West.

First quarter operating revenues increased five percent to $301.1 million from $287.3 million in 1984, while operating expenses of $278.1 million were down from $300.2 million in 1984.

Labor expenses for the first quarter included $2.6 million reserved for employee profit sharing. The employee owners of Western hold 32 percent of the company's common stock. Each one has played a key role in the company's success and will participate in an annual profit sharing plan as a result of a program begun in 1983. Western is the first airline to permanently restructure its labor costs through the collective bargaining process. Through the Western ESOP and employee profit sharing plan, the people who produce the success of the company will participate in the benefits of that success.

During the first quarter, Western announced a major expansion of the schedule at our Salt Lake City hub. Starting April 1, daily departures at Salt Lake City increase by 32 percent, to 108 from 84. This expansion in 28 current markets will continue to 116 daily flights in June.

The added flights will give Salt Lake City travelers more departure choices in both the West and the Midwest and provide increased connecting opportunities for passengers originating in other cities.

The additional flights are achieved by increasing utilization of Western's existing planes and expanding the fleet. Two used Boeing 737-200 twinjets have been acquired and three new Boeing 737-300 are being delivered in the spring.

We are also accelerating to November and December of this year acceptance of three 737-300s which had been scheduled for delivery in 1988 and three more scheduled for delivery in 1986. Operation of nine of the new 737- 300s will greatly improve the utilization of this quieter, more fuel-efficient aircraft.

The company is off to the best start in Western's 59-year history, but the industry is volatile, marked by excessive capacity, an abundant supply of new personnel and constant downward pressure on the fare structure. Although the momentum of the first quarter is expected to continue, your management is committed to keeping costs down and meeting the challenge of the competitive marketplace in order to be consistently profitable for the long rather than short term.

I'll add one note concerning the utilization of our current aircraft. Several of the revisions to the pilot contract took a while to make their full impact on scheduling the fleet and the pilot hours. We began to feel the benefits in the first quarter; however, the biggest impact was felt in the summer schedule of 1985.

In the above letter to shareholders we mention the 737-300's. The first was delivered the end of March, 1985. It was checked over in Los Angeles and on March 29th, it was flown to Salt Lake City for a dedication ceremony. What I didn't know was to whom it was being dedicated. When the flight arrived we had a platform and podium set up for speeches from some guests; who included Jerry Grinstein, Victor Brown and the Airport Director, Louis Miller.

Grinstein was his usual fluent self and as he finished his speech the captain leaned out the window and pulled the "speed tape" off the side of the nose exposing the name, "Larry Lee." The aircraft was dedicated to me.

This caught me totally by surprise. While the naming of the plane could easily be kept a secret, what followed amazed me. Jerry then asked that my family come out onto the field to join me as I received this tribute. Out marched Margie, Mother Lewis and the whole family; no one was missing except our sweet Daddy, Clay Lewis, who had recently passed away.

Bob Wylie, vice president Boeing sales, presented Margie with a key to the 737-300 and a beautifully encased copy of a plaque that was mounted at the entry of the aircraft. It was difficult for me to imagine how all my family had been smuggled into SLC and housed at the Hotel Utah without my having even a hint of what was going on. My secretaries, Karen Jepson and Juanita Robbins played a big part in this and deserved most of the credit.

This was all written up, with appropriate pictures, in both of the Tribune and the Deseret News. At the meeting of the board of directors on May 9, 1985, I advised them I would retire at the end of the year. The summary of my statement, as contained in the minutes of that board meeting, reads as follows:

> Mr. Lee began by stating that he wished to address the board personally on the subject of management succession. He stated that he believed he had accomplished the three basic goals he had outlined when he first became president and chief executive officer some two years ago, in particular his goals of putting in place a first rate top management team and a true management

succession plan. He stated that having done so, he did not feel he should stand in the way of Messrs, Grinstein and Wilson continuing to direct the company's [future] progress. After stating his sincere appreciation for all of the board's support, he indicated his plans to retire at the end of this year and his intention to announce those plans at the Shareholders' Meeting later that day.

Prior to this Shareholders' Meeting I had met with the head of each union to make sure they felt comfortable with this announcement. While they felt it was premature, I reminded them that the time and effort I had put in as their CEO was the equivalent of four years in the first two . I also advised them I had no intention of leaving the board of directors and would function as chairman of the executive committee until Western had a clearer vision of how the next few years would be.

I don't mean to make so much of my relationship with the unions, but you have to recall the Teamsters still held an ax over my head. I talked to both Benning and his boss, Marv Griswold, and they agreed to remove the clause from their agreement that bound me to Western. Their original concern over Jerry had long since disappeared; it was just that they felt they deserved some longer continuity of management at the top.

The Shareholders' Meeting on May 9th went well and my announced retirement was graciously accepted without too many questions from the shareholders in attendance.

This was the last board meeting for Bishop Victor Brown. He had turned 70, which was an automatic requirement to give up his seat. He became a "Director-Emeritus" and was honored at the luncheon at his beloved Hotel Utah following the Shareholders' Meeting.

Vic and I had been friends for some time, but over the past four years we became very close to one another. He was my most trusted friend and would remain so until his death. You may recall my comments about his desire to have me meet with Gerald Grinstein in the late fall of 1982. He had a strong sense that Jerry had potential beyond his work as an attorney in Seattle.

As I have said, I had these same feelings as I became better acquainted with Grinstein. He was not the usual lawyer type - the sort who is the butt of so many jokes. Jerry had a relaxed attitude around any person, be it a ship cleaner or a senator. Each of us must learn the vocabulary of a business and that was my task as a teacher these past two years. I now believed he had completed graduate school and deserved to receive the honors that would flow to him from his risky decision to join me in this great adventure. I felt very comfortable in the decision I had made. I only wish I was as comfortable with the way Robin Wilson was approaching his role as chief operating officer.

Wilson was acting more like the CEO than the COO. He was not getting into the depth he should with each department and I could predict this would become a problem with Grinstein. I knew Jerry would not tolerate any condition that would undermine his authority - I think he'd learned that lesson with Dimitriadis.

The key was to hold the management team together for as long as possible as we were now being seen by other airlines as a success story and the vultures who had been hovering to snatch our aircraft, gates and landing slots when we went bankrupt, were now working hard to keep up with our expansion in the West.

The old adage that "success breeds success" was never truer than in our case. With The Partnership and CAP in place, we were not only getting good press, but our stock had now risen 80% higher than when the shares were issued to the employees at the time "The Partnership" was implemented. In addition, our debt equity ratio had gone from 8 to 1 to an enviable position of 4 to 1. The gates of financing were now open and we felt confident that many of the "pricey" deals we had floated to get us by would be paid off before certain detrimental triggers were pulled.

Some of this "good press" was coming from the aviation oriented media, but we were also receiving positive input from some of the national business media. For example, in January 1986 the magazine, Business Week, published an article ranking some nine hundred companies with respect to various types of financial improvement during 1985. Western Airlines, Inc. was ranked number one among all those companies in terms of growth in the market value of its stock during the year. This is what I referred to as "getting the bride finely arrayed to attract a suitable groom."

By now I knew Western would have to find a merger partner, preferably American Airlines or Delta Air Lines. Our route structure lined up with these carriers much better than any others. My preference was American, but I knew they would have less interest in us than Delta as they already had a stronger presence in the western part of the United States. One advantage with American was that we each had our exclusive terminals in Los Angeles and they were side by side.

Another reason for my feelings relating to a merger was that our traffic for 1985 was hyped by the United Airlines strike, which began on May 17th. The following article was in the May 27, 1984 issue of Air Transport Magazine:

> Most airlines . . . recorded large increases in telephone reservations and passengers, with load factors leaping to the 80-90% ranges for direct competitors.

With the Salt Lake hub, we were in excellent position to accommodate the United Airlines traffic that was cancelled at their Denver hub. Without this added traffic we would not have had a record profit in 1985; nevertheless, with this added enhancement, '85 turned out to be the most profitable year in Western Airlines history.

What then gave rise to my concern? Western was "wrongsized" for the current low-fare competition in the west; an onslaught coming mostly from Southwest Airlines and America West Airlines. Even a resurrected Continental Airlines was cutting away at our traffic and lowering our yield per passenger.

Grinstein and I had several discussions on this topic and they led to our engaging the First Boston Corporation as financial advisors to examine various strategic alternatives to Western Airlines. We were mainly concerned that we could now be seen as a primary target for a takeover. We reported this to Western's board of directors at our meeting on July 30, 1985. This was strictly exploratory to make sure we were covering all the bases as there was a flurry of route purchases and other similar activities occurring within the industry at this time.

First Boston had put in a great deal of time working with our finance and legal departments to see what Western could do to protect itself from predators in the marketplace. Grinstein was doing most of the work in guiding their efforts and he had them make a report to the board. The minutes of our meeting reflect their input:

> At Mr. Lee's request, Mr. Grinstein described his view of a changing industry, in which consolidations were taking place as anticipated and in light of which the company had engaged The First Boston Corporation to advise Western and its board and its shareholders and employees in the event of a takeover attempt. Mr. Grinstein introduced Messrs. Ed Robinson and Jim Connor of First Boston Corporation and Andrew E. Bogen of Gibson, Dunn & Crutcher and asked that they present a summary of their observations to the board.
>
> Mr. Robinson described changes which have occurred in the mergers and acquisitions environment, from a situation where acquisitions were being made for strategic business purposes to a situation involving a new class of acquirers, who are motivated frequently by short run economic interests and may have little or no interest in the assets or the management of a target company. He described several means of acquisitions, including tender offers, "bear hugs" and "creeping tender offers," wherein shareholders may not have the chance to sit back and consider all alternatives. He indicated that First Boston would urge the company to do all that it can to have time and ability to act in the best interests of its shareholders. He emphasized that financing was available for acquisitions and that it is important for a company to know and understand its inherent value, and he described various methodologies for such evaluation.
>
> Mr. Connor recounted that historically there had been little merger and acquisition activity in the regulated era of the airline, but that subsequent to deregulation the market had seen great fluctuations in airline stock values. Both internal and external buyers had appeared on the scene with various reasons for buying, both offensive and defensive. He stated there were several reasons why Western might be attractive to a prospective

buyer, including its name, its cost structure, its location and its equipment. Mr. Bogen tracked judicial developments which had resulted in the rules of the takeover game having been changed. He emphasized that the greatest danger to a company like Western was not the traditional tender offer, but rather creeping types of tenders and related examples of stock acquisition.

He described for the board various types of anti-takeover measures, including some charter provisions which he stated might be reasonably helpful in certain circumstances although they would need shareholder approval. Such measures typically include a classified board of directors, super-majority provisions and prohibitions on shareholder consent without a meeting. He indicated that many institutional shareholders automatically opposed these kinds of provisions. Additionally, he described a relatively new idea which was being considered in conjunction with Delaware council, First Boston Corporation, the New York Stock Exchange and the company's management, whereby a shareholder acquiring more than ten percent of the company's common stock would need board or shareholder approval to acquire more than ten percent, or have limited voting rights for such shares in excess of ten percent. He described progress toward preparing a form of proxy which might allow for an early special Shareholders' Meeting at which shareholder approval would be sought for those provisions the company would like to have in its charter. He stated that on balance the proposal to require board of director or shareholder approval for acquisitions in excess of ten percent might be received favorably, since the concept of giving shareholders the right to vote might hopefully avoid a "knee jerk" reaction which many institutional holders have had to defensive provisions in company charters. He stated that when preliminary work was completed, they would expect to return to the board with specific suggestions for such a Shareholders' Meeting.

The reason I placed this rather long dissertation in my personal history is that this is such a dramatic change from Western's position of a couple years ago and no single person accomplished this kind of a turnaround. We went from a "no-one-wanted-us" airline to one which sought protection from a takeover. As a company we had now developed a great team spirit and it was highlighted right up to the board room where union leaders, outside directors, and management worked together to secure the company's future.

I should mention that earlier in the year we had brought a new member on the board from Mexico City. When Miguel Blasquez died, we asked Jorge Valencia, our VP in Mexico, to give us his input as to who we might get to replace him. With Western's heavy presence in Mexico, we felt we wanted to continue this tradition of having a top executive from that area.

We found the desirable qualities we needed in Jose Carral, senior vice president Bank of America in Mexico and Executive VP of the Mexico/U.S. Chamber of Commerce. He was a fine addition to the board. These outside directors were now receiving a fee and stock; they had been working for free these past five years. Well, not exactly free, they were getting positive space passes for themselves and their families. Some of them found this to be more worthwhile than the fees.

While Western still had many challenges ahead, the day-to-day operations of the company rolled on at a less frenetic pace and we all enjoyed getting a second wind. I kept my office at LAXGO and our rental at Marina del Rey.

After forty-three years I was finally going to be able to retire from Western Airlines. With the exception of having to work for Neil Bergt for a couple of years, it had been a good career. Most of those with whom I had grown up in the airline were now gone, but never forgotten.

On January 21, 1986, I presided over my last board meeting. At the conclusion of the meeting the following report was made by the "compensation and management succession committee:"

> Mr. Stuart, chairman of the committee, reported that the committee met that morning and considered several matters, the first of which was the resignation of Mr. Lee as chairman, effective January 31, 1986. He stated that committee recommended that

the board accept the resignation with regret and asked the secretary to read a proposed resolution saluting Mr. Lee upon his retirement. Upon motion made and seconded, the following resolution was unanimously adopted:

RESOLVED, that Western Airlines, Inc. and its board of directors salute Larry Lee for his forty-three years of service to America's Senior Airline. During which time he rose from ramp employee and baggage loader to chairman of the board and chief executive.

For his attention to the details of quality that have made this airline unmatched in service and reputation.

For his commitment to home, family and community and his fellow man, by which he has always provided an example to follow.

For his loyalty to the employees of this company, to whom he has always given his highest priority.

For his integrity, above all, which enabled him to see this company through its darkest hours and to guide it into a new era of profitability and respect.

For these reasons, the people of Western Airlines, Inc. honor Larry Lee, and express their gratitude and admiration for all he has done.

Mr. Stuart further presented the committee's recommendation that the board instruct the secretary to have the resolution suitably inscribed, framed and presented to Mr. Lee, and to express the board's consensus that upon his retirement as chairman, Mr. Lee be designated 'Chairman Emeritus.'

Gerald Grinstein was then installed as chairman and chief executive officer effective January 31, 1986.

I remained on the board as chairman of the executive committee and a member of the planning and compensation committees.

At this meeting Lawrence H. Hecker was elected and appointed vice president flight operations and the flight attendants were once again added back into this division of the company.

Topper Van Every was elected to the position of vice president inflight services. That was my old job, the one I accepted when I left the industrial relations department. Jerry Grinstein had asked my opinion on this move and I counseled him not to do it as it was not the type of work Topper wanted. I gave him Topper's background, beginning with his being hired by Western upon his graduation from the University of Arizona. I told Jerry that Topper had asked that I not consider him for work with large groups of employees and felt he was at his best when he heading up departments with mostly administrative projects.

Grinstein persisted in this. His main argument was that Topper was the only one he could trust who had experience in that department. He said it would only be for a short while and he would then move him to another position. When Jerry talked to Van Every, Topper gave him about the same information I had outlined and Jerry promised it would be a short-time interim move. Well it did turn out to be a short time, but there was to be no other move than the boot out the door. It brought back visions of Neil Bergt and his hatchet.

The afternoon of the above mentioned board meeting Jerry came to my office and stated, "Robin Wilson has just fired Topper Van Every." I couldn't believe what I was hearing. I reminded him of Topper's not wanting that job and being talked into it on the basis that Jerry would look after him. The dawn broke as Jerry recognized the significance of what I had just said. I truly felt Jerry was sorry about this event, but he felt he was between the proverbial rock and hard place as Wilson had made it clear there was no place in his lineup for Topper. We were to later learn that Wilson did not like anyone to tell him he was wrong. Topper always told it as he saw it and one could pretty well count on his opinions being correct.

I remind you again that George Kamats, Neil Bergt's senior VP of operations had once called me in Salt Lake City to complain about the inadequacies of most of those with whom he was working at the general office.

He said, "Topper Van Every is the only one around here who has his head screwed on right. I don't know what I'd do without him."

My only purpose for writing about this event is that it was the only real sour note that was to occur during my last three years at Western Airlines. I had watched Topper's capabilities contribute to the growth of the company in so many ways. Without his expertise, we would never have been successful in being the first airline to implement IBM's Passenger Airlines Reservation System, (PARS). We would not have become one of the most efficient carriers in airline food and beverage service. Many of the improvements in our security and procurement functions were the result of his capability and he had to endure the wrath of those whose house he had to clean up in the process of implementing better procedures; this included several slashings of his tires and harassment to his family.

Of greatest importance, there would not have been the timely opening of our Western hub in SLC had it not been for Van Every organizing the whole project for Harold Achtziger and others who had to get their personnel and equipment relocated in time to meet the startup summer schedule change of May, 1982. Topper's office was papered with his "bubble charts" that diagrammed each event and date leading up to May 1st of that year. This was by far the biggest reorganization of flight and ground services ever to occur in any airline at that time. Of all the people on my project team, Topper was the most important and performed the best. His field counterparts took the bows, but they would have been lost without Topper's maps.

The aircraft interiors, seats galleys, etc., became the state of the art as a result of his personal involvement with vendors. For example, several of his plans for the interiors of the Boeing 767's in service today can be traced to his work with Boeing when Western was to receive that aircraft. The engineers at Boeing's design department were even calling Topper to get his opinion on changes other airlines were requesting.

I believe it was in this area that Topper began butting heads with Robin H. H. Wilson. Robin considered himself the expert in the "inflight" field and Topper was deemed "uncooperative" due to his trying to get Robin on the right track.

This was to be the first of several error's Wilson made that ultimately led to his being terminated by Grinstein; this particular error being, not having the courtesy to discuss the termination of a corporate officer with the chairman of the board and CEO prior to taking that action. I don't believe there was a high level of trust toward Wilson from that day forward.

I have added this vignette to my personal history as Topper was definitely a part of my success story; he was a great lieutenant.

Western gave me two nice "sendoffs," one in the large hangar at LAXGO and the other in the new concourse at Salt Lake International Airport. The one in Los Angeles caught me totally by surprise. Jerry had invited me out for lunch and when we returned he said there was something he wanted to show me in the hangar. We opened the back door from the second level and moved to the stairs. As I looked down I saw a sea of people and they all began to clap. Jerry had set this up and I'll never know how they kept it a secret from me.

Our daughter-in-law, Laura, had flown down from Salt Lake City with Alison, and Stacy was there with Jared and Gail. There was the goodbye speech from me and then four-year old Alison took over the mike and began relating her latest story. One of the gals from accounting had her in tow and Alison was really enjoying her new-found stardom. I had to take the mike away from her amid loud shouting that she wasn't finished with her story.

Everyone had their piece of cake and drink and as they headed back to work I shook hands with as many as possible. There were hundreds that attended and they represented a cross-section of every part of Western Airlines.

The other party in Salt Lake City was held in the new "D" concourse at the down time between the afternoon hubs. It occurred on January 29, 1986. The Salt Lake Tribune reported the following:

Western Employees Honor Retiring Chairman

On the same day Western Airlines' employees honored the company's retiring chairman Lawrence H. Lee at the Salt Lake City International Airport, the airline reported the highest annual profit in its 60-year history.

Mr. Lee, honored by about 350 employees Wednesday in a special ceremony marking his years of service to the airline, is credited with having been one of those instrumental in bringing the company back from the brink of financial disaster in 1983 by inaugurating a "competitive action" or recovery plan.

The program included adoption of a partnership program giving employees a stock-ownership position in the company and setting up a profit-sharing program in return for pay reductions.

Mr. Lee, who began his career with Western Airlines as a baggage loader in Salt Lake City in 1943, retires Friday. But he will continue to serve on Western's board of directors and as chairman of the board's executive committee.

He also will serve as chairman of the airline's Help Utah Businesses or HUB Council, a community organization that decides who will be the recipients of free Western Airlines passes.

Wednesday's party for Mr. Lee included presentations of plaques and mementos to him from Airport Manager Lou Miller on behalf of him and the Salt Lake City Airport Authority, flight attendants, pilots and two other Western employees, Donna Frazier and Al Katsilas.

Employees also signed a larger banner, which read, "Larry Lee. We love you. 1943-1986."

Later Wednesday, Western Airlines reported unaudited 1985 record net earnings of $67.1 million. The results for the company's 1985 fiscal year marked a $96 million turn around from the $29.2 million loss suffered by the airline in 1984.

Both of these experiences were appreciated and it gave me a chance to thank each of those who had contributed to our success. I recognize that it takes leadership to bring about this type of achievement; however, a coach can only plan and inspire, it is the team that wins - we had a winning team.

Jerry Grinstein had given me my consulting orders. He wanted me to be his representative in Salt Lake City and to be involved with the top people there to keep them apprised of Western's hub activities.

Western was giving away considerable free transportation to many of the not-for-profit organizations in Salt Lake City and it had gotten out of control. Therefore, in 1984 I formed what I called the HUB Council. The acronym, "HUB," stood for "Help Utah Business." This organization was made up of several entities; the arts, medical, new commerce, conventions and skiing. We appointed an individual to head each of these "spokes" in the hub. Overseeing this organization were three people. I was the chairman, ex-Governor Scott Matheson and Spencer Eccles, head of First Security Bank, were the two vice chairmen.

Each of the chairpersons for the various functions would receive requests that supported their non-profit traffic needs. These were reviewed at that level, prioritized and submitted to the executive committee for approval, or adjustment. This took all the heat off Western having these piece-meal requests coming at them on a too-frequent basis. With this came the proclamation that we would not be giving any cash contributions to any of them. They were happy and the company no longer had an albatross around its neck.

The Help Utah Business Council got a lot of good press and it helped solidify our image as the "home-town airline." I did not spend a great deal of time in Salt Lake City until I retired. The board of directors of Western Airlines had given me a six-year consulting contract that included a small salary, office, secretary and car. I moved from my temporary office in the Beneficial Life Building to the new Eagle Gate Tower.

Bishop Victor L. Brown had just been released as Presiding Bishop in the LDS Church and his counselors were also released. Karen Jepson was secretary to one of the counselors, Elder Richard Clarke, and he was leaving to preside over a mission in Africa. I offered Karen a job as my SLC administrative assistant to run the HUB Council in my absence. In this role she did an excellent job.

The year of my retirement, 1986, was very active for Western Airlines and for the board of directors. The First Boston Corporation, and others we had brought into the loop, were doing a good job of advising us on potential partners. Jerry and I knew that our main goal was to bring Western to the point where it would appear to be a bride ready for marriage.

Western was on a sound footing for the immediate future, but the low-cost carriers were still gaining strength and, as predicted, would be able to price their product at fares much lower than ours. When that happened we would be back in the red and again facing the possibility of bankruptcy. Even though Jerry would have liked to see Western go it alone, we knew we needed to merge with a carrier that had a strong financial record. At that time, Delta was the most financially-strong airline in the industry.

In March, 1986, Western employed the services of Dillon, Read & Co. as financial advisors in matters relating to mergers and acquisitions. Davis, Polk and Wardwell represented us on legal issues pertaining to this subject. We also had Morrow & Co. performing a "stock watch," in case of an attempt to acquire Western.

By spring of 1986, rumors of potential merger partners with Western were widespread. There had been no comment from Western and there was other "industry consolidation" talk in progress.

During this period we were able to restructure more debt and open a greater line of revolving credit. Finance and legal were doing a grand job of getting the past high cost of debt behind us.

Immediately following my retirement, Jerry authorized me to have Thayne Robson, head of the Department of Economics at the University of Utah, lead a study on the financial impact Western was having on Salt Lake City and the State of Utah. This was published in March 1986, and became the basis for much of the work I did in Salt Lake to tell the Western story. As I recall, the study indicated our presence was contributing over six-hundred million dollars a year to Utah.

This was a great story to tell and gave me a chance to have luncheons at the Alta Club with groups of the "movers and shakers" to solidify their understanding of our contributions to their businesses and various ventures. Thayne, may he rest in peace, was at my elbow on many of these occasions to answer questions relating to this study.

While there were several "recognitions" given to Western and to me personally during the foregoing period, I'll just mention two;

The first was in Los Angeles and was presented by the Chief of Police, Daryl Gates, and the Los Angeles Police Department. It was a certificate of merit reading:

Certificate of Appreciation to Lawrence H. Lee in grateful recognition of the exemplary support and cooperation extended to Narcotics division personnel assigned to the division International Airport office

Mr. Lee, president and chief executive officer, Western Airlines, has provided the direction and set the tone for airline employees to follow in providing outstanding cooperation with divisional detectives. His voluntary efforts have resulted in significant arrests and confiscations of narcotics intended for local or national distribution. Mr. Lee unfailingly has maintained the liaison essential to the Department's enforcement program at this major distribution location.

Narcotics division's detectives are joined by all the men and women of the Los Angeles Police Department in commending and thanking Lawrence H. Lee for his distinguished service to professional law enforcement.

This was a tastefully-designed certificate of appreciation with the silver and gold Police Officer badge at the top and the gold seal of the City of Los Angeles. It was followed by another certificate of appreciation from the Los Angeles City Council for the same type of deeds and was presented personally by Pat Russell, President of the Council. It read about the same as the certificate from Chief Gates.

This recognition really did not reflect my work while I was CEO; rather it was for the work that I did with the ground services staff during the period that I was senior vice president of ground and inflight services. With all of our flights in and out of Mexico, we were very vulnerable to smugglers, even among airline and airport personnel.

The second event occurred on July 24, 1986. Even though I had recently retired as chairman of Western Airlines, the "Days of '47" committee asked me to be the Grand Marshal at the "Days of '47" events. I elaborated more about this event in my "family history."

Back to the events at the general headquarters in LAX. At the Western Airlines' board of director's meeting held August 19, 1986, the board issued their final "whereas" for me.

> WHEREAS, Lawrence H. Lee has served with distinction as a member of this board of directors during the last three years, in addition to serving more than forty years as a dedicated employee of this Corporation, from ramp employee to President and Chairman; and

> WHEREAS, he has now chosen to resign from this board to accept a call from his church, once again exemplifying his selfless nature; and

> WHEREAS, his counsel will be sorely missed in the deliberation of this board.

> NOW THEREFORE, this board recognizes by this resolution and gratefully salutes the dedication and contribution which Lawrence H. Lee has provided, and wishes him all the best as he embarks on his newest challenge.

It was unusual that I did not attend this last board meeting. However, my not wanting to be at this meeting was the reason for the premature resignation. It was to be the meeting when Jerry would announce our decision to be a merger partner with Delta Air Lines, Inc. As it turned out, that meeting was delayed a few weeks and was held on September 9, 1986.

As early as mid-1985, around the time we brought in First Boston Corporation, we began having contacts from other airlines and related entities regarding possible mergers or marketing agreements. As I mentioned, Grinstein, as the new CEO, handled this. In due course, we examined or actually had discussions with: Air Cal, Alaska, American, Braniff, Delta, Frontier, Northwest, PSA, People Express, Piedmont, TWA and USAir. The examinations or discussions were in terms of merger or acquisition or marketing alliances.

Two of these potential transactions rose above the others, American and Delta. As mentioned earlier, my hope was that American would show more interest, but their CEO, Crandall, could not see the potential this merger would provide. To this day, I don't think he was right. Many of the same positive factors prevailed as those we had considered at the time we had tried to merge with American and had been turned down by the "regulated airline governance."

Delta would provide an easier transition as the pilots would merge within the same union, ALPA. The discussions with Delta were fairly extensive during March and April of 1986. The major hang-up was that Delta wanted the ability to have a "second look" six months later with potential to renegotiate the transaction if circumstances had changed. This was not acceptable.

As Jerry and I had discussed with the employees, and what had become a major selling point during the CAP meetings, Western was wrong-sized to compete over the long run. We were disadvantaged both in size and geographical location. We were squeezed from both sides. We could not emulate the advantages that the giant carriers had at that time, which basically allow them to control a large portion of available traffic, nor could we match the flexibility enjoyed by low-cost carriers such as America West, Southwest or the re-structured Continental. The carriers could squeeze from below.

Grinstein fired Robin H. H. Wilson, as predicted. We had brought in Don Lloyd-Jones, who had once served as president of American Airlines. He was on the property as a consultant. When Wilson left, Grinstein made Lloyd-Jones the president and COO. That gave him someone to oversee the day-to-day operations while he concentrated on merging Western.

On August 29, 1986 Grinstein and Lloyd-Jones flew to Atlanta to meet with Delta's Chairman, Dave Garrett. They presented a concept of a marketing agreement to Delta, but it was made clear that Delta's interest was in acquiring Western Airlines. From that point on, the merger crystallized.

Dillon, Read, the firm that was advising us on potential partners, noted that their in-depth study of a merged Western and Delta indicated this would be a sound combination. In fact, all the parties we had advising us on this merger termed it a formula for success. Since I had been in and out of what was going on with Delta, Jerry filled me in on what he was planning to do at the September 19th meeting.

Western had been offered two seats on Delta's board of directors. One of those would be filled by Archie Boe; that was Delta's request. Jerry approached me on taking the other seat. He said I had earned it. I turned it down, but I felt this was a very magnanimous gesture by Grinstein. I told him he had earned the seat and he should take it. He did, and that was a good thing. If he hadn't, he wouldn't have been there years later to take over the leadership of Delta when it was self-destructing.

By October 1986, Western's stock price stood over $11.75 for 20 consecutive days. That met one of the conditions of a major loan guarantee and the company was able to transfer $100 million from debt to equity. Western's debt/equity ratio was one to one. I can't recall what that ratio was when I agreed to become the CEO, but it was horrible. During that time-frame our stock had been as low as two and five-eighths, and was now at the merger-pegged price of $12.50. This represented one of the biggest turnarounds in airline history.

It seemed my job was done. All that I had promised to do for Western had now been completed. This led to my decision to vacate my seat on the board of directors prior to a vote on Delta. I felt I would by tied to the company for another year if I didn't move at this point. A shareholder suit that included Western's board was filed shortly after the merger announcement. While it was felt to be without merit, it could still have kept me from accepting a mission call from our LDS Church.

One of the best summaries of the last ten years of Western Airlines' history was written by Captain Art Cornelius and Flight Attendant, Teri Carroll. This article was published in a magazine commemorating Western's sixtieth anniversary:

I was in inflight training on Western's fiftieth anniversary and remember being overwhelmed with a great sense of pride in the company, says Art Cornelius. The hangars were spotless, we had the best maintenance in the industry and the future held so much promise. There was a move underway to deregulate the airlines, but no one knew what that meant or much cared.

A lot of apathy existed toward deregulation actually happening. Most people assumed that the airline business would go on as it had for the last 50 years. In the fall of 1978, the womb of protection disappeared: The airlines had to compete under deregulation.

Overnight the whole industry changed, adds Teri Carroll. To say we were in shock would be an understatement. It was like working with a blindfold on. The most noticeable difference was the type of passengers that were now flying. We were used to experienced business flyers. Deregulation seemed to create another group of travelers who didn't understand the nature of our business. We went from five flight attendants covering 120 passengers to four trying to serve 140 people-many of whom had never flown before. The public's expectations just weren't realistic. I had women actually get quite upset that I wouldn't babysit their children or serve lunch on a 35-minute flight.

By the end of 1981, everyone at Western felt the impact of deregulation when we were asked to take a one-year 10 percent pay cut. People were frustrated. We were flying at full capacity but losing money. The media had us in the grave and started to shovel dirt on us. It was hard to take because we knew how to do our jobs.

Two years ago I didn't think Western was going to survive, continues Art. The company was losing $1 million a day. Some positive steps had already been taken. A hub was established in Salt Lake, changing our old linear routes, which dated back to when the M-2s used to deliver mail, to a feeder system. The choice of a Salt Lake hub over Denver had already grown in significance, but the threat of bankruptcy kept this from becoming clear. I kept thinking of the time our crew walked past the Braniff offices when they went bankrupt and the image of those people sobbing or just staring blankly out the window stuck with me. They just ran out of time. I wondered if we would too.

Western was only days away from extinction. If we didn't give those concessions in 1984 then this airline would have bought the farm. Everyone finally came to realize that Western started with people, not airplanes or ledgers. We're Western Airlines and we're the ones who will make it go. The key is to pull together and share in the company because we're investing in ourselves.

We climbed out of the grave, adds Teri. Our face was a little dirty, but we made it out. More than anything else the concessions instilled confidence in the financial community that Western knew how to run a deregulated airline. Attitudes began to change. Five years ago the attitude was, 'I could have a job here until I'm 60.' Today people realize their career growth is tied to the company. People work much harder than before, but feel much better about their jobs. We're beating the odds and it's just a great feeling to see furloughed people coming back and new faces being added.

Deregulation caught us off guard. We weren't prepared for the problems it caused, but we'll be ready from now on. Despite the hardships, I wouldn't want to go back to a regulated industry. Flying isn't exclusive anymore and in the long run Western will do better. Someday we'll be able to look back on this decade and see the good it produced, even though it was at a cost to family, career and financial goals.

Our place in the history of the airline industry hasn't been written, says Art. I think that the jury is still out on the success of deregulation, but the possibilities for Western are as wide open as they were 60 years ago, and the challenge is still there: to operate America's best commercial airline.

Thus ended my forty-three years with Western Airlines, which was indeed, "The O-o-n-ly Way to Fly." It was a career of pride and pain, pride in the great service we had rendered and pain at seeing its demise. The day I finally departed Western's corporate headquarters in Los Angeles was one of the saddest days of my life. I couldn't help dwelling on the future of our 10,000 employees. While I knew they would be better off with Delta than going it alone at Western, I also knew they were in for a culture shock.

Delta had always considered itself the "family" Airline - one big, happy family. Only the pilots belonged to a labor union and that spoke well for the other employees. Nevertheless, the workforce was spoon fed and could not make the kind of decisions relating to day-to-day operations that Western's personnel were used to doing. We, even with five unions, were more of a family than they would ever be. It was that family spirit, "one for all and all for one," that put us in the financial shape which made us attractive to Delta.

Concurrent with my departure from Western, Margie and I received a call from our Church to serve a one-year mission in London, England. Part of our duty there would be to work on a celebration of the 150th anniversary of the LDS Church's first missionary efforts in the British Isles. This was timely as I would not be around to watch Western disappear into Delta. We left for England shortly after the merger was announced. That call from our church turned into three years in England. While there, we were asked to preside over the England Leeds Mission that was headquartered in Leeds. This was all volunteer work.

While we were in England, Tom Greene, Western's vice president and general counsel, sent me the following epitaph he had written:

A FINAL WISH

March 1987

In everyone's life there are a few select occasions when the human spirit cries out to preserve the moment. When we look back upon younger days we remember that feeling in relation to lighter moments...the first car, the winning touchdown, the high school prom. As we mature, the moments inevitably take on a more serious note... graduation from college, a wedding day, the birth of a child.

There is one occasion, however, which for young and old alike creates a different reaction. When we experience the death of a relative or a close friend, we seek not to freeze that moment in time but rather to reconstruct those earlier times of pleasure. We talk of "living a full life" and of "life going on" and of what the deceased "would have wanted."

Companies die too. We are fond of reminding ourselves that corporate entities are only shells but clearly they have personalities of their own and just as clearly those personalities reflect the combinations of people and purposes which make up each of them.

And so it is with Western Airlines. This company will be no more and we are overwhelmed with a nostalgia which pressures us to remember the good times and to understand why this company's personality can mean so much. Certainly it lived a full life: the oldest airline, humble beginnings, colorful people, record losses, record profits, new routes, new airplanes, regulation and deregulation, love affairs and would-be mergers, near-bankruptcies and partnerships.

Surely we should be gratified that the death is of natural causes; it is not the mercy killing that it would have been just a few years ago. Western Airlines is passing on with class and dignity, its burial with honors befitting its heroic efforts. And life does go on and this unique company, if it could express a final wish, would want the lives of us who mourn it to go on as well, with joyful memories and a secure knowledge that a fortunate few really knew what it meant to be "The Only Way to Fly."

TWENTY-ONE YEARS LATER
2008

I am currently doing the final editing of the recorded highlights of my airline history. I could not send the document to the bindery without a few final notes on the current condition of the commercial aviation industry.

Where the "legacy carriers" will go from here is the question in the minds of all their CEO's as each tries to keep his company from winding up on the scrap pile. As to Delta Air Lines, their competitive action plan is based on a merger with Northwest Airlines. This is to be completed and, hopefully, approved by the end of the year with Delta being the surviving carrier.

Earlier, I had mentioned that Jerry Grinstein had taken the board seat at Delta at the time of the Western/Delta merger. He served as a strong member of that board through some tough periods that required several changes in management. Finally, faced with the threat of bankruptcy, their board of directors asked Jerry to take over as CEO to see if he could bail out the company. Had the pilots cooperated in a timely manner, he might have accomplished this task. However, they did not and it was necessary for him to preside over Delta's "reorganization."

Grinstein indicated to the board that he would not stay on after Delta came out of bankruptcy and, now being in his mid-seventies, he has resigned and severed ties with them; much the same as I had done with Western. When he left, he had several million dollars coming to him in compensation and he turned all that money over to the employees to fund a Delta Air lines organization that would help those employees who were having severe financial problems.

The way Jerry handled all this placed him on an even higher pedestal with the ex-Western employees, those who had vocally supported him prior to and during the bankruptcy. It is surprising how many of them are still working at Delta.

The Delta pilots finally came around when Jerry did a superb job of leading a battle to stave off an unwelcome overture from US Air to purchase Delta while they were yet in bankruptcy. As one might expect, given his past history, he did a masterful work with the legislators and agencies in Washington.

As to the airline industry as a whole, it is in serious trouble. The price of jet fuel has skyrocketed and the industry is presently losing billions of dollars a year. The fare increases and pricing gimmicks cannot keep up with rising costs. Coming out of bankruptcy, Delta's stock had been pegged at $23.25 a share and it was recently as low as $4.50. Other airline stocks have gone even deeper than this. The industry has too many seats in the air and the six major airlines, now called "the legacy carriers," are still unable to compete within the United States with the "low-cost carriers."

Jerry Grinstein increased Delta's international flying where the yield was higher. The new president, Richard Anderson, has kept this trend going and, by merging with NWA, will have the number one world-wide airline. While Jerry and I agree with the concept, we do not see the cultures of Delta and NWA working out in the short run. The only thing that could ease this situation would be a very dire aviation condition wherein the workforce would see they must give their full cooperation or they will die. For the sake of all these employees, I hope they can pull it off.

One last comment, I have perceived a culture at Delta that still tries to tie to the "good-ole-boy" southern traditions - staid mores that should have disappeared when Delta discovered it was really as vulnerable to economic change as any other legacy carrier. They are now, or shortly will be, an amalgamation of Chicago and Southern, Northeast, National, Pan Am, Western, Republic and Northwest. The original "Delta" is a very small part of this conglomerate and the various cultures are now incorporated in such a way as to force management to take a much wider view of all human factors. That requires a management blend at the top that is both "humane" and yet tough enough to make changes while not getting bogged down in the minutia of change. Delta Air Lines was never able to do this in a timely manner. Maybe the assortment of these various airline personnel, procedures and cultures will breed the sturdy mongrel that outlives the once extolled thoroughbred.

THE END

Photo credit: Josh Lee

In memory of Mama and Daddy, who both passed away in 2017, just 3 months apart, after 71 years of marriage. Their hard work and loving relationship were an example to everyone around them.

-Laura Lee, Editor

Larry Lee in his white overalls, leaning against
a DC-3 nose stand. Salt Lake City Airport, circa 1944.

Larry Lee at Alta Ski Resort, Alta, Utah, circa 1944

Larry and Margie at the Desert Inn, Las Vegas, Nevada, circa 1950

Larry Lee, circa 1983

At the dedication of the "Larry Lee", March 29, 1985, with (left to right) Louis Miller, Jerry Grinstein, Victor L. Brown, and Robin H. H. Wilson

BOARD OF DIRECTORS

Fred Benninger*
President
Tracinda Corporation
Las Vegas

Archie R. Boe
Retired President
Sears, Roebuck & Co.
Chicago

Victor L. Brown*
Presiding Bishop
The Church of Jesus Christ
of Latter-Day Saints
Salt Lake City

Joseph T. Casey
Executive Vice President
Chief Financial Officer
Litton Industries
Beverly Hills

Gerald Grinstein*
Chief Executive Officer
Western Air Lines, Inc.
Los Angeles

Walter J. Hickel
Chairman of the Board
Hickel Investment Company
Anchorage

John A. Kammermeyer
Air Line Pilots Association
Los Angeles

Bert T. Kobayashi Jr.
Kobayashi, Watanabe,
Sugita and Kawashima
Attorney-at-Law
Honolulu

Lawrence H. Lee*
Chairman of the Board
Western Air Lines, Inc.
Los Angeles

Charles Levinson
International Trade
Unionist and Economist
Geneva

Susan Edwards Pace
Chairwoman
Western Air Lines Master
Executive Council
Assoc. of Flight Attendants
Los Angeles

Spencer R. Stuart*
Chairman of the Board and
Chief Executive Officer
InveQuest Incorporated
Dallas

James J. Shields
National President
Air Transport Employees
Los Angeles

Robert H. Volk
Chairman and Chief
Executive Officer
Martin Aviation, Inc.
Santa Ana

Robin H.H. Wilson
President and Chief
Operating Officer
Western Air Lines, Inc.
Los Angeles

* Executive Committee

The Board of Directors of Western Airlines,
as seen in the 1984 Annual Report to Shareholders

The minutes of the Western Airlines Board meetings that Larry kept, as well as other supporting documentation, can be found at the University of Utah's J. Willard Marriott Library, Special Collections, entitled the "Lawrence Howard Lee Papers." As a family, we wanted these materials to be made available to the public for future generations of Utahns, students, airline employees, and those in business management and labor relations, that all might profit and find a path through turbulent times.

-Laura Lee